KING ARTHUR

MEDIEVAL BRITISH LITERATURE
AND
MODERN CRITICAL TRADITION

KING ARTHUR

MEDIEVAL BRITISH LITERATURE
AND
MODERN CRITICAL TRADITION

ANDREW BREEZE

UPPSALA BOOKS

London

UPPSALA BOOKS

London, England

www.uppsalabooks.com

Copyright © Uppsala Books 2025

ISBN 978-1-961361-24-9 Hardback

ISBN 978-1-961361-25-6 Paperback

CONTENTS

1. Preface 1

2. Arthur's Historicity 1485-2025 5

3. How Arthur's Fame Reached Wales from North Britain 35

4. Who Was Merlin? 55

5. *Mabinogion* Tales 71

6. Geoffrey of Monmouth 107

7. Laʒamon's *Brut* 137

8. *Sir Gawain and the Green Knight* 169

9. The Alliterative *Morte Arthure* 199

10. *The Awntyrs off Arthure* 223

11. Sir Thomas Malory's *Morte Darthure* 239

12. Afterword 267

PREFACE

Many books have been written about Arthur since (according to the chronicles) he died like a hero in 537 at *Camlan* or Castlesteads, a Roman Wall fort near Carlisle in north-west England. But, right or wrong, *King Arthur* is unlike any of them. In its first chapter is set out evidence for Arthur as a sixth-century British warrior fighting other North Britons in what is now southern Scotland and the Borders. It challenges (one hopes) the orthodoxy promulgated since the 1970s on Arthur's being legendary. Not so. Like Queen Boudica or Joan of Arc or Abraham Lincoln or Winston Churchill, Arthur was a person who not only existed, but knew how to fight. As if that were not enough, in the seventh chapter we move forwards to views of Professor Ann W. Astell on *Sir Gawain and the Green Knight*, and how it was composed no earlier than October 1386 and no later than December 1387. We can go further. In that chapter the case is made for the *Gawain* Poet as Sir John Stanley (1350?–1414), Cheshire magnate, who would have written the poem in late 1387 for that year's Christmas celebrations at Chester Castle. Stanley thus emerges as a great artist, one of the score or so of England's supreme poets: a contemporary of Chaucer (whom he knew) and in some ways his superior. Besides these are (less contentious) chapters on Arthurian traditions in Britain from their beginnings up to Malory's *Morte Darthure*.

Apart from the above, one may say more on how the book has been written and on how it can be used. The form of construction

1

is simple, but (one hopes) comprehensive. Texts dealt with are limited to British poetry and prose. The great Arthurian romances from medieval France or Germany or elsewhere on the European Continent are (unfortunately) no part of it. Instead, the ten chapters make up a survey of Arthurian tradition in Britain, from the earliest Welsh-Latin annals and chronicles to eleventh- and thirteenth-century *Mabinogion* texts, Geoffrey of Monmouth's pseudo-history of the twelfth century, and English poems and prose from the thirteenth century to 1485 (with Caxton's edition that year of Malory's *Morte Darthure*). As for the approach, it does not consist of a reading of these texts, but of commentary on them, especially from the early twentieth century onwards.

Four advantages emerge from this. The first is that, within each chapter, a thorough bibliography of discussion will be found. Readers can go from the notes to previous accounts of Arthurian texts, where an attempt has been made at completeness and inclusiveness. Nothing has there been deliberately omitted, either in those notes or in material cited in those notes; but, if work of importance has been left out, then nobody wishes to know about it more than the present writer.

The second point is that, by a study of reception by previous scholars and critics (that is, of secondary material in the light of our original sources in Latin or Welsh or Middle English), a pattern emerges. Earlier writers often had insights which later ones show themselves unaware of. An instance would be for *Sir Gawain and the Green Knight*, with John H. Fisher in the USA, or Derek Brewer and John Stevens in Cambridge, together defending the poet's conservativism. They did not regard him as subversive, as a critic of Camelot's worldly values or of Arthur himself. In this they differed from many commentators of the last thirty years or so. But their attitude is surely vindicated by research since the late 1990s on the poem's Cheshire origins.

The third aspect is more general. It is that of Arthur himself. His representation by writers in medieval England and Wales is this book's central theme. Each author naturally made Arthur in his own image, or (better) in the light of his views on conflict, power, kingship, justice, nationality, women. So we find Arthur in a remarkable development from a sixth-century North British commander and patriot, to a boisterous Dark-Age Celtic ruler and hero, to a High Medieval fount of justice and courtesy. It is a pattern unfolding as one goes from chapter to chapter. Despite that, Arthur the man of war is there from beginning to end. His origins as a North British fighting man of the 530s can be traced even in the Arthur of Malory, writing more than nine centuries later.

A fourth advantage of the above lies in books to come. In their encounters with Arthurian texts, future authors will respond with their special attitudes and values. For all time, books and articles can thus be added to those cited in our ten chapters. Some of what those (yet unwritten) documents say will be new and illuminating; some of it, less so; and it may be that what is claimed is on occasion found to repeat (unwittingly) what was noticed long ago.

So, there is much in *King Arthur* to provoke argument. Reactions will be varied. Which way up the spun Arthurian coin lands, as regards propositions in the book, will (of course) be a matter of interest.

CHAPTER ONE

ARTHUR'S HISTORICITY 1485-2025

Arthur's historicity has been disputed regularly from the fifteenth century to the twenty-first. Two points emerge from analysis of it. First, there was no real advance for most observers between the age of Richard III (when William Caxton took on the matter) and that of Charles III. Second, material for a solution has yet been in print (if unnoticed) since 1926, when William J. Watson published his classic monograph on Scottish place-names. On a long march from 1485 to 2025, then, we find plenty of the misleading and the misled, occasionally relieved by the insights of certain gifted scholars (including Heinrich Zimmer, O. G. S. Crawford, Sir Frank Stenton, K. H. Jackson, Rachel Bromwich, David Woods). More cheeringly, the subject demonstrates how even the toughest problems can yield (in A. E. Housman's phrase) to 'coherent thought and consequent reasoning'.

So the conclusions will be these. Arthur existed, being a brave and successful warrior (not a king); he was neither Welsh nor Cornish, but a North Briton, fighting other Britons between Firth of Clyde and North Sea; he was not a Romanized cavalry supremo defeating Saxons up and down Britain (an illusion of R. G. Collingwood, Oxford historian); and he had nothing to do with the British victory of Mount 'Badon' (= Braydon, north Wiltshire) in 493, instead dying a soldier's death in 537 at (after a proposal of

1935 by O. G. S. Crawford) *Camlan* or Castlesteads, on Hadrian's Wall, near the old Roman city of Carlisle.

That said, we begin our study proper with England's earliest printer. In his edition of Malory, Caxton (d. 1491) faced up to assertions that 'there was no suche Arthur', all accounts of him being 'fayned and fables'. He countered them with 'evidences to the contrary' supplied by various 'noble jentylmen' who told him of Arthur's tomb at Glastonbury; the mark of his seal 'in reed waxe' at Westminster Abbey; relics of his knights at Dover Castle and elsewhere; 'at Wynchester the Rounde Table'; and at Caerleon in South Wales the 'grete stones' and royal vaults of Camelot itself. The whole text makes interesting reading.[1] Informants of the 1480s used archaeology to support their case and did not suffer from negativism.

By Henry VIII's time the polemic was shriller, Arthur's champion now being John Leland (d. 1552), king's antiquary. On the other side was the Italian humanist Polydore Vergil (d. 1555), Leland's sceptical *bête noire*. Leland's proofs were literary ones, differing from those of Caxton. Crucial amongst them is the list of Arthur's Twelve Battles in the ninth-century *Historia Brittonum* (formerly attributed to Nennius), with Leland (reasonably) styling its author as *bonae et antiquae fidei scriptor*, a writer old and trustworthy. Leland gave those battles as on the rivers Glen, Dugles (four times), Bassas; in the Caledonian Forest; at the Fortress of Guinion, City of the Legion, Strand of Traitheurith, Hill of Agned; and at Mount Badon, *in quo multi corruerunt uno impeto Arthurii*, in which a host fell at a single onslaught of Arthur.[2] In that reckoning, 'Badon' was Arthur's supreme triumph.

In 1544, then, priceless evidence for the historical Arthur entered print. It was a huge advance. Unfortunately, spelling out its meaning still had to wait almost five hundred years. As a sample of the discourse in between, we turn to Theophilus Evans (1693-1767), Welsh ultra-Protestant cleric, whose *Drych y Prif Oesoedd* or 'The Mirror of Ancient Times' is a masterpiece of (unwitting) comedy, with Evans representing British history in the same (if now unconscious) spirit as his contemporary Hogarth depicted English parliamentary elections. Evans, naturally, gave anti-Arthurians short shrift. Do the English deny Arthur's existence? It is because Arthur was their implacable foe. Hence their disparagement. Yet bardic references to Arthur and his tomb at Glastonbury offer proofs 'clear as the rising sun', which only some captious scoffer (*ambell geccryn enllibus*) will have the neck to deny.[3]

For those, however, who did not relish historical tub-thumping, nothing could be done until the advent of critical texts and historical philology. That was to be the achievement of nineteenth-century Britons and Germans. To the first we owe an edition by John Williams (1811-62) of Welsh-Latin annals, including this one for 537: *Gueith Camlann, in qua Arthur et Medraut corruere; et mortalitas in Brittania et Hibernia fuit.*[4] It means 'The Battle of Camlan, in which Arthur and Medrawd fell; and there was a great loss of life in Britain and Ireland.' If *Historia Brittonum*'s battle-list is one vital Arthurian text, this entry (in a tenth-century compilation) is another. It has yet been dismissed as a late fabrication, and thus unreliable; some also locate its *Camlan* in Wales. Such views are easily rebutted. A late forger would not mention Medrawd, a personage utterly obscure until the twelfth century (when Geoffrey of Monmouth made him out as Arthur's treacherous nephew). Nor does location of *Camlan* in Wales explain why Welsh bards were so vague on its whereabouts; a difficulty removed if it was in faraway North Britain. Finally, the entry's factual nature is vindicated by that *mortalitas*, also recorded in Irish annals, and part of a world-wide famine of 536-7 (known too from Chinese and Byzantine sources) due to a mega-eruption of late 535 located in the Americas or Iceland. The cubic miles of ash and sulphur pumped into the upper atmosphere obscured the sun and produced a 'volcanic winter' (as noted in 2010 by David Woods) of crop failure and starvation. If the annal is right on a calamitous famine, it will be right on a calamitous battle.

John Williams promoted knowledge at his rectory in remote Llanymawddwy, south Gwynedd; so, later on, did professors in Imperial Berlin. In his *Nennius Vindicatus* (1893), Heinrich Zimmer (1851-1910) drew attention to a third source for the historical Arthur, the bearing of his name by sixth- and seventh-century Celts, after whom it lost currency. Thereafter the great Theodor Mommsen (1817-1903) brought out (1894) a subsidiary edition of *Historia Brittonum*, republished (in 1898) as part of a complete *Monumenta Germaniae Historica* volume. Zimmer and Mommsen had impact. Citing the first, Alfred Nutt (1856-1910) commented on how 'at the close of the sixth and beginning of the seventh centuries' we find princes called Arthur, including one (who died in about 630) from south-west Wales and another (killed allegedly in 596 or perhaps 590) from Gaelic Scotland. After that the name disappears from the records.[5] The implication is obvious. *Arthur* (from Latin *Artorius*) is a rare form. If Arthur were a mere Celtic sprite, it is hard to see why sons of kings were given his name for a while, and then not so. If, however, he really lived in the early sixth century, the objections vanish. As with 'Napoleon' amongst nineteenth-century Italians or South Americans, 'Arthur' was an appellation in vogue, then out of it.

Sir John Rhŷs (1840-1915) thereupon noted how the historian Gildas (493-570) mentions the victory of 'Badon' (in 493) but 'says nothing whatever about Arthur there or anywhere else': a telling silence. Less satisfactory were Rhŷs's refusal to pin the real Arthur down geographically, and his taking him as perhaps 'successor of the Count of Britain', a Roman title. Rhŷs yet correctly explained *Arthur* from Latin *Artorius*, citing H. C. Coote as the first to point this out, in his *The Romans of Britain* (1878).[6] So, further progress.

Sir John Lloyd (1861-1947) was a more substantial scholar than Rhŷs. He saw how a Latin etymology for *Arthur* indicated a real man and not one from 'the realm of myth'. But he still tended to regard him as the victor of 'Badon', proposing that Gildas's failure to name him was merely one of that writer's quirks. Beyond that it was hard to go, except to place Arthur's wars 'in the South and East' of Britain.[7] Lloyd's bafflement came from everyone's inability to answer Where? for the ninth-century battle-list published in 1544. In similar mood was Hugh Williams (1843-1911), editor (in 1899-1901) of Gildas. 'Attempts to fix the chronology based on such hazy narratives cannot be trusted' was his verdict.[8] Application of Celtic philology and a willingness to emend scribal corruption were (as argued below) to be the only solutions.

In that context, two books of the 1920s supply a new beginning. First, most of those twelve battles can be related to toponyms listed by Watson. Significant for *Dubglas* below are Douglas Water, near Lanark; for 'Bassas', Cars*tairs* (south-east of Lanark), but also *Tarras* Water, Eskdale (near the border with Cumbria); for *Guinnion*, Carwinning, a hillfort near Dalry, north Ayrshire; for the 'City' of the Legion, *Karig Lion* 'Legion(s) Rock' by the Antonine Wall, West Lothian; for *Tribruit*, Dreva, on the Tweed west of Peebles; for 'Agned' Hill, *Pennango* 'Death Hill', near Hawick, Borders.[9] These can be compared with the battle-catalogue published by Sir Edmund Chambers (1866-1954) from Mommsen's edition. The forms are: Glein, Dubglas (in the region of 'Linnuis'), Bassas, Caledonian Forest, Fortress of Guinnion, City of the Legion, Strand of Tribruit, Hill of Agned, Mount Badon. Better readings, then, than Leland had in 1544; if still requiring correction after Watson and others. Chambers has much else of interest, such as comment on Caxton's unease about Arthur as perhaps due to the monk Ranulf Higden (d. 1364), whose world-history Caxton had published in 1482; even if Higden, like the Yorkshire canon William of Newburgh (1136-98), was in his time a mere 'solitary voice' in nay-saying Geoffrey of Monmouth (d. 1155) and his fabrications.[10] So it was in Caxton's time that doubts started to gather, never departing until now.

Thanks to Watson and Chambers, the material was now easy of access. The machine had been assembled. To it can be added apparatus from a monumental glossary by John Lloyd-Jones (1885-

1956). In listing toponyms edited by Mommsen, it has surprises. Welsh *Baddon* 'Badon' was a form quite unknown to the bards until Geoffrey of Monmouth's inventions seduced them. This despite its supposedly being Arthur's greatest triumph. On the other hand, the bards never forgot the débâcle of Camlan. That tradition was authentically Arthurian. Take also *Dubglas* in 'Linnuis', the latter routinely understood as Lindsey, even though Lincolnshire has no River Douglas for one battle, let alone four. Lloyd-Jones's entry for Middle Welsh *Cludwys* 'men of Clyde, Strathclyders' permits emendation of 'Linnuis' to Old Welsh *Clutuis*; which points to conflicts on Strathclyde's south-east frontier by Douglas Water, a barrier of major strategic importance.[11] Welsh native tradition has, therefore, nothing on Arthur as Badon's victor, but much on his death at *Camlan*; while another bardic form locates four other engagements on the banks of Douglas Water, near Lanark, Scotland.

Progressing through the 1930s, we discover further clues, plus a major historical error. Amongst the former was derivation of the Twelve Battles list from a vernacular 'catalogue poem'; also noted are those princes (including sixth-century Artúr of the Argyll region), who show *Arthur* as an appellation then 'familiar throughout' Celtic Britain, even though before the sixth century it is 'practically unknown'.[12] As regards battle-list poems, others survive in early Welsh and (for the sake of credibility) naturally allude to real places, not fairyland ones. Working in Sweden, the great toponymist Eilert Ekwall published entries on Braydon, near Swindon, and the River Glen, Northumberland.[13] The forms are pre-English, and we argue that the former was the 'Badon' of 493, while the latter is widely recognized as where Arthur's first engagement was fought. It cannot be emphasized too much that 'Badon' is impossible as a Celtic form. Emend to *Bradon-* and we not only have something which makes sense, but can locate it at the hillfort of Ringsbury, near Braydon, Wiltshire.

Now for an Oxford University red herring. The culprit is R. G. Collingwood (1889-1943). He said (rightly) that the battle-list is 'genuine'. Its toponyms are not the work of a 'forger'. Yet almost none has a site 'established beyond controversy'. Therefore (now veering close to error) he assumed that they do not belong to 'any one part of Britain' (true as regards 'Badon' in the south, against the other eleven). Collingwood (now plunging over a historiographical cliff) thus took them to show Arthur as 'commander of a mobile field-army' in the best Roman style, and perhaps holding the revived Roman office of *comes Britanniarum*, Count of the Provinces of Britain. Arthur was thus presented to an admiring public as 'the last of the Romans', the energetic leader of swift-moving British cavalry squadrons, a man endowed with the spirit and acumen of an Alexander.[14]

The effects of this were lamentable. Analysis below of the idea's long-drawn-out decline will be instructive, even if aspects of it are not dead even now, such as Arthur's supposed use of cavalry in Roman style. This despite Kenneth Jackson's firm dismissal in 1969 of the notion. All the same, it was neither the first defective notion on Arthur nor the last. The fame that it acquired contrasts with the obscurity to which research by others was consigned. One of them concerns 'Badon'. We say again that the form is meaningless and unCeltic. Not so the Welsh place-name element *brad* 'treachery, betrayal', applied to woods and other haunts of thieves.[15] But no attention was paid to what *brad* might mean for 'Bad-'. All the same, enlightenment was to come from a fourth item in Arthur's dossier, the declaration on a North British hero in elegies (of 603-4?) that he glutted crows with the flesh of enemies, *ceni bei ef arthur*, 'though he was not Arthur', supreme warlord.[16] Of the same period is comment on the name of Braydon Forest as 'pre-English' but 'obscure', and on Ringsbury Camp, which crowns a hill overlooking the forest.[17] That hillfort, near both Braydon and the Roman road from Winchester to the old British capital of Cirencester, will be where 'Badon' (or, rather, Bradon) was won and lost in 493, with a West Saxon attack crushed to such effect that the British gained a half-century respite from English aggression.

Meanwhile, the Collingwoodian Arthur went his dashing way, this 'rather ingenious' interpretation being warmly accepted by one writer.[18] Better, however, was admission by Henry Lewis (1889-1968) after O. G. S. Crawford (1886-1957) that the *Camlan* of 537 was very probably on Hadrian's Wall; even if Lewis repeated the (now obsolete) view of *Camboglanna* as Birdoswald, not Castle-steads.[19] A further Northern symptom, of the sixth-century prince Arthur of Gaelic Scotland, whose brother had the still more British name Rhiwallon ('he of kingly power'), was also given philological attention.[20]

Research during the 1950s increased in quantity, if not always quality; for it presents trapdoors and stepping-stones alike. In an admirable survey, Sir Thomas Kendrick (1895-1979) set out the post-medieval disintegration of Geoffrey of Monmouth's Arthur, despite attempts by Leland and others to shore him up; he noted too how Higden's earlier scepticism got under the skin of his trans-lator, John Trevisa (d. before 1402), a Cornishman, who thought Higden's views on Arthur were not 'worth a bene'.[21] Modern doubts were then provided by Kenneth Jackson (1909-81). He was then cautious on whether Arthur was 'a leader of the official Ro-man kind' or merely a Celtic 'tyrant' like Vortigern, declaring that in either case 'nothing useful can be said' on the question, even if Collingwood had 'ably' defended the former view. (Jackson was later rather more curt on the subject.) As for the British triumph of 'Badon' in around 'the year 500', it was perhaps at Badbury (near Swindon), where 'the British leader may or may not have been' Arthur.[22] Jackson never addressed in print the objection that *Bad-bury* is an English form, whereas the 'Badonicus mons' of Gildas (writing in 536) must represent a British one. Badbury and the like are here thus irrelevant.

Other views were presented by Rachel Bromwich (1915-2010), Jackson's former student and (like Collingwood) a future object of his acerbity. Her account was businesslike. Aneirin's *Gododdin*, composed after a heroic North British defeat in 603 (?) by the English at Catterick (today in North Yorkshire), demonstrates Northern traditions of Arthur 'at an early date'. Although she could make little of the Twelve Battles, she took some as against 'rival British factions' (not the Anglo-Saxons), attributing the 'ambiguity of their names' to their being 'corrupted forms' of toponyms in North Britain.[23] With justification, Rachel Bromwich put her money on Arthur as a Northerner. Jackson's response was icy. On the hypothesis of Arthur as 'a chief of northern Britain' and his battles as 'all fought in the north', he asserted that philological evidence 'does little to support it'. This even though he referred both to the British names Arthur and Rhiwallon in the family of Aedhán (d. 608), king of Scottish Dál Riada, as also traditions of a sixth-century marriage with a Welsh princess (called Lluan and from the Brecon region).[24] Jackson was a far greater scholar than Rachel Bromwich. But on this matter she was right, and he (for once) wrong.

Now for Sir Winston Churchill (1874-1965) and how Arthur's legend went to the depths of his romantic patriotism. Despite acknowledging the Twelve Battles as in 'scenes untraceable', he interpreted Arthur as one who (like himself) 'kept the light of civilization burning'. Fully understanding the case for 'Badon' as fought in Wiltshire about the year 500, he (with reason) snorted at the timidity of scholars unable to say whether Arthur even existed, riposting 'This is not much to show after so much toil and learning.' Less wisely, he swallowed Collingwood's view of Arthur as 'a new Count of Britain' and 'commander of a mobile field army' which trounced Saxons wherever they came forth.[25] Such a figure, a trained cavalryman and strategist combating barbaric German invaders, was too much for Churchill (who did just that himself) to resist. Still, Churchill's knowledge of war gave his remarks an edge not found in assertions by lesser beings like ourselves.

Commentary of the later 1950s varies. R. S. Loomis (1887–1966) cited J. S. P. Tatlock and Jackson for the sources as Aneirin's *Gododdin* (of 603-4?), *Historia Brittonum* (829-30), *Annales Cambriae* (of 955?), but neglected the earliest testimony of sixth-century royal baptisms.[26] Less happily, the entry in an (otherwise) excellent collection of lives (with the archaeologists Glyn Daniel and Stuart Piggott amongst the contributors) presented the Collingwoodian Arthur, 'Roman of the Dark Ages', not a king but a 'Romano-British general' who commanded a 'special force or task force' against Saxon aggressors, despite which he fell at *Camlan* amongst 'Briton fighting against Briton'.[27] Geoffrey Ashe (1923-2022), veteran Arthurian, offered a similar mixture of sound and unsound. The *Historia Brittonum* battle-list is authentic. 'A fabricator would have given familiar names', not ones 'unrecognizable'. In contrast were his views (after Rhŷs and Collingwood) on the term *dux bellorum* ('leader in battles') there applied to Arthur, and its supposed links with Roman *Comes Britanniarum* or *Comes Litoris Saxonum*, making Arthur a latter-day Count of Britain, or of the Saxon Shore.[28] We shall reject this as a chimaera; *dux bellorum* will instead be clumsy Welsh-Latin for *penteulu*, captain of the royal host, an officer subordinate to kings alone, for he held a position of high status and trust (as medieval Welsh law-tracts make clear), which was of purely Celtic origin. It had nothing to do with Roman government or military organization.

Nora Chadwick (1891-1972) tended to minimalism, dismissing claims by the French historian Ferdinand Lot (1866-1952) for a northern Arthur as 'not admissable', because the sites of his battles are 'virtually unknown'.[29] More authoritative than Ashe was Kenneth Jackson, whose chapter on Arthur is still the best starting-place for enquirers. He said this. We do not know if Arthur is historical, 'but he may well have existed.' *Arthur* is certainly from Latin *Artorius*. It is not a Celtic form. (So, a fifth proof for Arthur as a real person.) Less fortunately, Jackson ignored the grave difficulties of English *Badbury* from British-Latin 'Badon'; while

Gildas's curious failure to mention Arthur is brushed aside. Gildas (we hear) no more needed to tell his readers that Arthur was victor at Badon than an English bishop of 1860 was obliged to describe Waterloo as 'won by the Duke of Wellington'. (But if Arthur died in 537, as stated by Welsh annals, he would not have been at 'Badon' in 493.) Better, however, were Jackson's details on Arthur in the seventh-century *Gododdin*, and on his name as already given in baptism to four or five British and Scottish princes active in around the year 600. As for the Twelve Battles, 'a great deal of nonsense has been written' on them. For Badbury and 'Badon', Jackson again failed to see objections solvable only by emendation. 'Urbs Legionis is certainly Chester'; yet Jackson did not see this toponym as a *lectio facilior*, corrupting that of some obscure northern locality. The 'Caledonian Forest' was in Strathclyde, not the Scottish Highlands (this will be correct). The *regio Linnuis* of the River Douglas 'is probably Lindsey in Lincolnshire'. (But Lincolnshire has no River Douglas.) Then came a brilliant suggestion, providing a sixth proof for the historical Arthur. A recension, in an eleventh-century Vatican manuscript, of *Historia Brittonum* from the year 944 has *Mons Breguoin* as helping locate 'Mons Agned'; and Jackson took *Breguoin* as perhaps High Rochester, Northumberland, site of the Roman fort of *Bremenium* (a 'place on a roaring stream'). We can go further. It shows a Welshman of the 940s regarding Arthur as a North Briton, and rather accurately so, for we place 'Mons Agned' at *Pennango* ('hill of death') near Hawick, Borders, and hence not far from High Rochester. Jackson did comment positively (it was 'ingenious and by no means impossible') on Crawford's 1935 identification of *Camlan* with *Camboglanna*, a fort on Hadrian's Wall. He then referred acidly to Collingwood's proposals for Arthur as Roman commander, which he styled an 'imaginative' proposition; while (at the time) he was yet restrained on Arthur as instead a 'chief of the North', where he urged caution, given the darkness shrouding locations for the Twelve Battles.[30] The whole chapter is revealing on a very great scholar's strengths and weaknesses. Even one of Jackson's calibre could be tripped up by preconceptions (such as Arthur's presence at 'Badon'). His knowledge of the Celtic languages yet allowed insights denied to most of us, ignorant of those languages.

Thomas Jones (1910-72) of Aberystwyth, a careful and industrious researcher, likewise presented a mixture of acceptable and unacceptable. Arthur's existence 'can no longer be denied'. His name indicates 'Roman influences'; he perhaps held a 'military post' for defending post-Roman Britain.[31] Yet the Yarrowkirk inscription (discussed below) in southern Scotland allows another interpretation of Roman *Artorius* and Celtic *Arthur*. As for the Twelve Battles, there is a thorough review of them by Count Tolstoy. Of particular value is his locating the Caledonian Forest, after Kenneth Jackson and the Scottish humanist Hector Boece (1465-1532), 'where the county boundaries of Peebles, Lanark, and Dumfries meet', near the headwaters of Clyde and Tweed.[32] The conflict was in the Southern Uplands, not the Scottish Highlands.

If Collingwood's Arthur-the-Roman-Commander was a trapdoor or Wrong Turning of the 1930s, here is another one, of the early 1960s and again concerning *dux bellorum*, chief of battles. Citing the Dutch philologist A. G. van Hamel (1886-1945) for a parallel here in Irish *rígféinnid* ('leader of a *fiann* or band of warrior-hunters'), the Rees brothers saw Arthur as equivalent to the Irish hero Finn, leader of the Fenians and also 'one who defends his country against foreign invaders'.[33] There is a problem. Arthur existed. Finn is completely legendary. But the remark opened the door on a lubricated slope for the notion that Arthur and Finn are both figures of folklore, equally fictitious. The short-term advantage was evident. It forestalled embarrassing questions on failure to locate those twelve conflicts. Arthur as a pan-Brittonic champion, no more historical than Hercules or Robin Hood, was thus a useful cover. He did not exist, so neither did his battles. No need to try and find where they were, then.

One turns with relief from such nebulous thinking to a North British monument of Arthur's time. West of Selkirk in southern

Scotland is an inscription of the early sixth century, reading HIC MEMORIA PERPETUA / IN LOCO INSIGNISIMI PRINCIPES NUDI DUMNOGENI / HIC IACENT IN TUMULO DUO FILII LIBERALI or 'This is the eternal memorial; in this place lie the most illustrious princes Nudus and Dumnogenus. Here lie in the grave the two sons of Liberalis.'.[34] It tells us more than we might expect. These people were chieftains, otherwise unknown. They were Christians, the epitaph echoing other Christian ones from Italy and North Africa. While Liberalis had a good Latin name, those of his sons Dumnogenus ('he born of the world') and Nudus were British. In short, their tomb demonstrates the hybrid of Latin and Celtic that North Britain was in the early sixth century; age of Artorius or Arthur. No obligation then to see him as Roman commander or cavalry leader or Britain's national defender. Also in the refreshing world of the actual are editions of genealogies mentioning prince Arthur, son of Pedr. His great-grandfather was the Dyfed ruler Vorteporix, amongst the royal targets in 536 of Gildas's invective; in another pedigree is the name of Lluan, said to have married in the sixth century into the house of Dál Riada, Scotland, and distantly connected with Arthurian tradition.[35] The younger Arthur, active in the early seventh century, demonstrates the Northern Arthur's fame in Wales less than three generations after his death.

After that, a return to the quagmire of the Twelve Battles. Ashe's later report on it offers old errors with some advances. The conflicts 'seem to be widespread'. 'Linnuis' is 'probably' north Lincolnshire. The Caledonian Forest is midway between Carlisle and Glasgow; *Tribruit* was likewise in 'the Scottish Lowlands' (better, Southern Uplands). While *Badbury* is English, it could be from 'a Celtic "Badon"'.[36] (But no such form exists.) In such chaos, a rational view of Arthur's enemies was impossible. That did not stop him from cantering into the pages of a respected volume, where he is a commander of squadrons, his title *dux bellorum* 'a memory of late Roman military titles', and 'his mounted forces' having deadly effect on Saxon infantry.[37] Bishop Hanson, contrasting Nora Chadwick (unsure of Arthur's existence) with her late husband H. M. Chadwick (who thought Arthur born in Devon or thereabouts between 450 and 470), naturally spoke of a need to 'suspend' judgement here on details.[38]

Thereafter Jackson had a final chance to aim his verbal howitzer at the shade of Collingwood and at Rachel Bromwich. For the former's 'romantic and eloquent account' of Arthur as commanding 'a sort of Horse Guards or Dragoons', he retorted that there is 'not the slightest real evidence that Arthur, if he ever existed, had anything to do with cavalry.' For the latter, who took Aneirin's *Gododdin* as indicating North British origins for Arthur, he riposted that 'Arthur was the great national hero of the entire British people, and there is therefore no logic whatever in the idea.'.[39] Why, one wonders, was Jackson was so implacable a foe to the Northern Arthur?

While Jackson was pummelling Arthur the Northerner, Proinsias Mac Cana (1926-2004) was busy converting him into a Celtic myth. The Irish folklore warrior Fionn or Finn had (he declared) 'obvious similarities to the British Arthur. Both defended their countries against foreign enemies and overcome fearsome monsters. Both invaded the Other World and both are hunters.'[40] Mac Cana, accelerating down an incline prepared by van Hamel and the Rees brothers, could not distinguish a phantasmal dragon-slayer from a man with a Latin name who died near Carlisle in 537 CE. But we should.

In the 1970s came a proliferation of popular academic work on Arthur, together with sober and serious remarks (sometimes by the same writer). In the foreground was the archaeologist Leslie Alcock (1925-2006), whose best-selling study contains much information on post-Roman Britain and two huge fallacies. Fallacy number one comes in a map of Arthur's battles, with 'Badon' placed at no fewer than six possible points, from Dorset to Lincolnshire. Better than 'Badon' were the Caledonian Forest,

Camlan, Breguoin, Glein. They all (despite hedging on the first and last) are rightly situated (in south-west Scotland, Cumbria, Northumberland). But with uncertainty there and elsewhere, no compelling image of Arthur could emerge. Alcock did, however, offer a solution on why Welsh annals put 'Badon' in 516, when we argue for 493: because of 'dislocation' in the copying of dates 'from one Easter Table to another'. As for fallacy number two, it was his association of Cadbury Castle in south-east Somerset with Camelot. At the time he considered the identification 'a happy one'.[41] One sees why. It did wonders for archaeological fund-raising and general ballyhoo. But it soon attracted professional attacks on Alcock and eventually (in 1995) his humiliating retraction (see below).

The year 1971 brought opinions by others. May McKisack (1900-81) outlined sixteenth-century attitudes to Arthur. Humphrey Lhuyd (d. 1568) of Denbigh was a true Renaissance humanist, except here, when 'no doubt inevitably, his critical sense deserted him' and he defended Geoffrey of Monmouth against all comers. But Robert Fabyan (d. 1513) of London had already questioned accounts of Arthur's victories in France; John Rastell (d. 1536) went further, as on Westminster Abbey's supposed seal of Arthur (adduced by Caxton); John Stowe (d. 1605) accepted Geoffrey's inventions wholesale; Ralph Holinshed (d. 1580), recording Arthur's 'twelve great victories', still rejected other feats as 'beyond credit'; while Richard Carew (1550-1620), patriotic Cornishman, was quite certain on Arthur's birth at Tintagel, Cornwall.[42] Sir Frank Stenton (1880-1967) had a single (but judicious) phrase on Arthur, as perhaps 'a less imposing figure' in actuality than in legend.[43] Charles Thomas (1928-2016), citing work by Thomas Jones, moved Arthur 'firmly to North Britain', with *Camlan* in 537 on Hadrian's Hall, and nowhere near Cadbury, claimed as 'Camelot' on 'the strength of a post-medieval folk-tale' (which was Thomas's swipe at Alcock's archaeological circus down in Somerset).[44] Like Alcock, Thomas was to change his mind; in both cases for the wrong reasons.

Important finds at that Cadbury are described together with remarks on how archaeological facts and 'historical inferences' about the British hero 'come together with the symbolism of Camelot'.[45] Another best-selling book, by the London classicist John Morris (1913-77), has become a still more impressive ruin. For all its learning, it is really a magnificent historical novel, with Arthur a 'just and powerful ruler who long maintained in years of peace the empire of Britain', which 'his arms had recovered and restored' from and after Saxon conquest.[46] Morris's unblinking assurance was to be shattered by a terrible historical storm.

Before that, another historical fact (based upon a 1953 paper by Nora Chadwick). It concerns Artúr, a prince not British but of the Gaelic dynasty ruling Scotland's Atlantic coast. According to the Latin life of St Columba (d. 597) by Adhamhnán (d. 704) of Iona, Artúr died in 596; but 590 seems a likelier date. This warrior, his name 'of rare occurrence' (and his mother a Welsh princess?), was born before about 570 and had a brother called Rhiwallon (d. 629), where the form is purely Brittonic (not Gaelic or British-Latin).[47] Artúr offers a precious clue. In 570 or so, many people not only remembered Arthur (d. 537) but had actually met him, especially in Strathclyde. Artúr's name dates from a mere thirty years or so after Arthur's floruit. It is the oldest evidence for the historical Arthur. It also supplies an answer to a comment of Peter Hunter Blair (1912-82), on how 'Arthur's fame was great in the sixth century, although we do not know why.'[48] It will be due to Arthur's victories for Strathclyde against the Gododdin (of southeast Scotland) and men of Rheged (Cumbria and the north Solway coast).

After Arthur-the-Roman (of Collingwood) and Arthur-a-hunter-warrior-like-Finn (of Rees and Rees) and Arthur-the-Somerset-warlord (of Alcock) came a fourth (and equally untrue) acquired identity: Arthur-the-non-existent, this last thanks to a celebrated 1977 paper of David N. Dumville (1949-2024). With reason, he demolished the extravagances of Alcock and Morris;

without reason, he concluded that there is no historical evidence whatever for the British champion. This despite early genealogies, annals, chronicles, vernacular poetry. Like Collingwood, Dumville created an idea long influential. It appeared too late for one essential guide, where its author yet stuck to her guns on Arthur the North Briton, also directing readers to Thomas Jones's work on Welsh tradition, if spoiling the effect by associating Arthur with Welsh *arth* 'bear'.[49] Yet *Arthur* is from Latin *Artorius*, an uncommon form. It is not of Celtic origin. If it were, the champion would have namesakes in early Welsh and Breton. Another correction (after M. W. C. Hassall) is on *Camboglanna*, now taken not as Birdoswald but Castlesteads, seven miles west of it on Hadrian's Wall.[50] That was where Arthur fell. For older rethinking (in Latin prefaces by Welsh humanists) we encounter on the one hand John Caius (1510-68) of Cambridge, praised as Arthur's champion against Polydore Vergil, and on the other an admission on how many Arthurian legends are no part of history.[51]

The fallout of Dumville's 1977 essay was widespread. One archaeologist now found himself 'even less confident' on events in fifth-century Britain.[52] Charles Thomas also flinched (without need, we shall argue). Having in 1971 placed Arthur's death on Hadrian's Wall in 537, he then waved the white flag, quoting Dumville's assertion that 'there is no historical evidence about Arthur' and adding 'Any sane person would agree. These enticing Will-of-the-wisps have too long dominated, and deflected, useful advances in our study.'[53]. In like vein was James Campbell (1935-2016) of Oxford. Dismissing Aneirin's *Gododdin*, *Historia Brittonum*, *Annales Cambriae* (while also ignoring both Arthur's Latin name and the genealogies) as 'unlikely to derive from contemporary materials', he snapped the lid shut on what he termed 'the rather ridiculous' interest in identifying the 'real' Arthur.[54] Yet these men (two archaeologists, one historian) were none of them competent in the Celtic languages: an unfortunate lack.

Then came a voice from the grave. In a posthumous work, John Morris (1913-77) again held high his image of Arthur: 'the last Roman emperor in Britain, heir to the island emperors who had been enthroned since Honorius' decree in 410', etc.[55] Small wonder that J. N. L. Myres (1902-89) was irate. He declared (with perfect truth) that there is no evidence for Arthur's 'playing any decisive part' in fifth-century Britain, and attempts to prove that he did show 'total disregard' for the historical sources.[56] Wallace-Hadrill likewise cited with approval Dumville's paper and Thomas's insistence that Arthur should be removed from 'models of fifth-century Britain'.[57] In that, all three (Dumville, Thomas, Myres) were right. Arthur (d. 537) had nothing to do with Mount 'Badon' in 493 or anything else of the fifth century.

But they went too far. It meant that for nearly forty years Arthur was banished from historical discourse. Lloyd in 1911 understood Arthur's Latin name as that of a man, not a fairy; the Chadwicks in 1932 saw the twelve battle-toponyms as denoting real places, and Celtic princely baptisms as indicating a real hero of the sixth century; Ashe in 1957 and Jackson in 1959 insisted on those battles as genuine, and not some forger's invention. All that counted for nothing. From now on comes a litany of the historical Arthur as (supposedly) irrecoverable. Even *Camlan* was not exempt. Its site was 'impossible to determine'. It need not have been on Hadrian's Wall (with *Camboglanna* taken as Birdoswald, despite Rivet and Smith's earlier acceptance of it as Castlesteads), but anywhere 'throughout Britain'.[58] The editors did not reflect that the choke-point of a Roman fort and gateway is an apt location for conflict; that *Historia Brittonum*'s Vatican recension of 944 has Arthur in North Britain; and that, if *Camlan* had been in Wales, it is strange that the bards knew nothing of it.

The most prominent anti-Arthurian was to be Dr Oliver Padel (b. 1948), writing (after van Hamel, Rees and Rees, Mac Cana) of Arthur the mythical hunter-warrior, like the Finn of Gaelic folklore. He was (we are told) no 'historical' figure of the fifth-sixth centuries, merely a 'pan-Brittonic figure' of wonder-tales.[59] That had the unfortunate result of removing the Twelve Battles and much else from debate by dismissing them as anything actual. Alcock himself then ate humble pie, maintaining that 'the Arthur/Camelot attribution' was a 'reasonable inference' in the 1960s, before 'sustained minimalist criticism' began with Dumville in 1977.[60] At this time attention was drawn to an earlier writer who grappled with knotty evidence: Sir John Price (d. 1555), stoutly defending Geoffrey of Monmouth against the 'calumnies' of Polydore Vergil.[61]

Not much more helpful is the statement in a popular guide that Arthur 'may have had a real original'.[62] After that, Dr Padel, for whom Arthur was a 'legendary war-leader' whose battles 'cannot be identified'.[63] Ken Dark then published careful analysis of Artúr and his namesakes of the fifth-sixth centuries.[64] Compare an aside by Sir Rees Davies (1938-2005) on Arthur, whoever 'he was or was not', in stained glass as All Souls College.[65] Even at Oxford, nobody could explain the champion's identity. Compare too an argument of over five centuries previous. In his account of Gawain, Sir Thomas Malory (d. 1471) actually wrote how 'all men may se the skulle of hym' at Dover Castle; a passage not in his sources.[66] Was Malory troubled by critics, as Caxton would be in 1485? Then, once more, Dr Padel on the Twelve Battles, assuring readers that 'safe identification is impossible for the most part'.[67] In contrast are remarks by a great Cambridge scholar on medieval confidence in Arthur. Geoffrey of Monmouth's inventions 'soon came to lie at the heart of vernacular and even Latin textual culture in England'; Arthur as presented by Geoffrey was 'held to be historically real' and 'no figure of the imagination'.[68]

The fog of negativism chilled (alas) even the work of N. J. Higham (b. 1950). On the battle-list and Welsh battle-poems he opined that, while some took it to 'confer historicity' on Arthur, it was better not to treat the catalogue 'as historical in any modern sense of the word'; and his book closes with an entire section on

'The Rise and Fall of the "Historical" Arthur'.[69] Higham yet studied the material with care, unlike Professor Derek Pearsall (1931-2021), who (mis)informed readers on *Historia Brittonum*'s account of Arthur 'killed in the triumphant and last charge at Mount Badon (516)'.[70] The Artúr of sixth-century Argyll was then discussed in detail, together with the Welsh princess married earlier on into Artúr's family.[71] Although the chapter offers important ammunition against Arthur denial, it had no effective influence. As for those battles, Martin Aurell (following Higham) considered their names 'empruntés à la tradition des bardes' rather than 'inventés'.[72] That (alas) does not get us far. But there was progress on background. In a useful volume, *Camlan* and *Breguoin* and the *Cludwys* (who had Douglas Water within their territory) are correctly marked.[73] Such precision differs from what occurs elsewhere, as when we read how 'it is difficult to speak with any greater certainty about the "historical" Arthur than that he may have been a military leader who succeeded, before his death at the battle of *Camlan*, in delaying the advance of the conquerors.'[74] Better is an archaeological miscellany, especially for discussion of early Christian inscriptions.[75] Their Celtic-Latin texts belong to the Celtic-Latin-Christian world of Arthur himself.

At this point, an epoch-making paper from the Irish Republic. By relating Gildas's allusion (chapter 93) to a *densissima nebula atraque nox*, a thick mist and black night obscuring the whole island of Britain, David Woods of Cork at a stroke dated this text to mid-536 and Mount 'Badon' to 493, with Gildas writing after a volcanic cloud appeared in the northern hemisphere, but before the famine which it produced (on which Gildas is silent).[76] One infers too that Arthur (d. 537) was not present at 'Badon' in 493. More helpful than further dismissal of *Historia Brittonum*'s conflicts as no means 'to establish Arthur's historicity in a recognizable form, let alone distinguish his role and/or his dates.'[77] Books by enthusiastic amateur Arthurians have not so far been cited. Whatever their other merits, they help make us think why we believe what we do; even if few are likely to follow one such volume (by a hospital endocrinologist) in asking 'Re Artù era un veneto?' and then using the resemblance of Venice (Italy) and *Venedotia* or Gwynedd (Wales) to reveal Arthurian sites.[78] As for Professor Charles-Edwards (b. 1943), he is silent on the Historical Arthur or *Camlan* or David Woods's paper of 2010, which (unfortunately) leaves in confusion the dates of 'Badon' and Gildas alike.[79]

Remaining work may be summarized thus. In one study is the assertion on the battle-list that 'THE LOCATIONS OF ALL OF THESE BATTLES ARE UNKNOWN AND UNKNOWABLE.'[80] Dr Padel likewise again declared that 'safe identification is impossible for the most part'.[81] Against this, one amateur scholar made two reasonable points on the annal for 537: its very 'terseness' demonstrates its historical nature; while the other annals refer to 'historical people in historical activities', and so, therefore, will this one.[82] The *mortalitas* of the same entry was a real (and dreadful) event. In 2015 was published a paper (based mainly on Watson's book of 1926) locating every one of the engagements attributed to Arthur, with all but four of them in what is now southern Scotland, with one identification (*Guinnion* = Carwinning, north Ayrshire) the result of a suggestion by Dr Tim Clarkson.[83] Thereafter another paper, developing arguments of David Woods in 2010 for 536-7 as years of a volcanic winter, so that the North British conflicts would probably represent cattle-raids by Arthur and Strathclyders in a time of famine.[84] They made Arthur first a Strathclyde hero, then a legend.

Discussion since then has been thus. The Twelve Battles feature with a caution on them as 'difficult to identify'.[85] They were then the subject of a complete book on the question 'ob es eine historische Person mit Namen Arthur überhaupt gegeben hatte.'[86] Its author's use of photographs and map-inserts (obtained at some expense) make it a model for future researchers on the subject, whatever one thinks of his conclusions. As for earlier controversy, we are reminded by an Oxford monograph that George Buchanan

(1506-82), Scottish humanist, was a stern critic of Geoffrey of Monmouth (much as he was of Franciscans or Mary, Queen of Scots).[87] Simon Esmonde-Cleary proclaims himself 'very sceptical' on the Arthur of history (without giving details on why).[88] Not sceptical at all is another writer, again presenting supposed links between the Veneti of north-east Italy and Welsh *Venedotia* or Gwynedd, a domain 'connected with the dynasty of King Arthur'.[89] Sceptical once more is Nick Higham, despite relaying up-to-date research on Arthur's conflicts.[90] In an entire volume, he never once accepts Arthur as a real person.

Another battle, that of Leland versus Polydore Vergil, has been looked at afresh.[91] Gildas has been edited and translated with unexpected views on the text as not of 536, but 708.[92] Opinions on Arthur as a purely 'legendary' and 'pan-Brittonic' figure occur in a book on the Cornish.[93] Remarks on early Arthurian tradition likewise have nothing on the British commander who fell near Carlisle in 537.[94] Frankest of all is the admission of one editor that 'a putative historical Arthur is not the concern of this volume'.[95] Nothing to be learned there, then. A book of 2020 has chapters on 'Badon' in 493 and *Camlan* in 537.[96] Genealogies with the seventh-century Arthur of West Wales, as also the sixth-century Princess Lluan who found a husband in Scotland, are now re-edited.[97] He and *Camlan* are mentioned too in another collection, also mute on *Camlan*'s site and implications.[98] A further reference to the twelve battles is again silent on their date and location.[99] Whether Arthur should be found on 'historiographical radar' is doubted in a Cambridge textbook.[100] Why?, one wonders. But the writer does not stay for an answer. After that, however, change: for Peter Field of Bangor has declared his belief in Arthur as 'a real person'.[101] So we end with a new era. Earlier scholars (especially Zimmer, Crawford, Bromwich, Dark) will be vindicated. The whole subject (especially for *dux bellorum* as equivalent to Welsh *penteulu*, captain of the royal host) is once more dealt with in a book.[102]

We end by repeating conclusions set out by various writers cited above. Arthur existed, as a commander (not a king) fighting other Britons (not the English) in what are now southern Scotland and northern England; his position as *dux bellorum* is equivalent to Middle Welsh *penteulu* 'captain of the royal host' and has nothing to do with any Roman title; his battles would be on behalf of Strathclyders against their British neighbours in 536-7, and related to cattle-raids during the famine of a volcanic winter; these soon made him a hero in Strathclyde, and then a legend; he did not command cavalry, a form of warfare unknown in Britain of the Dark Ages, as pointed out by Jackson in 1969; nor had he anything to do with the British triumph of 493 over the West Saxons at 'Badon' (or, better, Braydon), in Wiltshire.

POSTSCRIPT. Since the above was written there has come to hand Bernard Mees, *King Arthur and the Languages of Britain* (London, 2025). It is a book of the first importance. While one may disagree with (for example) points in it concerning battle-locations, its author is yet sure of Arthur's historicity, even if observing (in his preface) that he does 'not expect to change the minds of professors who have spent the last thirty years or more telling their students that King Arthur never existed'. Correct. But the rest of us may take notice and scrutinize what he has to say.

Notes

1. William Caxton's preface in Thomas Malory, *Le Morte d'Arthur* (Westmestre, 1485), signatures Ai-iii.

2. John Leland, *Assertio Inclytissimi Arturi, regis Britanniae* (Londini, 1544), fol. 3a.

3. Theophilus Evans, *Drych y Prif Oesoedd* (Y Mwythig, 1716), 92-4.

4. *Annales Cambriae*, ed. John Williams 'Ab Ithel' (London, 1860), 4.

5. Alfred Nutt, *The Celtic Doctrine of Rebirth* (London, 1897), 7.

6. John Rhŷs, *Celtic Britain*, 3rd edn (London, 1904), 236-9.

7. J. E. Lloyd, *A History of Wales* (London, 1911), 125-6.

8. Hugh Williams, *Christianity in Early Britain* (Oxford, 1912), 350.

9. W. J. Watson, *A History of the Celtic Place-Names of Scotland* (Edinburgh, 1926), 354, 363, 366, 383-4, 386-7, 458.

10. E. K. Chambers, *Arthur of Britain* (London, 1927), 130-1, 239.

11. John Lloyd-Jones, *Geirfa Barddoniaeth Gynnar Gymraeg* (Caerdydd, 1931-63), 48, 101, 149.

12. H. M. Chadwick and N. Kershaw Chadwick, *The Growth of Literature: The Ancient Literatures of Europe* (Cambridge, 1932), 155, 161-2.

13. Eilert Ekwall, *The Concise Oxford Dictionary of English Place-Names* (Oxford, 1936), 58-9, 189.

14. R. G. Collingwood and J. N. L. Myres, *Roman Britain and the English Settlements*, 2nd edn (Oxford, 1937), 322.

15. R. J. Thomas, *Enwau Afonydd a Nentydd Cymru* (Caerdydd, 1938), 3-4.

16. *Canu Aneirin*, ed. Ifor Williams (Caerdydd, 1938), 49, 343.

17. J. E. B. Gover, Allen Mawer, F. M. Stenton, *The Place-Names of Wiltshire* (Cambridge, 1939), 11, 40.

18. A. H. Williams, *An Introduction to the History of Wales: Prehistoric Times to 1063 AD* (Cardiff, 1941), 73.

19. *Brut Dingestow*, ed. Henry Lewis (Caerdydd, 1942), 275.

20. T. F. O'Rahilly, *Early Irish History and Mythology* (Dublin, 1946), 362.

21. T. D. Kendrick, *British Antiquity* (London, 1950), 14.

22. K. H. Jackson, *Language and History in Early Britain* (Edinburgh, 1953), 116, 199.

23. Rachel Bromwich, 'The Character of the Early Welsh Tradition', in *Studies in Early British History*, ed. N. K. Chadwick (Cambridge, 1954), 83-136.

24. K. H. Jackson, 'The Britons in Southern Scotland', *Antiquity*, xxix (1955), 77-88.

25. W. S. Churchill, *The History of the English-Speaking Peoples: The Birth of Britain* (London, 1956), 46-7.

26. R. S. Loomis. *Wales and the Arthurian Legend* (Cardiff, 1956), 180.

27. Anon., 'Arthur', in *People: A Volume of the Good, Bad, Great & Eccentric Who Illustrate the Admirable Diversity of Man*, ed. Geoffrey Grigson and C. H. Gibbs-Smith (New York, 1957), 8.

28. Geoffrey Ashe, *King Arthur's Avalon: The Story of Glastonbury* (London, 1957), 74-5.

29. N. K. Chadwick, 'Early Culture and Learning in North Wales', in *Studies in the Early British Church*, ed. N. K. Chadwick (Cambridge, 1958), 29-120.

30. K. H. Jackson, 'The Arthur of History', in *Arthurian Literature in the Middle Ages*, ed. R. S. Loomis (Oxford, 1959), 1-11.

31. Thomas Jones, 'Arthur', in *The Dictionary of Welsh Biography Down to 1940* (London, 1959), 14-15.

32. Nikolai Tolstoy, 'Nennius, Chapter Fifty-Six', *The Bulletin of the Board of Celtic Studies*, xix (1960-2), 118-56.

33. Alwyn Rees and Brinley Rees, *Celtic Heritage: Ancient Tradition in Ireland and Wales* (London, 1962), 70.

34. K. H. Jackson, 'Angles and Britons in Northumbria and Cumbria', in J. R. R Tolkien *et al.*, *Angles and Britons: O'Donnell Lectures* (Cardiff, 1963), 60-84.

35. *Early Welsh Genealogical Tracts*, ed. P. C. Bartrum (Cardiff, 1966), 4, 10, 15.

36. Geoffrey Ashe. 'The Arthurian Fact', in *The Quest for Arthur's Britain*, ed. Geoffrey Ashe (London, 1967), 27-57.

37. Sheppard Frere, *Britannia: A History of Roman Britain* (London, 1967), 382.

38. R. P. C. Hanson, *Saint Patrick: His Origins and Career* (Oxford, 1968), 20.

39. K. H. Jackson, *The Gododdin: The Oldest Scottish Poem* (Edinburgh, 1969), 85-6, 112.

40. Proinsias Mac Cana, *Celtic Mythology* (London, 1970), 115.

41. Leslie Alcock, *Arthur's Britain* (London, 1971), 62, 55, 163.

42. May McKisack, *Medieval History in the Tudor Age* (Oxford, 1971), 57, 95, 97-8, 113, 118, 141.

43. F. M. Stenton, *Anglo-Saxon England*, 3rd edn (Oxford, 1971), 3.

44. Charles Thomas, *Britain and Ireland in Early Christian Times* (London, 1971), 38-42, 117.

45. Leslie Alcock, *'By South Cadbury is that Camelot...': The Excavation of Cadbury Castle 1966–1970* (London, 1972), 193.

46. John Morris, *The Age of Arthur* (London, 1973), 116.

47. John Bannerman, *Studies in the History of Dalriada* (Edinburgh, 1974), 90-1, 99.

48. Peter Hunter Blair, *An Introduction to Anglo-Saxon England*, 2nd edn (Cambridge, 1977), 30.

49. Rachel Bromwich, *Trioedd Ynys Prydein*, 2nd edn (Cardiff, 1978), 274-6, 544-5.

50. A. L. F. Rivet and Colin Smith, *The Place-Names of Roman Britain* (Princeton, 1979), 293-4.

51. *Rhagymadroddion a Chyflwyniadau Lladin 1551-1632*, tr. Ceri Davies (Caerdydd, 1980), 26, 51.

52. Peter Salway, *Roman Britain* (Oxford, 1981), 485, 501.

53. Charles Thomas, *Christianity in Roman Britain to AD 500* (Berkeley, 1981), 245.

54. James Campbell, 'The Lost Centuries: 400-600', in *The Anglo-Saxons*, ed. James Campbell (Oxford, 1982), 20-3, 26-44.

55. John Morris, *Londinium: London in the Roman Empire* (London, 1982), 340.

56. J. N. L. Myres, *The English Settlements* (Oxford, 1986), 15-16.

57. J. M. Wallace-Hadrill, *Bede's 'Ecclesiastical History of the English People'*: *A Historical Commentary* (Oxford, 1988), 21.

58. *Culhwch and Olwen*, ed. Rachel Bromwich and D. Simon Evans (Cardiff, 1992), 84-5.

59. O. J. Padel, 'The Nature of Arthur', *Cambrian Medieval Celtic Studies*, xxvii (1994), 1-31.

60. Leslie Alcock, *Cadbury Castle, Somerset* (Cardiff, 1995), 6.

61. Ceri Davies, *Welsh Literature and the Classical Tradition* (Cardiff, 1995), 61.

62. Norris J. Lacy and Geoffrey Ashe, *The Arthurian Handbook*, 2nd edn (New York, 1997), xiii.

63. O. J. Padel, 'Arthur', in *The Blackwell Encyclopaedia of Anglo-Saxon England*, ed. Michael Lapidge, John Blair, Simon Keynes, Donald Scragg (Oxford, 1999), 48.

64. Ken Dark, 'A Famous Arthur in the Sixth Century?', *Reading Medieval Studies*, xxvi (2000), 77-95.

65. R. R. Davies, *The First English Empire* (Oxford, 2000), 2.

66. Andrew King, *'The Fairie Queene' and Middle English Romance* (Oxford, 2000), 118.

67. O. J. Padel, *Arthur in Medieval Welsh Literature* (Cardiff, 2000), 4.

68. D. H. Green, *The Beginnings of Medieval Romance* (Cambridge, 2002), 172.

69. N. J. Higham, *King Arthur: Myth-Making and History* (London, 2002), 145, 146, 218-66.

70. D. A. Pearsall, *Arthurian Romance* (Oxford, 2003), 3.

71. Ann Dooley, 'Arthur of the Irish', in *Arthurian Literature XXI; Celtic Arthurian Material*, ed. Ceridwen Lloyd-Morgan (Cambridge, 2004), 9-28.

72. Martin Aurell, *La légende du roi Arthur* (Paris, 2007), 84.

73. John T. Koch, *An Atlas for Celtic Studies* (Oxford, 2007), maps 21.2, 21.3.

74. Anon., 'Arthur', in *The Welsh Academy Encyclopaedia of Wales*, ed. John Davies, Nigel Jenkins, Menna Baines, Peredur I. Lynch (Cardiff, 2008), 37-8.

75. *St Ninian and the Earliest Christianity in Scotland*, ed. Jane Murray (Oxford, 2009).

76. David Woods, 'Gildas and the Mystery Cloud of 536-7', *The Journal of Theological Studies*, lxi (2010), 226-34.

77. N. J. Higham, 'The Chroniclers of Early Britain', in *The Arthur of Medieval Latin Literature*, ed. Siân Echard (Cardiff, 2011), 9-25.

78. Piero Favero, *La Dea veneta* (Udine, 2012), 161.

79. Thomas Charles-Edwards, *Wales and the Britons 350-1064* (Oxford, 2013), 217.

80. Guy Halsall, *Worlds of Arthur* (Oxford, 2013), 67.

81. O. J. Padel, *Arthur in Medieval Welsh Literature*, rev. edn (Cardiff, 2013), 3.

82. Flint Johnson, *Evidence of Arthur* (Jefferson, 2014), 17.

83. A. Breeze, 'The Historical Arthur and Sixth-Century Scotland', *Northern History*, lii (2015), 158-81.

84. A. Breeze, 'Arthur's Battles and the Volcanic Winter of 536-537', *Northern History*, liii (2016), 161-72.

85. Tim Clarkson, *Scotland's Merlin* (Edinburgh, 2016), 108.

86. Kurt Liebhard, *Suche nach dem historischen Arthur* (Weissenthurn, 2016), 32.

87. Harriet Archer, *Unperfect Histories: The 'Mirror for Magistrates', 1559-1610* (Oxford, 2017), 57.

88. Simon Esmonde-Cleary, 'Lyonesse', in *Arthur, la mer et la guerre*, ed. Alban Gautier, Marc Rolland, Michelle Szkilnik (Paris, 2017), 15-29.

89. Piero Favero, *King Arthur's Tribe* (Udine, 2017), 43.

90. N. J. Higham, *King Arthur: The Making of the Legend* (New Haven, 2018), 287-8.

91. John J. Thompson, 'Re-Imagining History Through the English Prose Brut Tradition', in *'L'Historia regum Britanniae' et le'Bruts' en Europe: Production, circulation et réception*, ed. Hélène Tétrel and Géraldine Veysseyre (Paris, 2018), 345-73.

92. *Llythyr Gildas a Dinistr Prydain*, ed. Iestyn Daniel (Bangor, 2019), 77, 101.

93. S. J. Drake, *Cornwall, Connectivity, and Identity in the Fourteenth Century* (Woodbridge, 2019), 58-9.

94. Mark Williams, 'Magic and Marvels', in *The Cambridge History of Welsh Literature*, ed. Geraint Evans and Helen Fulton (Cambridge, 2019), 52-72.

95. Ceridwen Lloyd-Morgan and Erich Poppe, 'Introduction', in *Arthur in the Celtic Languages*, ed. Ceridwen Lloyd-Morgan and Erich Poppe (Cardiff, 2019), 1-10.

96. A. Breeze, *British Battles 493-937: Mount Badon to Brunanburh* (London, 2020), 1-24.

97. Ben Guy, *Medieval Welsh Genealogy* (Woodbridge, 2020), 334, 340.

98. Huw Pryce, 'Chronicling and Its Contexts in Medieval Wales', in *The Chronicles of Medieval Wales and the March*, ed. Ben Guy, Georgia Henley, O. W. Jones, Rebecca Thomas (Turnhout, 2020), 5-32.

99. Matthew Strickland, 'Undying Glory', in *Writing Battles*, ed. Rory Naismith, Máire Ní Mhaonaigh, E. A. Rowe (London, 2020), 39-75.

100. Rory Naismith, *Early Medieval Britain* (Cambridge, 2021), 89.

101. P. J. C. Field, 'King Arthur: Hero or Legend?', in *The Arthurian World*, ed. V. Coldham-Fussell, M. Edlich-Mutt, Renée Ward (London, 2022), 25-34.

102. A. Breeze, *The Historical Arthur and the 'Gawain' Poet* (Lanham, 2023), 3-37.

CHAPTER TWO

HOW ARTHUR'S FAME REACHED WALES
FROM NORTH BRITAIN

If the Arthur of history was a North Briton, raiding other Britons during 536-7 in southern Scotland and beyond, how did traditions of him spread? In short, how did the Arthurian legend start? Here again is ground to be broken. Uncertainty on where Arthur lived (or whether he even existed) has numbed real understanding of the question. Yet, if Arthur's Northern identity is secure, the progress of his fame becomes intelligible. It projects light as well upon previous commentators, some of them edging towards the truth, others away from it.

Fundamental here are Northern aspects of sources from Wales: the Middle Welsh text of Aneirin's *Gododdin*, *Historia Brittonum*, *Annales Cambriae*, genealogies. So much appears in a curt Welsh–Latin annal for 537, on *Gueith Camlan, in qua Arthur et Medraut corruere*, 'The Battle of Camlan, in which Arthur and Medrawd fell.'[1] The context is Northern, not Welsh. Had Arthur's death at *Camlan* been in Wales (as some imagine), it would be strange if the Welsh forgot that. Also strange is the obscurity of Medrawd. Nobody in Wales remembered who he was, making it easy for Geoffrey of Monmouth (d. 1155) to blacken his name (although in later Scots tradition his reputation was rather better, as noted below: suggesting that he was remembered in the Scottish Borders, where he will have campaigned with Arthur himself).

Further information comes from Welsh and Irish genealogies. Heinrich Zimmer in 1893 drew attention to 'Arthur' as a name given to Britons and Scots as early as the sixth century, after which it went out of fashion. They included an Artór of Dál Riada (roughly, the Argyll region of Scotland), who was killed in 596 (or 590?), and (from Dyfed, in south-west Wales) an Arthur son of Pedr, active from 600 to 630 or so. Zimmer's observations were soon taken up.[2] They show Arthur as known to the Welsh by about 580, when Pedr of Dyfed called his son after the Northern hero.

This is extraordinary. As early as the sixth century, Arthur was famous in Wales. His legend there was already beginning. It brings us to Sir John Rhŷs (d. 1915), who in the best Oxford manner offered a mixture of the valuable and obtuse. Despite noting Arthur's Seat (a pocket mountain in Edinburgh) and the like in Scotland, he yet regarded Arthur as belonging to all Britons, from Brittany to Cornwall to Strathclyde.[3] This, alas, gets us nowhere. Better was Sir John Lloyd (d. 1947), who from the 'vagueness of Welsh tradition' on Arthur rightly eliminated Wales as a 'theatre of his deeds', but could otherwise do no more than locate his battles as somewhere between Lincolnshire and the English Channel.[4] Hence the scepticism of Hugh Williams (d. 1912). For him, the Arthur of the ninth-century *Historia Brittonum* is a pious warrior-king created by the 'poetic tradition' of Powys and Bangor and 'the Cymry of Cumbria'.[5] Williams correctly saw the context as mythical, not historical. Yet he failed to see how, within that mist of glory, an informed eye can make out rocks of fact.

From the 1920s, gifted philologists began pointing out those facts. William Watson (d. 1948) related Arthur to 'the north' on the basis of Arthur's Seat and other sites, which he thought trustier evidence than the quagmire of the Twelve Battles.[6] His reasoning was sound. Arthur gave his name to places in Scotland; fifth-century southerners like the Ambrosius named by Gildas (493-570) or the Vortigern of *Historia Brittonum* (829-30) did not, despite their renown (as Emrys or Gwrtheyrn) in Wales. Conclusion:

Arthur was a North Briton whose fame travelled south. That is why we find Arthur as a figure of folklore in southern Scotland, unlike Ambrosius or Vortigern, both active in south Britain.

Sir Edmund Chambers (d. 1954) produced a volume full of insights, although he modestly disclaimed any special knowledge of Celtic. For the Twelve Battles, he therefore limited himself to reproducing the passage on them from the admirable edition of Theodor Mommsen (d. 1903), together with the failure of others to make sense of it.[7] In contrast were H. M. Chadwick (d. 1947) and N. K. Chadwick (d. 1972), each an expert on the languages of early Britain, so that their comments have special weight. They drew attention to Welsh copies of Northern genealogies (of Strathclyde rulers and others), demonstrating that *Historia Brittonum* and *Annales Cambriae* have different sources as regards Arthur's battles (because *Camlan* figures in the second, but not the first). They also derived *Historia Brittonum*'s battle-list from a (lost vernacular) 'catalogue poem', like ones in Welsh that trumpet royal victories; and they discussed other material in *Historia Brittonum* on Taliesin and Aneirin as Northern bards active in about 600 CE. That Welsh interest in the history of the 'Old North' they dated to the ninth century, when scholars in Wales used written records 'perhaps mainly from Strathclyde', and in any case no later than about 800 CE. They mentioned too (in puzzled terms) Aneirin's *Gododdin*, related to some 'disastrous battle fought against the English' of Northumbria. As for Arthur, while they agreed with Zimmer on genealogies as proof of his sixth-century fame, they dismissed lore on his battles and so on (in Scotland, Powys, south Britain) as not 'a historical record'.[8] So there is light and dark. While the Chadwicks well understood the Northern aspects of Welsh genealogies and historical texts, they did not grasp that Aneirin's *Gododdin* and the Arthurian battle-list are, once again, Northern documents preserved in Wales.

Quite unlike the commentary by the Chadwicks was the enthusiastic conjecture of R. G. Collingwood (d. 1943) on how

Arthur was a leader entrusted with a Roman 'military command' to combat Germanic invaders up and down Britain.[9] Arthur is not short of legends and Collingwood provided him with a new one. How different was Sir Ifor Williams (d. 1965), whose epoch-making edition of Aneirin's *Gododdin* has a two-fold importance for Arthur. First, Williams proved that the text is of Northern origin, being elegies for warriors of the Gododdin (a British people of Lothian and Tweeddale, whom the Northumbrians finally conquered in 638). Aneirin laments those who fell in an attack on the Northumbrians at *Catraeth* (= Catterick, Yorkshire), perhaps in the year 603. Aneirin's verses, preserved in Middle Welsh form, are thus a further Northern export to Wales. Second, they have a precious allusion to Arthur. Aneirin tells how one grim champion 'glutted ravens' on those that he slew, *ce ni bei ef arthur*, 'though he was not Arthur'.[10] Even if Williams said little here, critics have made up for that. We can say now that it accords with Arthur as a North Briton (even if its terseness on Arthur implies that he was not a Gododdin man. Aneirin would have said far more of him otherwise). It is also evidence for his historicity. Aneirin mentions fighting men by the score, but never anyone mythical.

In the post-war period we again find progress, stasis, relapse. Kenneth Jackson (d. 1991), restrained on Arthur ('nothing useful can be said about him here'), was more forthcoming on Aneirin's *Gododdin* as representing a 'last effort' of northern Britons to 'crush the advancing power of Deira' at Catterick. He referred as well to the victory in 603 of Bernicians over the Scots of Dál Riada.[11] That bloodbath of 'Degsastan' (as Bede calls it in his *Ecclesiastical History*, book one) may have occurred near Dawyck, Upper Tweeddale, where a conspicuous *stan* or monolith remains to this day. The raid on Catterick perhaps belonged to the same campaign, with the Scots and Gododdin making a two-pronged attack on Northumbria. If so, it dates Aneirin's *Gododdin* to 603 or soon after.

Thereafter Wales's links with North Britain received fuller treatment, so that Rachel Bromwich (d. 2010) took Arthur as the 'outstanding instance' of a Northern hero whose feats were later transferred in Wales.[12] Her views kindled the wrath of Kenneth Jackson (her former teacher). Even at the time, in what is (all the same) a classic paper, he wrote icily of how 'philological evidence' did 'little to support' this notion. (Quite untrue, we think.) He was yet clear on other Northern material in *Historia Brittonum*, such as the saga of Urien, who between about 570 and 590 ruled the kingdom of Rheged (east Cumbria and beyond); was praised by Taliesin (some poems survive); and who died by treachery near Lindisfarne, on the Northumberland coast.[13] But Jackson remained implacably opposed to the Arthur of *Historia Brittonum* as also from the 'Old North'.

For a bizarre Welsh transformation of Arthur's identity, we have the (eighth-century?) 'Spoils of Annwfyn', a poem narrating his attack on the Other World.[14] In juxtaposition to such wild tales is modern doubt. Nora Chadwick had cautious remarks on the 'Northern Section' (chapters 57-65) of *Historia Brittonum*, dating its composition to 'the seventh century' and noting how it comes straight after the account of Arthur's battles (chapter 56). But she saw no need to connect the two, the twelve engagements having 'virtually unknown' locations.[15] They could not (she imagined) be proved as northern. This is unfortunate. The 'Northern Section' (chapters 57-65) has high authority, being of the late seventh century, well before compilation of *Historia Brittonum* in 829-30.

If the battle-list were also of the seventh century (or even sixth?), its authority for an Arthur of the 530s would increase. It would take us at a stroke from the ninth century to the seventh. It may have been still older. Forms such as 'Bassas' for *Tarras* (near Car*stairs*?) or 'Linnuis' for *Clutuis* 'men of the Clyde' show corruptions greater than those of the 'Northern History'. The text has also suffered interpolations, with 'Badon' as a spurious addition, for Arthur (d. 537) could not in 493 have besieged West Saxons at a hillfort near Braydon, north Wiltshire.

Jackson (like Nora Chadwick, his ex-teacher), likewise rejected a link between the battle-list and the 'Northern History' following it, declaring further that nothing was certain about the historical Arthur, 'not even his existence'; Jackson yet admitted 'certain possibilities, even probabilities' for him as a real person, including that lost 'panegyric poem' on his Twelve Battles and other oral literature.[16] No word, however, on the North as scene of those triumphs. Despite that, Thomas Jones (d. 1972) was confident on Arthur as a real person, even if one who by the ninth century was the subject of 'many folktales' in Wales.[17] One of those tales is known from *Historia Brittonum*, on a stone in mid-Powys with a (supposed) footprint of a hound, made while Arthur was hunting the boar Twrch Trwyth. The motif is a common international one.[18] So the contrast between such popular fantasies and the (vanished) battle-poem's circumstantial detail is obvious. By 830, then, Arthur was protagonist of a Welsh saga, which is known in full from the epic of 'Culhwch and Olwen', composed in the 1090s. Whereas this *Mabinogion* tale alludes to place-names galore, all known to the Welsh, the names of Arthur's battles were so unfamiliar that some have been corrupted by scribes (such as 'Linnuis' or Lindsey, a blundering version of *Clutuis* 'men of the Clyde'). They will be genuine historical testimony (as even Jackson conceded) and not invented; they will be from North Britain, on which the Welsh displayed both curiosity and vagueness.

In another classic paper, Jackson gave expert analysis of *Historia Brittonum*'s chapters 57-65. We can still learn much from his study, especially on his attitude to Arthur, because he rejected chapter 56 as 'probably not part of the Northern History', having convinced himself that its matter was not demonstrably from North Britain, unlike that of 57-65, based on a seventh-century chronicle which perhaps incorporated notes 'for the sixth and early part of the seventh century' by Rhun (son of the Urien Rheged praised by Taliesin in the 580s), a cleric who in 627 (although Bede ignores his presence) baptized Edwin of Northumbria.[19] If, as we argue, Arthur's combats lay between Forth and Clyde and the Wall of Hadrian, it suggests that the battle-list was of similar early date; even if one writer added to it 'Badon' (= Braydon, Wiltshire), a British victory of 493 in which Arthur (d. 537) had no part.

Verses cataloguing victories of Cynan Garwyn, father of Selyf (d. 616?), bring us close to the structure and vocabulary of *Historia Brittonum*'s ghost-poem.[20] As for Arthur of Dyfed (580?-630?), whose father admired the northern Arthur (and whose great-grandfather Vorteporix was in 536 denounced by Gildas), he now figures in a convenient handbook.[21] The list of Twelve Battles is also translated with the remark on them as 'likely to be genuine' (which is true) and probably 'widespread' (which is false).[22] There is a lesson in other Northern texts, the sixth-century poems by Taliesin on Urien: Taliesin never mentions Arthur, implying that men of Rheged had no love of him; yet Brewyn (the Roman fort at High Rochester, Northumberland) is alluded to. This is singular, because *Historia Brittonum* texts at Rome and Paris cite it to locate 'Agned', Arthur's eleventh conflict.[23] It is yet another Northern symptom in *Historia Brittonum*. One notes too how, High Rochester being in Gododdin territory, it is small wonder if they did not hero-worship Arthur, who will have raided their territory as he did that of Rheged.

If Arthur was one formidable adversary, so was Kenneth Hurlstone Jackson; and one of the last stones hurled by him was at Rachel Bromwich, erstwhile his pupil. In his translation of Aneirin's *Gododdin* he made two points. One we accept, that the text of the elegies reached Wales 'from Strathclyde', as did the 'Northern History' and genealogies already discussed, all part of a Welsh ninth-century 'particular interest' in the Old North. (John Koch in 1997 was to say much more on this.) The other we deny, where Jackson (echoing Sir John Rhŷs) found 'no logic whatever' in using Aneirin's aside on Arthur 'to support the theory that he was a

Northern leader', he being 'national hero of the entire British people, from Scotland to Brittany.'[24] But our locating of Arthur's campaigning in North Britain will flatten that. Nor did Jackson ever perceive that Aneirin's Arthur is a professional killer (respected even by his foes), quite unlike the legendary hunter or pious crusader or raider of the Other World in later Welsh tradition. The line by Aneirin (dating from 603?) has an authenticity or credibility absent from later accounts, both ecclesiastical and secular.

In an influential volume, Leslie Alcock (an archaeologist) made a game attempt to deal with the historical texts. While conceding that the battle-catalogue might belong to the 'Northern British History', he still considered a 'firm answer' unlikely; and, even if a northern provenance were proved, that 'would not in itself make Arthur a Northern Briton', because the 'History' contains reference to Maelgwn (d. 547) and Cadwallon (d. 633), both of Gwynedd.[25] His points were reasonable. But most of them must now go. All the same, while the Twelve Battles passage will ultimately be from Strathclyde, it has suffered corruption and tampering, with Northern place-names misunderstood, 'Badon' added, and the whole wrenched from the context of North Britain into that of repelling Saxon invaders. Finally, while it might perhaps have come together with the 'Northern History', it was surely no actual part of it. Its textual history would be separate. Hence the corruption of its toponyms, when those of the 'History' are well preserved. They were discussed by Ifor Williams, who yet steered clear of chapter 56's philological minefield.[26] On that, he remained silent.

Other Welsh interest in the 'Old North' is seen in the annals. If *Historia Brittonum* is of Gwynedd, the annals are of greater Dyfed, where a chronicle incorporating Arthurian and other information from North Britain was started at St Davids in the late eighth century. Despite many a 'close parallel' between the annals and *Historia Britttonum*, they 'used independently' their common source. Neither was 'directly derived' from the other.[27] These conclusions of Kathleen Hughes (d. 1977) tally with those of Nora Chadwick, as (for instance) on how *Camlan* in 537 was present in one text only. If Leslie Alcock was a (good) archaeologist posing as a historian, John Morris (d. 1977) was a professional classicist and (too good) historical novelist. Arthur as Britain's last Roman emperor (developed after Collingwood), shows how unbridled imagination will lead a good scholar wrong with confidence. So we learn little from his statement on chapter 56 as from 'a poem that was already old'.[28] In contrast are careful entries on Artúr (d. 596?), prince of Dál Riada in Gaelic western Scotland, and Domnall Brecc (d. 642?), king of Dál Riada. The former indicates the lustre of the name 'Arthur'.

The latter was killed (near Falkirk) by Strathclyders, whose bards produced a grim stanza on how 'ravens gnawed' the late king's head. Surviving as an interpolation in Aneirin's *Gododdin*, it implies that the entire text was transmitted to Wales via Strathclyde, picking up this verse on the way.[29]

Rachel Bromwich rightly described Arthur as a Northerner whom tradition relocated in Wales (like Taliesin the poet, or Tristan, lover of Isolde); and wrongly as fighting the Angles of east Yorkshire and as possessing a name to do with Welsh *arth* 'bear'.[30] He never fought anywhere near the Humber; his name is of pure Latin origin, from *Artorius* (as Jackson pointed out, after Rhŷs and others). Problems of Aneirin's *Gododdin* as a genuine North British document (on a noble defeat of 603?) are examined by Thomas Charles-Edwards, who finds that while 'historical arguments' show it as 'authentic', they conflict with linguistic ones, its texts having in transmission been thoroughly 'modernised'.[31] (But John Koch was to challenge that in 1997.) A convenient version of the 'Northern History' in *Historia Brittonum* may be noted.[32] It does not include the chapter 56 before it, evidently felt to have a separate origin.

The quandary of historians on *Historia Brittonum* and early poetry was indicated by Wendy Davies, writing of how much in the first was 'not yet sufficiently understood' and much of the second remained 'exceptionally uncertain in many respects'.[33] Such were attitudes in the early 1980s, as with Professor David N. Dumville (1949-2024), who described *Historia Brittonum* (for example) as 'a pseudo-historical work', so that (he declared) the political context of work by Taliesin and Aneirin 'effectively eludes our grasp'.[34] All the same, wholesale transfer to Wales of traditions on Urien or Taliesin or Llywarch the Old or others from North Britain is clear enough.[35] Arthur will be of their number.

Professor Dumville's scepticism found a disciple in Dr Oliver Padel (b. 1948), who thought that 'it is unnecessary to postulate a historical person' as Arthur, who is better taken as purely legendary, a 'pan-Brittonic figure of local wonder-tales'.[36] Once again, the universal Arthur of Rhŷs in 1904 or Jackson in 1969. No Northern provenance. Dumville's 'sustained minimalist criticism of the historicity of Arthur' impacted Leslie Alcock, making him eat humble pie on the whole subject; he also took seriously Dumville's notions on Aneirin's *Gododdin* as composed 'around the middle of the sixth century'.[37] That makes no historical sense. In about 550, the Northumbrians were no threat. By 603 and the bloody English victory of 'Degsastan' (near Dawyck in Upper Tweeddale?), it was another story.

Information on sixth- and seventh-century princes called after Arthur is set out in an excellent paper.[38] In the later sixth century, the feats of Arthur (d. 537) were surely sung not just in Strathclyde but Dál Riada and West Wales; and then faded. Why that happened is yet left unexplained.[39] More on this (and the North-South movement of tradition) when we come to 2013 and later statements on the question. Nor does Professor N. H. Higham budge from disbelief in Arthur. Verses on Arthur's twelve conflicts are attributed to a poet 'writing in Gwynedd'. (Why a Gwynedd man and not a North Briton is not explained.) The list is then termed 'impenetrable' and thus 'cannot be treated as historical'.[40] Higham's doubts emerge again in French guise, as in his relating

Arthur 'avec l'Exode et le Livre de Josué' and their deeds of war.[41] But it is no substitute for genuine source criticism.

Northern symptoms appear all the same on a useful map, with (editorial hesitation notwithstanding) the Arthurian *Camlan* (in Cumbria) and *Brewyn* (in Northumberland) correctly marked.[42] *Camlan* is in *Annales Cambriae*, *Brewyn* in *Historia Brittonum*, so that each is an independent witness; which is significant. James Fraser bolsters the North British cause by relating sixth-century events in *Historia Brittonum*'s 'Northern Chronicle' to those of 'panegyric poetry' by Taliesin.[43]

Four books of 2010-11 indicate the continuing issues. While Arthur is never mentioned in the first, places linked with Urien are. His rule over late-sixth-century Cumbria sparked conflicts with both Strathclyders and Northumbrians.[44] So the poems and chronicles on Urien will be historical (for all the doubts of some) and Northern.

The second book has an unexceptionable account of *Historia Brittonum*.[45] The third cites one writer's belief on Taliesin's 'The Battle of Gwen Ystrad' as of the eleventh century, not the sixth.[46] This can be given short shrift, the bard having detailed knowledge of places near Winster, Cumbria, of no interest to a late forger.

In similar vein are attempts to discredit *Historia Brittonum* and *Annales Cambriae*, because the 'rhetorical style' of the former will (supposedly) 'count against' its historicity on Arthur; while the latter, if 'arguably' containing Northern sources, will (allegedly) hardly be 'chronologically accurate' on Arthur's death in 537.[47] That even though it is perfectly accurate on the British and Irish famine (not 'plague') of 537 (as pointed out in 2010 by David Woods of Cork). Although a fourth writer naturally (given his subject) has almost nothing on the present matter, he does show how Strathclyde legends of hermit-sages influenced Welsh concepts of Merlin.[48] (On which see the next chapter.)

An Oxford volume has careful analysis of Northern material in *Annales Cambriae* and *Historia Brittonum*, including Arthur's battles.[49] But nothing on Arthur as a sixth-century warrior. Not careful is another Oxford book, with comments on possible 'snippets of sixth-century fact' in *Historia Brittonum* that are supposedly yet 'impossible now to disentangle' from the 'propaganda' and 'myth' around them.[50] Its Twelve Battles are again marginalized as (allegedly) having a 'legendary quality', as does the allusion to Arthur in Aneirin's *Gododdin*.[51] In a collection on how Dark-Age Scotland was perceived in Wales is much on Taliesin and Aneirin, plus the 'historical Arthur' as amongst the 'casualities' of 1970s revisionism.[52] A conclusion not difficult to refute.

The North Britons appear in a study by Tim Clarkson, who (with reason) questions various orthodoxies, even if he still shares the prevailing lack of confidence in the sources. The poems of Taliesin are 'too late to be used' for valid historical enquiry; the Urien praised by the bard cannot be 'associated with any place on the modern map'.[53] Poet and ruler (unjustifiably) vanish in Cumbrian mist. In 2015, some such mists were (?) dispelled when Arthur's genuine battles were given locations between Forth and Tyne.[54]

Amongst consequences is one for Aneirin's *Gododdin*, where its allusion to Arthur acquires a pointed sense. He will be a Northern hero in a Northern poem. That counts against scepticism relayed by Dr Clarkson, on how nothing in the *Gododdin* text need predate 'the ninth century'.[55] Not so. Arthur figures there not as the pious wonder-worker of the ninth-century *Historia Brittonum*, but as an effective killer, admired grudgingly even by his *Gododdin* foes. It underlines the difficulties in challenging orthodoxies. A long analysis of *Historia Brittonum* includes rejection of the battle-list as in no way 'a record of historical events' and thus 'neither near-contemporary nor authoritative'.[56] Why? If it is not archaic and thus 'authorititive', we should not here find obscure places in Scotland itemized; their very obscurity underlined by scribal corruption of forms; or later interpolations of the 'monkish' kind. Implication: our material is, in essence, early and Northern and secular. That is why Welsh monks of the ninth century consistently misunderstood it.

An important study of 1997 by John T. Koch is summarized by Helen Fulton. It can be modified on the basis of what we say above. Aneirin's laments for the fallen at *Catraeth* or Catterick (in 603, when Dál Riadans fought Northumbrians at 'Degsastan' on the Upper Tweed?) were for more than a century commemorated orally. A written version then 'must have existed' in Strathclyde from before 638 (when the *Gododdin* were finally conquered by Northumbrians). One such written text reached Wales 'around 655 or 656' and another in the 870s, the latter surviving as the more (not less) 'archaic' stratum in the Book of Aneirin.[57]

By analogy, the battle-list in *Historia Brittonum* may thus have reached Wales in the seventh century as an actual poem circulating in Wales, rather than as a Latin synopsis in the ninth (even if the point can, perhaps, not be proved either way). As for the Gododdin hero who glutted ravens with his foes 'though he was not Arthur', Koch is cited again on the verse as no 'interpolation'. The words are Aneirin's.[58] Arthur died in 537; by 603, it seems, a poet thought him a fighting man *sans pareil*. Almost all of this is progress. Aneirin's verses (of 603?) were, apparently, read in Wales of the 650s. That puts them more firmly within the realm of the historical, with a written copy existing close to the events described in it.

Less helpful is comment on the British victory of 'Badon' (an error for 'Braydon') in 516 (an error for '493') as won by Arthur (who never came near the place) carrying the Cross of Christ on his shoulders (when he did no such thing). This is what we read in *Annales Cambriae*, and it is related to the statement in *Historia Brittonum* on how Arthur at the fortress of *Guinnion* (which Tim Clarkson regards as Carwinning, a hillfort near Dalry in southwest Scotland) bore on his shoulders an image of Mary, Mother of God. Quoting a 2015 paper by Ben Guy on *Historia Brittonum* as 'pseudohistory', the authors relate these twin allusions to symbols on 'sixth-century Byzantine' shields.[59] This may be so. But it is a pity that they said nothing on the correct date or site of 'Badon' or *Guinnion*, or Arthur's relation to each. It would show the texts as more historical than imagined. There is relapse too in a 534-page study of genealogies, including ones from Strathclyde, as also that of Arthur son of Pedr in West Wales.[60] But no mention of what that might mean for Arthur. Unfortunate too are expressions in a student handbook on whether Arthur can be placed on 'the historiographical radar' at all.[61] Such views block discussion on how Arthur's fame spread. Still worse is disparagement of those 'attempting to historicize King Arthur'.[62]

After all this, Peter Field of Bangor then strode to the rescue with his belief on how the early evidence 'suggests that Arthur was a real person'.[63] As for the 'Northern History' in *Historia Brittonum*, there is a professional account of it in another volume (if with some errors, such as placing *Maserfelth* in 642 at Oswestry in Shropshire, and not at Forden, Powys).[64] Although Arthur never figures in the last book, it still provides a basis on which to build. There is also now an extended account of Arthur's raids in what are now southern Scotland and northern England.[65]

Our survey is at an end. It allows these conclusions on Arthur and diffusion of his renown. Over the centuries, the Britons of Wales never forgot their kinsfolk of North Britain. Arthur fell in 537, after a spectacular war-record during a terrible famine. In about 580, Pedr of Dyfed called his son after this valiant commander. In the 650s, Aneirin's *Gododdin* was read in Wales, its text including reference to Arthur, fighting man. In the 790s, annals were copied (from Northern and other sources) at St Davids, with (false) ascription of the British victory at 'Badon' in 516 (*recte*, 493) to Arthur, and (correct) mention of his death in 537 at *Camlan* on the Wall of Hadrian. In 829 or 830, compilers in Gwynedd assembled legendary material on him from the Powys region, together with an archaic account of his victories, placed before a seventh-century 'Northern Chronicle'. Nearly three centuries after his death, we discover Arthurian fact and fiction therein well contrasted. On the one hand is the Arthurian legend, assuming its standard form. He now belongs to Wales as a hunter, a protagonist of saga, a raider on the Other World, a saintly Christian in combat, the victor of 'Badon'. On the other, still faintly be seen, is Arthurian fact, of his victories at places in North Britain, his status as *dux bellorum* or *penteulu* ('chief of the royal warband'), his fighting for some kings and against others, and his eventual death on the Roman Wall.

A final point. What were the sources of *Historia Brittonum*'s chapter 56, and how were they transmitted? It is certainly of Northern origin. Only a North British bard, perhaps of the sixth century, would know the circumstances of Arthur's feats. But the material hardly came to ninth-century Gwynedd together with the 'Northern History'. Its toponyms are more corrupt than those there; it relates Arthur to 'Badon' in south Britain, a subject of small interest to Strathclyders. The corruptions and interpolations instead indicate a Strathclyde text reaching Wales at an early date. (If it had come from the North in the ninth century, Strathclyders would have preserved its name-forms better, including one on themselves as *Clutuis* or *Cludwys*, 'people of the Clyde'.) It seems that a poem on Arthur reached Wales early on, was copied and miscopied, and was (much later) put into Latin guise, complete with bogus reference to Saxons and 'Bradon' and an image of the Blessed Virgin on Arthur's shoulders and his slaughter of foes by the hundred. They would be due to Welsh monks and not any Strathclyde bard. In this, too, then, we see how the Welsh took on Arthur the North Briton, and sped his legend on its long and fabulous course.

Notes

1. *Annales Cambriae*, ed. John Williams 'Ab Ithel' (London, 1860), 4.

2. Alfred Nutt, *The Celtic Doctrine of Rebirth* (London, 1897), 7.

3. John Rhŷs, *Celtic Britain*, 3rd edn (London, 1904), 237-8.

4. J. E. Lloyd, *A History of Wales* (London, 1911), 126.

5. Hugh Williams, *Christianity in Early Britain* (Oxford, 1912), 351.

6. W. J. Watson, *The History of the Celtic Place-Names of Scotland* (Edinburgh, 1926), 129, 208-9.

7. E. K. Chambers, *Arthur of Britain* (London, 1927), 168-204, 238-9.

8. H. M. Chadwick and N. K. Chadwick, *The Growth of Literature: The Ancient Literatures of Europe* (Cambridge, 1932), 151-72.

9. R. G. Collingwood and J. N. L. Myres, *Roman Britain and the English Settlements*, 2nd edn (Oxford, 1937), 321, 322.

10. *Canu Aneirin*, ed. Ifor Williams (Caerdydd, 1938), 49.

11. K. H. Jackson, *Language and History in Early Britain* (Edinburgh, 1953), 116, 199, 212, 213.

12. Rachel Bromwich, 'The Character of the Early Welsh Tradition', in *Studies in Early British History*, ed. N. K. Chadwick (Cambridge, 1954), 83-136.

13. K. H. Jackson, 'The Britons in Southern Scotland', *Antiquity*, xxix (1955), 77-88.

14. R. S. Loomis, *Wales and the Arthurian Legend* (Cardiff, 1956), 131.

15. N. K. Chadwick, 'Early Culture and Learning in North Wales', in *Studies in the Early British Church*, ed. N. K. Chadwick (Cambridge, 1958), 29-120.

16. K. H. Jackson, 'The Arthur of History', in *Arthurian Literature in the Middle Ages*, ed. R. S. Loomis (Oxford, 1959), 1-11.

17. Thomas Jones, 'Arthur', in *The Dictionary of Welsh Biography* (London, 1959), 61-2.

18. K. H. Jackson, *The International Popular Tale and Early Welsh Tradition* (Cardiff, 1961), 117.

19. K. H. Jackson, 'On the Northern British Section in Nennius', in *Celt and Saxon*, ed. N. K. Chadwick (Cambridge, 1963), 20-62.

20. I. Ll. Foster, 'The Emergence of Wales', in *Prehistoric and Early Wales*, ed. I. Ll. Foster and Glyn Daniel (London, 1965), 213-35.

21. *Early Welsh Genealogical Tracts*, ed. P. C. Bartrum (Cardiff, 1966), 10.

22. Geoffrey Ashe, 'The Arthurian Fact', in *The Quest for Arthur's Britain*, ed. Geoffrey Ashe (London, 1968), 27-57.

23. *The Poems of Taliesin*, ed. Ifor Williams (Dublin, 1968), 86.

24. K. H. Jackson, *The Gododdin: The Oldest Scottish Poem* (Edinburgh, 1969), 65, 112.

25. Leslie Alcock, *Arthur's Britain* (London, 1971), 83.

26. Ifor Williams, *The Beginnings of Welsh Poetry* (Cardiff, 1972), 42-3, 51-3, 72-3.

27. Kathleen Hughes, 'The Welsh Latin Chronicles', *Proceedings of the British Academy*, lix (1973), 233-58.

28. John Morris, *The Age of Arthur* (London, 1973), 116.

29. John Bannerman, *Studies in the History of Dalriada* (Edinburgh, 1974), 90-1, 99-103.

30. Rachel Bromwich, *Trioedd Ynys Prydein*, 2nd edn (Cardiff, 1978), 274-7, 544-5.

31. T. M. Charles-Edwards, 'The Authenticy of the *Gododdin*', in *Astudiaethau ar yr Hengerdd*, ed. Rachel Bromwich and R. Brinley Jones (Cardiff, 1978), 44-71.

32. *English Historical Documents c. 500-1042*, ed. Dorothy Whitelock, 2nd edn (London, 1979), 261-3.

33. Wendy Davies, *Wales in the Early Middle Ages* (Leicester, 1982), 206, 210.

34. D. N. Dumville, 'Early Welsh Poetry: Problems of Historicity', in *Early Welsh Poetry*, ed. B. F. Roberts (Aberystwyth, 1988), 1-16.

35. Jenny Rowland, *Early Welsh Saga Poetry* (Cambridge, 1990), 75-119.

36. O. J. Padel, 'The Nature of Arthur', *Cambrian Medieval Celtic Studies*, xxvii (1994), 1-31.

37. Leslie Alcock, *Cadbury Castle, Somerset* (Cardiff, 1995), 6, 119.

38. Ken Dark, 'A Famous Arthur in the Sixth Century?', *Reading Medieval Studies*, xxvi (2000), 77-95.

39. O. J. Padel, *Writers of Wales: Arthur in Medieval Welsh Literature* (Cardiff, 2000).

40. N. J. Higham, *King Arthur: Myth-Making and History* (London, 2002), 145, 146.

41. Martin Aurell, *La Légende du roi Arthur* (Paris, 2007), 84.

42. J. T. Koch, *An Atlas for Celtic Studies* (Oxford, 2007), map 21.3.

43. J. E. Fraser, *From Caledonia to Pictland: Scotland to 795* (Edinburgh, 2009), 126.

44. Tim Clarkson, *The Men of the North* (Edinburgh, 2010), 74-5.

45. E. D. Kennedy, '*Historia Brittonum*', in *The Encyclopedia of the Medieval Chronicle*, ed. Graeme Dunphy (Leiden, 2010), 790-1.

46. Mark Williams, *Fiery Shapes* (Oxford, 2010), 78-9.

47. N. J. Higham, 'The Chroniclers of Early Britain', in *The Arthur of Medieval Latin Literature*, ed. Siân Echard (Cardiff, 2011), 9-25.

48. Patrick Sims-Williams, *Irish Influence on Medieval Welsh Literature* (Oxford, 2011), 15.

49. T. M. Charles-Edwards, *Wales and the Britons 350-1064* (Oxford, 2013), 353, 355.

50. Guy Halsall, *Worlds of Arthur: Facts and Fictions of the Dark Ages* (Oxford, 2013), 72.

51. O. J. Padel, *Writers of Wales: Arthur in Medieval Welsh Literature*, rev edn (Cardiff, 2013), 4, 6.

52. John T. Koch, 'Waiting for Gododdin', in *Beyond the Gododdin*, ed. Alex Woolf (St Andrews, 2014), 177-204.

53. Tim Clarkson, *Strathclyde and the Anglo-Saxons in the Viking Age* (Edinburgh, 2014), 28, 29.

54. A. Breeze, 'The Historical Arthur and Sixth-Century Scotland', *Northern History*, lii (2015), 158-81.

55. Tom Clarkson, *Scotland's Merlin* (Edinburgh, 2016), 29.

56. N. J. Higham, *King Arthur: The Making of the Legend* (New Haven, 2018), 188, 189.

57. Helen Fulton, 'Britons and Saxons', in *The Cambridge History of Welsh Literature*, ed. Geraint Evans and Helen Fulton (Cambridge, 2019), 27-51.

58. Nerys Ann Jones, 'Arthurian References in Early Welsh Poetry', in *Arthur in the Celtic Languages*, ed. Ceridwen Lloyd-Morgan and Erich Poppe (Cardiff, 2019), 15-34.

59. K. Dark and C. Dark, 'Carrying the Cross in *Annales Cambriae*', *Studia Celtica*, liv (2000), 75-80.

60. Ben Guy, *Medieval Welsh Genealogy* (Woodbridge, 2020), 334.

61. Rory Naismith, *Early Medieval Britain* (Cambridge, 2021), 89.

62. S. J. Joyce, *The Legacy of Gildas* (Woodbridge, 2022), 5.

63. P. J. C. Field, 'King Arthur: Hero or Legend?', in *The Arthurian World*, ed. V. Coldham-Fussell, M. Edlich-Muth, Renée Ward (London, 2022), 25-34.

64. Rebecca Thomas, *History and Identity in Early Medieval Wales* (Cambridge, 2022), 78-9, 140-6.

65. A. Breeze, *The Historical Arthur and the 'Gawain' Poet* (Lanham, 2023), 3-37.

66. A. Breeze, 'Who Was King Arthur's Sir Modred?', *RILCE*, xxxix/1 (2023), 167-94.

CHAPTER THREE

WHO WAS MERLIN?

Arthur existed; Merlin did not. The Celtic sorcerer is pure legend. So we ask here who this famed non-person was and how all the fabrications on him come about.

We start in the 1840s with a dictionary of Welsh topography. It has much on Merlin and Carmarthen. The town is 'said to have been the birthplace of the celebrated Merlin, or Ambrosius, whose exploits were the subjects of the romances of earlier ages'; his mother was a local princess, but he allegedly took 'the name of Merddyn, or Merlin, from the place of his nativity' and spent much time in a nearby wood 'still called Merlin's Grove'; his skills in such sciences as mathematics and astronomy supposedly 'caused him to be regarded as a magician in the dark age in which he lived'.[1] That puts Merlin firmly in West Wales. A surprise, then, to read in Welsh-Latin annals of the Battle of *Arfderydd* in 573, when 'Merlinus insanus effectus est'.[2] *Arfderydd* was nowhere near Carmarthen. One wonders too how Merlin came to be in armed conflict, and why this information should appear first in a National Archives manuscript of about 1300, when it is absent from the earlier version in London, British Library, MS Harley 3859, copied in about 1100. We shall argue that it is a figment added by a scribe too much influenced by Geoffrey of Monmouth's forgeries.

In the early twentieth century, Sir John Rhŷs of Oxford said more on Carmarthen, making a point fundamental to Merlin's legend. The place-name, or specifically the -*marthen* part of it, is from British *Moridunum* 'sea fort, stronghold by the sea'.[3] In Bangor, the young Ifor Williams (editing the *Mabinogion* tale of Maxen Wledig) also related the name of Carmarthen or (in Welsh) *Caerfyrddin* to ancient *Moridunum* 'sea-fort'.[4]

Now for another comment on Merlin. He was believed to be a 'Strathclyde Briton' associated with North British rulers of the 570s; he is yet 'more mythical' than the bards Taliesin or Aneirin, his supposed contemporaries; unlike them, he does not figure in the ninth-century *Historia Brittonum*; and poems attributed to him are (at least in part) 'evidently late'.[5] So his dossier is suspect. Sir John Lloyd was even more sceptical. Observing that Merlin, unlike Taliesin or Aneirin, is not named in *Historia Brittonum* as a North British bard in the sixth century, he regarded his whole story as having 'a suspiciously mythical air' despite its fame in early Wales.[6] So Lloyd was a doubter. Ifor Williams, in an edition of Dafydd ap Gwilym and other fourteenth-century poets, then described Merlin as a supposed contemporary of Taliesin in about the year 600; later tradition made him out as a magician and prophet at the court of King Arthur.[7] Nothing on him as definitely historical, though.

After two scholars in Bangor, one from England. Sir Edmund Chambers, while claiming no special knowledge of the Celtic languages, wrote a serious and useful book on Arthur, where he said this on the fictions cooked up about Merlin by Geoffrey of Monmouth (d. 1155). For Chambers, Merlin was 'wholly a creation of Geoffrey's active brain', even if this was a 'hard saying' for Celticists who clung to the idea of his having really existed. Chambers pressed his point for no Merlin previous-to-Geoffrey as follows. Merlin's name 'is untraceable in any assured pre-Galfredian document' such as *Historia Brittonum* (ninth century), the Mabinogion tale of *Culhwch and Olwen* (eleventh century), or the *Four Branches of the Mabinogi* (early twelfth century). As for verse prophecies in the (thirteenth-century) Black Book of Carmarthen or (of about 1400) the Red Book of Hergest, these may postdate Geoffrey. Even the archaic dialogue (in the Black Book) of Merlin and Taliesin might be later than him. No confidence can be built on a reference to Merlin in the Welsh triads. As for Geoffrey's placing of Merlin 'at the gates of Carmarthen', Chambers thought that proved nothing. In short, he regarded Merlin as an invention of Geoffrey which was then taken up by the Welsh.[8]

In Cambridge, however, the Chadwicks used inconvenient facts to puncture the bold statements of Chambers, whom they yet with reason called a 'most careful and judicious' scholar. They made these comments. There is no vernacular life of Merlin or Myrddin, as there is for Taliesin (the wonder-tale of his encounters with the witch Ceridwen and King Maelgwn of Gwynedd). Instead is the Latin poem *Vita Merlini* by Geoffrey of Monmouth, and they were crisp on it. It is 'worthless for historical purposes'. What is said on Merlin in Geoffrey's *History* is 'likewise worthless'. Treating the whole question at length, they concluded that traditions of Merlin as a prophet predate Geoffrey, who (like Nostradamus) concocted obscure prophecies taken seriously for centuries. The Chadwicks hence defined Merlin as a Welsh seer connected with Carmarthen. It was Geoffrey who gratuitously identified him with the fifth-century hero Ambrosius Aurelius, also accepting traditions of him as the North British man-of-the-woods Lailoken, a warrior allegedly driven mad at the Battle of *Arfderydd* or Arthuret in 573. Of special interest in this context is discussion by the Chadwicks of *Cyfoesi*, a dialogue (in the Red Book of Hergest) of Merlin and his sister, which at their time of writing lacked an accessible translation. The Chadwicks noted references in its oldest part (of about 950?) to *Arfderydd* and other aspects of North Britain, together with additions alluding to twelfth-century politics.[9] In their view, thanks to Geoffrey, three people have been turned into one: the fifth-century Ambrosius Aurelianus of southern Britain, the sixth-century Lailoken of North Britain, and the legendary Merlin of Carmarthen, Wales.

The lucid analysis of the Chadwicks gained acceptance only slowly. In discussion of the Book of Taliesin as one of Wales's 'Four Ancient Books', Sir Idris Bell first styled Merlin a poet of the late sixth century, like Taliesin, but then 'if a real person at all' as a warrior who lost his wits at the Battle of *Arfderydd*, in 573.[10] In his edition of the seventh-century *Gododdin* (of 603, year of failed Celtic attacks on Northumbria?), Sir Ifor Williams took its reference to Merlin as 'the oldest allusion to the early poet'.[11] Later on, he was more cautious. In a classic study he said nothing on Merlin as an early bard, unlike Taliesin or Aneirin. However, in his account of *Armes Prydein*, 'The Prophecy of Britain', written (we believe) in 940 and foretelling a Welsh triumph over the English (humiliated that year at *Lego* or Leicester), we hear that all will be well, for 'Merlin (Myrddin) says so!' Praise of St David in the same poem points to origins in south-west Wales.[12] In the 1940s, then, Sir Ifor Williams proved that Merlin enjoyed fame as a prophet two hundred years before Geoffrey of Monmouth. Even so, the idea of Merlin the poet died hard. Listing the names of the earliest Welsh or Cumbric bards, John Lloyd-Jones still considered him as perhaps court-poet to Gwenddolau, the Northern ruler defeated at *Arfderydd*, near Carlisle, in 573.[13]

An advance came in 1951 with Jarman's edition of the *Colloquy of Merlin and Taliesin* in the Black Book of Carmarthen. He dated its language to the second half of the eleventh century. He also cited an 1892 paper of Egerton Phillimore on how the name of *Myrddin* or Merlin derives from that of *Caerfyrddin* or Carmarthen.[14] Together with *Armes Prydein* as a work of 940, he confirmed that Merlin predates Geoffrey, who, aware of him as a prophet, linked him with both Ambrosius Aurelianus (victor, it seems, in 493 at 'Mount Badon' or Braydon, near Swindon) and Lailoken the wild man of Scotland, and supplied him with pseudo-prophecies in Latin verse. But he did not invent everything, as Rachel Bromwich correctly observed.[15] Kenneth Jackson then drew attention to historical figures in traditions of Merlin. Rhydderch son of Tudwal was king of

Strathclyde in the time of St Columba, and so before 597; in the Welsh legend of Myrddin, he is linked with 'the mad Strathclyde prophet' who ended up as the Merlin of medieval romance.[16] Older views yet crop up in a 1955 translation of a 1944 volume, where Myrddin is still listed with early poets 'famous and influential in their day' so that we can be certain 'that Myrddin did live at some time (more than probably, in the sixth century) and was a poet'; nevertheless, we hear that not a line of his poetry survives.[17]

James Carney of Dublin said much on Irish parallels to the legend of Lailoken, but nothing to effect on Merlin's origins.[18] Kenneth Jackson (with some disobliging comments on Carney's defects as a scholar) then referred to Merlin as a prophetic wild man living in the forest of *Celydon*, Scotland, having been driven mad at *Arfderydd* in the 570s, according to 'Welsh poetry of the twelfth century'.[19] The remark brings us up with a jolt. If the statement is correct, it suggests traditions of Merlin and Scotland independent of Geoffrey of Monmouth. It needs looking at.

A fuller account of verses attributed to Merlin followed in 1959, where Jarman thought 'the identity of the Myrddin in the Welsh poems with the Lailoken of Scottish tradition' was certain; he yet ended with a call for 'comparative analysis of all the material' to answer unanswered questions.[20] So problems remained. A year later he declared that 'no historical person of the name of Myrddin' existed in sixth-century North Britain. Merlin's name derives from that of Carmarthen. He was also confident that the Northern legend of Lailoken, wild man of the woods, 'was brought to Wales at some time between the sixth and the ninth or tenth centuries' to be merged with traditions of Merlin.[21] The identification of the two, in Jarman's view, was not due to Geoffrey of Monmouth. We shall return to this question, but it is clear how between 1955, when Parry's history was published, and 1959, when Jarman gave his inaugural lecture, progress had been made in obliterating Merlin, sixth-century bard of North Britain. As for that allusion in Aneirin's seventh-century *Gododdin*, Kenneth Jackson took it as a late interpolation, Merlin belonging to 'a Welsh, not a Scottish, context'; even if his story of his madness in the woods 'came from Strathclyde to Wales' with his name being substituted for that of Lailoken.[22]

In 1972, Rachel Bromwich showed how ideas which have been discredited can all still for a while refuse to lie down. Jarman's dismissal of 1960 notwithstanding, she still opined that Myrddin was a historical poet of the North, citing publications of Sir Idris Foster and Sir Glanmor Williams to this effect, as also Sir Ifor Williams's much earlier note of 1938.[23] Remarks by the last on how Geoffrey of Monmouth may have used tenth-century Welsh prophetic poetry for ideas on Merlin then appeared in English.[24] An edition of Geoffrey's *Vita Merlini* reproduced Jarman's translation of the *Afallennau* 'Apple Trees' stanzas in the Book of Taliesin, together with his description of them as dating from between 850 and 1050.[25] They are hence evidence for the tale of Lailoken in pre-Norman Wales, and identification of him with Myrddin. There is further discussion of them by Simon Evans, who dated most of them to the twelfth century, with allusions to attacks on the Welsh by Normans and others.[26] Merlin was mentioned too by high-status bards before 1282. For Hywel ab Owain Gwynedd (d. 1170), Merlin was a poet who praised women; Prydydd y Moch (d. 1220) saw him as a prophet; but they both regarded him as a bard inspired by the *awen* or muse, like Taliesin or Aneirin. There are implications of poems lost, perhaps with love as their subject.

In 1978, Jarman returned to the fray. He gave a clear account of how Merlin's name derives from that of Carmarthen. He further stated that the legend of Lailoken migrated from (what is now) Scotland to Wales, the result being poems with 'one foot in Dyfed and the other in northern Britain'.[27] Result: even Rachel Bromwich admitted that Merlin was not a historical northern poet. He was yet even before 1100 identified with Lailoken, as shown by the language of the *Cyfoesi* 'Greetings' verses in the Red Book of Hergest and the *Colloquy of Merlin and Taliesin* in the Black Book of Carmarthen, while the nucleus of other poems is at least as old. They have nothing to do with Geoffrey of Monmouth.[28] This is important evidence.

A reminder on the afterlife of refuted statements is provided by a note on Gerald of Wales, informing readers on a supposed 'historical figure, Myrddin ap Morfryn, a Welsh bard in the sixth century'.[29] Better is the statement on the Welsh poems *Afallennau* and *Hoianau* that they 'reveal nothing of Geoffrey's influence' and are surely 'written before his time'.[30] As for British-Latin *Moridunum* 'sea-fort', it now has proper treatment in a standard work.[31]

In his edition of the Black Book, A. O. H. Jarman again gave the dating of the *Colloquy of Merlin and Taliesin* as the later eleventh century.[32] Jenny Rowland then provided an account of the *Cyfoesi* verses which is especially useful, because edited and translated versions of this dialogue of Merlin and his sister are not easy to find. She concluded from its list of rulers that its first part dated from the early tenth century, but that it was added to in the twelfth century.[33] The implications of this for the Merlin legend are obvious. Jarman gave a final statement in 1991. He listed six Welsh poems relevant to the Merlin legend, the most important being *Ymddiddan Myrddin a Thaliesin* ('The Dialogue of Myrddin and Taliesin'), *Yr Afallennau* ('The Apple Trees'), and *Yr Oianau* ('The Greetings'), all in the thirteenth-century Black Book together with *Cyfoesi Myrddin a Gwenddydd ei Chwaer* ('The Conversation of Myrddin and His Sister Gwenddydd') in the Red Book of Hergest, written in about 1400. The poems are much older than the volumes containing them. Their legendary matter predates their prophecies, and he observed that the 'setting of the Welsh legends of *Arfderydd* and Myrddin was ex- clusively northern' and that they must have 'migrated to Wales' at some date 'between the sixth century and the middle ages'. He went on to refine that, with the earliest material perhaps arriving 'the ninth or tenth century'. Jarman remained firm in his belief that Merlin was purely 'legendary', the evidence including the absence of his name from 'northern and Scottish tradition in general'.[34]

One might think that definitive. Debate yet continued. Brian Murdoch, drawing attention to *Prophetia Merlini*, composed in Latin verse about 1150 by John of Cornwall, thought it either based upon Geoffrey of Monmouth's *History*, or 'an original either in Cornish or Breton'.[35] Whether that is so we shall see later. As regards Merlin's supposed prophecies on a British *reconquista*, there are chilling remarks on these as 'a deadly threat to English supremacy' and thereby linked to the 'ghoulish' fate of Llywelyn the Last's body, its head stuck on a pole for display in the Tower of London.[36] A curious outcome of the Merlin legend is discussed inconclusively in a study of the Early Middle English *Brut*.[37] Also inconclusive as regards origins is a study of how his prophecies gained international influence.[38]

Far more important is a study by Oliver Padel, who faces up to difficulties in Jarman's treatment of the legend and suggests modifications of it: 'refining his scheme without radically reshaping it' and allowing that others might here wish to propose 'an altogether new theory'. The main problem is this. Why did Geoffrey of Monmouth in his *History* of the 1130s omit 'all trace of the northern wild man' for Merlin, when according to Jarman this aspect had long been known in Wales, as shown by the early poems?[39] We shall see how Padel's response has been dealt with by later critics.

In the meantime, older opinions went their way. On the question of origins, the late Martin Aurell cited Jarman for the legend as no older than the 570s, starting in Scotland 'pour se transférer vers le Pays de Galles' in the seventh or eighth century.[40] His account is clearer than that in a source from Wales itself. Its entry for Merlin correctly begins with him as a 'legendary poet and prophet', but becomes confused by then calling him a 'member of the court of Gwenddolau feb Ceido', who fell at *Arfderydd* in 573.[41] A legendary character cannot belong to a genuine ruler's court; and such a description goes flat in the face of Jarman's view that North Britons knew nothing of Merlin until they started reading Geoffrey of Monmouth in the twelfth century. Also confusing is James E. Fraser, associating *Arfderydd* in 573 with 'fictional and historical characters' including Merlin, but leaving it unclear which category Merlin belongs to.[42]

John Reuben Davies then responded to Oliver Padel's criticisms on the strange link between Glasgow's St Kentigern (d. 603) and St Asaph, Welsh cathedral city. The association will be a fabrication of Geoffrey, which was then taken up in accounts of Kentigern.[43] This was not then known to Tim Clarkson, who describes the Welsh poems as 'ninth-century compositions incorporating older material' (which is not what Jarman said).[44] Another summarized Padel's arguments on how Geoffrey of Monmouth may have merged prophecies attributed to Merlin; Latin traditions on Lailoken; and Welsh poetry concerning a Lailoken-like figure not yet named as Merlin.[45] This is more useful than another account, with frequent reference to Merlin's demonic origins.[46] Mark Williams puts Padel's views more clearly. Geoffrey wrote an account of Merlin in the late 1130s without knowing much of him. When he came to write the life of Merlin, it was probably then that 'the Welsh Myrddin and the northern wild-man tradition were fused by Geoffrey himself'.[47]

Padel's views are cited in passing by Sims-Williams.[48] They are also mentioned by Julia Crick.[49] So, too, with Fiona Tolhurst.[50] More significant is Charles-Edwards's account of *Cyfoesi* or the Conversation of Merlin and Gwenddydd (his sister) in the Red Book of Hergest. Merlin answers her questions, as teacher to pupil. There are references to him as wild man of the woods, to *Arfderydd*, and to Gwenddolau, ruler in North Britain. Charles-Edwards agreed with the Chadwicks in dating the core of the poem to the tenth century.[51] It is important evidence in the present debate. It suggests identification of Merlin with Lailoken long before Geoffrey.

A publication of the same year sharpens focus on this. While Charles-Edwards dates the *Cyfoesi* poem to the tenth century, because it lists Welsh rulers up to Hywel the Good, who died in about 950, Dr Padel dates it to perhaps the thirteenth.[52] Yet why should a thirteenth-century poet put together a 'prophecy' giving prestige to rulers three hundred years before him? Because Merlin in the *Cyfoesi* text is so similar to Lailoken, this seems to be fatal for

Dr Padel's view that the first person to apply the Lailoken legend to him was Geoffrey of Monmouth. Dating rules that out. In tenth-century Wales, Merlin will have been known as a hermit-prophet-poet of the woods contemporary with *Arfderydd* and Gwenddolau in the 570s. So we can advance with confidence. We can be sure that in Wales, long before Geoffrey, 'Myrddin had taken over the identity of Llallogen' or Lailoken.[53]

The priority of Merlin-Lailoken in Wales before Geoffrey is hence established. A North British tradition moved southwards, like those of Arthur or Taliesin. In the eleventh-century *Mabinogion* tale of Culhwch and Olwen, Arthur has a court in Cornwall, while the Taliesin of legend (alluded to by twelfth-century poets) is associated with King Maelgwn (d. 547) of Gwynedd. When we come to more recent writers, however, we shall be surprised. The evidence presented by Thomas Charles-Edwards might seem clear-cut. But it has not been noticed as it should be. The result is confusing statements by some writers.

For Count Tolstoy, the Welsh saga previous to Geoffrey depicts Merlin as a seer 'driven to frenzy' by battle near Carlisle, and fleeing northwards to the 'forest of Celyddon'.[54] John Bollard cites Oliver Padel on the so-called 'Myrddin' poems. While they may predate Geoffrey, Myrddin is 'not explicitly named in them'; it may thus be that Geoffrey was the first to attach Myrddin/Merlin to the wild-man tale.[55] Victoria Flood states that Geoffrey in the 1130s 'reworked and modified Welsh prophetic paradigms' for the prognostications which he attributed to Merlin.[56] Her vagueness does not help us much. Also vague is Helen Fulton, declaring that movement of 'traditions in both directions' between Wales and North Britain accounts amongst other things for Myrddin, whose *Afallennau* verses associate him with battle at *Arfderydd* in 573.[57] It implies that Geoffrey did not make the link for himself, despite citation of Oliver Padel, who thinks that he did. As for Gwyneth Lewis and Lord Williams, they cite the comment in the Welsh annals on Merlin's madness, apparently not realizing that it occurs in a manuscript postdating Geoffrey, and then remark that 'we have no further details of what must have been an early form of the legend' of Merlin as man in the woods 'retold' (significant word) by Geoffrey.[58]

Since the above was written, there has appeared an extended account of legends of Merlin and *Arfderydd* or Arthuret in 573.[59] Thereafter came analysis of prophecies attributed to Merlin and how their 'imperial imaginings' derive from 'a complex, and contested, construction of Britishness'.[60] But that tells us little on Merlin's origins.

It is time to conclude. There is a first general point. A definitive account requires analysis of the six Merlin poems, especially the *Cyfoesi* verses, and this is not easy to do, because the edition of the last cited by Thomas Charles-Edwards has not (at time of writing) been published. Nevertheless, work by him and Jarman allows four conclusions. First, that Merlin never existed. He is totally fictional, like the Snow Queen, or King Lud of Ludgate, London. As with King Lud and Ludgate, so also with Merlin or Myrddin and Carmarthen or Caerfyrddin. A character has been invented out of a place-name. Hence Merlin's associations with West Wales, as recorded by Samuel Lewis in 1844. Second, Lailoken may have existed, as a warrior fighting at *Arfderydd* in 573. Third, that traditions of Lailoken in any case had by the tenth century reached Wales, like those of other North Britons (Arthur, Taliesin, Llywarch the Old), where his legend was applied to Merlin. Fourth, that these traditions were exploited by Geoffrey of Monmouth in the twelfth century, who added inventions of his own and propelled Merlin to European fame, and even (in the world of US showbiz) the entertaining figure of *Camelot* and Walt Disney's *The Sword in the Stone*. Hence the unexpected link between the Merlin whose grave is located by the Tweed, southern Scotland; and the fantasy Merlin of cartoons from dream-factories in Hollywood.

Notes

1. Samuel Lewis, *A Topographical Dictionary of Wales: From Abbey to Llandyvrydog*, 3rd edn (London, 1844), 190.
2. *Annales Cambriae*, ed. John Williams ab Ithel (London, 1860), 5.
3. John Rhŷs, *Celtic Britain*, 3rd edn (London, 1904), 300.
4. *Breuddwyd Maxen*, ed. Ifor Williams (Bangor, 1908), 26.
5. J. C. Morrice, *A Manual of Welsh Literature* (Bangor, 1909), 3-4.
6. J. E. Lloyd, *A History of Wales* (London, 1911), 169-70.
7. *Cywyddau Dafydd ap Gwllym a'r Gyfoeswyr*, ed. Ifor Williams and Thomas Roberts (Bangor, 1914), 197.
8. E. K. Chambers, *Arthur of Britain* (London, 1927), 93-6.
9. H. M. Chadwick and N. K. Chadwick, *The Growth of Literature: The Ancient Literatures of Europe* (Cambridge, 1932), 105-14, 123-32, 454-8.
10. H. I. Bell, *The Development of Welsh Poetry* (Oxford, 1936), 17, 22-3.
11. *Canu Aneirin*, ed. Ifor Williams (Caerdydd, 1938), 188.
12. Ifor Williams, *Lectures on Welsh Poetry* (Dublin, 1944), 52-3.
13. John Lloyd-Jones, 'The Court Poets of the Welsh Princes', *Proceedings of the British Academy*, xxxiv (1948), 167-97.
14. *Ymddiddan Myrddin a Thaliesin*, ed. A. O. H. Jarman (Caerdydd, 1951), 46-7.
15. Rachel Bromwich, 'The Character of the Early Welsh Tradition', in *Studies in Early British History*, ed. N. K. Chadwick (Cambridge, 1954), 83-136.
16. K. H. Jackson, 'The Britons in Southern Scotland', *Antiquity*, xxix (1955), 77-88.
17. Thomas Parry, *A History of Welsh Literature* (Oxford, 1955), 10, 14, 27.
18. James Carney, *Studies in Irish Literature and History* (Dublin, 1955), 129-31.
19. Kenneth Jackson, 'The Sources for the Life of St Kentigern', in *Studies in the Early British Church*, ed. N. K. Chadwick (Cambridge, 1958), 273-357.
20. A. O. H. Jarman, 'The Welsh Myrddin Poems', in *Arthurian Literature in the Middle Ages*, ed. R. S. Loomis (Oxford, 1959), 20-30.

21. A. O. H. Jarman, *The Legend of Myrddin* (Cardiff, 1960), 22, 26.

22. K. H. Jackson, *The Gododdin: The Oldest Scottish Po*em (Edinburgh, 1969), 49.

23. Ifor Williams, *The Beginnings of Welsh Poetry*, ed. Rachel Bromwich (Cardiff, 1972), 125 n. 10.

24. *Armes Prydein*, ed. Ifor Williams (Dublin, 1972), xxx-xxxiv.

25. *Life of Merlin*, ed. Basil Clarke (Cardiff, 1973), 1, 235.

26. *Historia Gruffud vab Kenan*, ed. D. Simon Evans (Caerdydd, 1977), ccxxxviii-cxl, 57.

27. A. O. H. Jarman, 'Early Stages in the Development of the Myrddin Legends', in *Astudiaethau ar yr Hengerdd*, ed. Rachel Bromwich and R. Brinley Jones (Caerdydd, 1978), 326-49.

28. Rachel Bromwich, *Trioedd Ynys Prydein*, 2nd edn (Cardiff, 1978), 469-74, 559-60.

29. *Expugnatio Hibernica*, ed. A. N. Scott and F. X. Martin (Dublin, 1978), 313.

30. R. Wallis Evans, 'Prophetic Poetry', in *A Guide to Welsh Literature, Volume 2*, ed. A. O. H. Jarman and G. R. Hughes (Swansea, 1979), 278-97.

31. A. L. F. Rivet and Colin Smith, *The Place-Names of Roman Britain* (Princeton, 1979), 422.

32. *Llyfr Du Caerfyrddin*, ed. A. O. H. Jarman (Caerdydd, 1982), xxxiv.

33. Jenny Rowland, *Early Welsh Saga Poetry* (Cambridge, 1990), 291-3.

34. A. O. H. Jarman, 'The Myrddin Legend and the Welsh Tradition of Prophecy', in *The Arthur of the Welsh*, ed. Rachel Bromwich, A. O. H. Jarman, and Brynley F. Roberts (Cardiff, 1991), 117-45.

35. Brian Murdoch, *Cornish Literature* (Cambridge, 1993), 7.

36. R. R. Davies, *The First English Empire* (Oxford, 2000), 40.

37. Kelly M. Wickham-Crowley, *Writing the Future* (Cardiff, 2002), 108.

38. Catherine Daniel, *Les prophéties de Merlin et la culture politique* (Turnhout, 2006), 15.

39. O. J. Padel, 'Geoffrey of Monmouth and the Development of the Merlin Legend', *Cambrian Medieval Celtic Studies*, li (2006), 39-65.

40. Martin Aurell, *La Légende du roi Arthur 550-1250* (Paris, 2007), 155.

41. Anon., 'Merlin', in *The Welsh Academy Encyclopaedia of Wales*, ed. John Davies, Nigel Jenkins, Menna Baines, Peredur I. Lynch (Cardiff, 2008),

549.

42. James E. Fraser, *From Caledonia to Pictland: Scotland to 795* (Edinburgh, 2009), 128.

43. J. R. Davies, 'Bishop Kentigern Among the Britons', in *Saints' Cults in the Celtic World*, ed. Steve Boardman, J. R. Davies, Eila Williamson (Woodbridge, 2009), 66-90.

44. Tim Clarkson, *The Men of the North* (Edinburgh, 2010), 89.

45. Karen Jankulak, *Writers of Wales: Geoffrey of Monmouth* (Cardiff, 2010), 90-1.

46. Corinne Saunders, *Magic and the Supernatural* (Cambridge, 2010), 115.

47. Mark Williams, *Fiery Shapes* (Oxford, 2010), 103 n. 106.

48. Patrick Sims-Williams, *Irish Influence on Medieval Welsh Literature* (Oxford, 2011), 15.

49. Julia Crick, 'Geoffrey and the Prophetic Tradition', in *The Arthur of Medieval Latin Literature*, ed. Siân Echard (Cardiff, 2011), 67-82.

50. Fiona Tolhurst, *Geoffrey of Monmouth and the Feminist Origins of the Arthurian Legend* (New York, 2012), 164.

51. Thomas Charles-Edwards, *Wales and the Britons 350-1064* (Oxford, 2013), 337-9.

52. O. J. Padel, *Writers of Wales: Arthur in Medieval Welsh Literature*, rev. edn (Cardiff, 2013), 47.

53. Tim Clarkson, *Scotland's Merlin* (Edinburgh, 2016), 135.

54. Nikolai Tolstoy, *The Mysteries of Stonehenge* (Stroud, 2016), 495.

55. J. K. Bollard, 'The Earliest Myrddin Poems', in *Arthur in the Celtic Languages*, ed. Ceridwen Lloyd-Morgan and Erich Poppe (Cardiff, 2019), 35-50.

56. Victoria Flood, 'Early Tudor Translation of English Prophecy in Wales', in *Crossing Borders in the Insular Middle Ages*, ed. Aisling Byrne and Victoria Flood (Turnhout, 2019), 65-88.

57. Helen Fulton, 'Britons and Saxons', in *The Cambridge History of Welsh Literature*, ed. Geraint Evans and Helen Fulton (Cambridge, 2019), 26-51.

58. *The Book of Taliesin*, tr. Gwyneth Lewis and Rowan Williams (London, 2019), 214.

59. A. Breeze, *British Battles 493-937* (London, 2020), 25-34.

60. Victoria Flood, 'Prophecy and Place in the Arthurian Tradition', in *The*

Arthurian World, ed. Victoria Coldham-Fussell, Miriam Edlich-Muth, Renée Ward (New York, 2022), 69-82.

CHAPTER FOUR

MABINOGION TALES: *CULHWCH*, *BREUDDWYD RHONABWY*, THE THREE ROMANCES

Of the eleven Welsh narratives going under the heading of *Mabinogion*, five concern Arthur. They are *Culhwch and Olwen*, of the later 1090s; *Breuddwyd Rhonabwy* ('The Dream of Rhonabwy'), of the early 1220s; and the so-called Three Romances of Geraint, Owain (or else *Iarlles y Ffynnon*, 'The Lady of the Fountain'), and Peredur, all similar in style and of between about 1230 and 1280. The five are here discussed in three parts, with emphasis on two things: their image of Arthur, showing dramatic changes between the eleventh century and thirteenth; and when they were written, which is (for some) still problematic. Two aspects are fundamental. First is the archaic and Celtic, so that Sir John Rhŷs (d. 1915) could, for example, relate the Mabon of *Culhwch* (whom Arthur frees from imprisonment at Gloucester) to the Gaulish deity Maponos.[1] Second (in varying degrees) is the purely medieval, so that Lady Guest (d. 1895) could distinguish between the older stories, lacking reference to 'Norman customs, manners, arts, arms, and luxuries', and the others, together 'full of such allusions'.[2]

1. *Culhwch and Olwen*

We begin with *Culhwch*, oldest of the eleven *Mabinogion* stories, the next oldest (the *Four Branches of the Mabinogi*) being composed

71

some thirty years later. Culhwch is the protagonist; his bride-to-be is Olwen, as fair and delightful as her father (the giant Ysbaddaden) is menacing and repugnant. To win her hand, Culhwch must accomplish tasks set by Ysbaddaden, wherein he is helped by Arthur and his men, the high point being their wild chase across South and West Wales for Twrch Trwyth, a monstrous boar. So the plot is simple. Everything else is not, excepting social manners and customs (which are semi-barbaric), leaving us with the learning and exuberance (and frequent brutality) of an eleventh-century Rabelais. Nothing refined there (in contrast to the Three Romances discussed below). Like an Atlantic wave (which the author would often see, for he was surely a cleric composing his merry history for fellow-clerics in West Wales), the tale is ebullient, boisterous, turbulent.

Specific comment begins with Morrice. He combined the acceptable and the contradictory, the latter being a puzzling statement on how the earliest tales have no mention of Arthur (true of the *Four Branches*, quite untrue of *Culhwch*). Yet he rightly saw the Arthur sought by Culhwch as a 'prince of some distinction, but not yet a mighty emperor', adding that his court is still in Cornwall (and not the Caerleon of Geoffrey of Monmouth, writing in the 1130s). Morrice also observed (correctly) that *Culhwch* is the most archaic of the *Mabinogion* texts in its language and social attitudes, so that Arthur's presence 'may have been due to a subsequent writer' (an intriguing remark).[3]

Although Sir Edmund Chambers (d. 1954) claimed no skill in the Celtic languages, his survey of Arthurian literature remains admirable. He cited the 1913 edition of Joseph Loth for the text (wherein Arthur is a 'well-defined figure') as of 'the late eleventh or early twelfth century'. Despite being the 'folk-tale' of the Winning of the Giant's Daughter, it has traces of Norman influence, but nothing from Geoffrey of Monmouth (d. 1155) or his French imitators. Arthur, perhaps an 'accretion to the original story', is yet the same Arthur who, according to the ninth-century *Historia Brittonum*, hunted the *porcus Troit* or Twrch Trwyth. Chambers went on to summarize the narrative's bewildering medley of characters and incident.[4] Bewildering in a different way were remarks of W. J. Gruffydd (d. 1954) on how the story's Oldest Animals (blackbird, stag, owl, eagle) allude to an ancient Celtic 'Creation Myth'.[5] That does not help us much. At Cambridge the Chadwicks were more cut-and-dried, with a brief comment on the tale as (in their classification) a 'heroic' one.[6]

A different line was taken by Saunders Lewis, stressing (as a good Celtic nationalist) supposed Irish aspects of the text: the stereotyped formulas of dialogue; grotesque character-descriptions; outlandish incidents, as with the woman who nearly killed Cei (the later 'Sir Kay') by an over-friendly embrace; or the 'bardic' elaboration of set-pieces, such as the famous lyrical account of Olwen's beauty.[7] These presumed Irish symptoms still attract attention. Another Welshman (and sometime Labour MP) took another line, citing depiction of splendour, so that champions wear rings of gold and bear swords with gold hilts.[8] A third Welshman assembled ancient allusions to Twrch Trwyth, a boar with a strong whiff of Celtic paganism, and perhaps mentioned by Aneirin, a North British bard lamenting warriors slain (in 603 CE?) in a gallant but doomed attack on Northumbria.[9]

There is further excellent comment on *Culhwch and Olwen* in what remains the best and most scholarly translation. The author's 'gusto' in portraying a 'fantastic and primitive world' is brought out; but there is also special attention to Arthur. As in archaic poems from the Black Book of Carmarthen and Book of Taliesin, he is a 'folk hero, a beneficent giant' ridding the land of 'witches and monsters' and even (for the sake of plunder) raiding the Other World; and this 'rude, savage' protector of his people can still be glimpsed within the creations of Geoffrey of Monmouth or Sir Thomas Malory.[10] A most interesting continuity. Changes in ten centuries notwithstanding, the Arthur of fiction was ever a patriot and military commander; as was the Arthur of North Britain who fell near Carlisle in 537. He was no Romanized cavalry-commander taking on English invaders, but a Celtic *penteulu* or 'dux bellorum' or captain of the royal host who was a saviour during in the terrible famine-years of 536-7. There are also pertinent observations by Rachel Bromwich (1915-2010). She pointed out how the narrative of *Culhwch* is a 'skilful dovetailing of two folk-tale motifs', of the Jealous Step-Mother (as in the tale of Cinderella) and the Giant's Daughter; that it dates from about 1100; displays 'a love of catalogue and enumeration'; and shows 'the influence of Irish saga' (including much 'crude buffoonery').[11] Sir Thomas Parry (d. 1985) wrote in similar terms on the author's 'jesting strain' and love of 'luxurious descriptions' (evident from Olwen, who makes her entry in a 'flame-red silken tunic' and 'collar of red gold' with pearls and rubies), as well as of lists (including tasks to accomplish, or marvels at Arthur's court).[12] As for when it was written, a resumé of arguments sound or dubious by various Celticists has the conclusion 'about 1100'.[13] Ashe concurred, adding that the present text contains a non-Arthurian story 'artificially woven into the Arthurian ethos'.[14] Arthur had begun his long process of drawing doughty warriors or handsome lovers or bewitching ladies (in the case of Morgain la Fée, literally so) into orbit around him.

There is a convenient summing-up of opinion in an Oxford handbook, with a comprehensiveness and objectivity not found in later equivalents. Sir Idris Foster there rehearsed what has been said on folk-tale elements, hints of ancient Celtic mythology, alleged Irish parallels, a prodigality of allusion to early British heroes and adventures (many of them otherwise unknown), and a date of composition in about 1100.[15] Gwyn Jones similarly referred to the importance of *Culhwch* for three reasons: for the wealth of Celtic lore which it sets out or hints at; for its picture of Arthur as a 'fabulous barbaric chieftain of a barbarous fantastic court, a tremendous man of action', so unlike the 'idealized and devitalized' monarch of French and German romance; and for itself, an anonymous masterpiece, by turns brutal, curt, tender, lyrical; but always, whether in the 'gravely beautiful or the headlong gasconade', a text 'resourceful' and 'exciting'.[16] Which is well said.

Less impressionistic, but much more precise, was analysis by the great Kenneth Jackson (1909-91), demonstrating how so many folk-tales or popular tales in *Culhwch* (The Giant's Daughter, Six Go Through the World, The Magic Flight) have analogues in other languages, such as ancient Greek (with Jason and the Argonauts) or Sanskrit, or modern oral tradition in Scottish Gaelic.[17] Nothing particularly Welsh or Celtic, then, about their appearance in this *Mabinogion* text. They are part of the world's ocean of story. Jackson's insights are as brilliant and illuminating as the somewhat diffuse utterances of others are not.[18] As for dating, Simon Evans (d. 1998), who knew more about Middle Welsh than anyone else during the last five hundred years, put *Culhwch* within the second half of the eleventh century.[29] It is a pity that his reasoned conclusions are now somewhat neglected. In a chapter on 'fact', Geoffrey Ashe thus rightly saw our text as 'from the pre-Geoffrey era' and hence predating the 1130s.[20]

Then came comments on intriguing clues. In Aneirin's *Gododdin*, laments for North British warriors wiped out in a glorious (but catastrophic) attack on Northumbrians at Catterick (perhaps in 603, when Scots and Irish were massacred by other Northumbians at 'Degsastan' on the Upper Tweed), we find mention of both Arthur (d. 537) and Twrch Trwyth, although not yet linked.[21] While we cannot be sure that the latter reference goes back to the seventh century, it must be early. There are remarks elsewhere on this and other pre-Christian elements in *Culhwch*, as with Arthur's rescue of Mabon from captivity at Gloucester, 'obviously a designation for the Other World'.[22] In admirable translations of passages (lyrical, savage, wild), Jackson placed the original in the tenth century.[23] Few now accept this. Foster revisited the text with emphasis on its archaic aspects (in Celtic paganism or Irish saga), also remarking on how its author never decided who the real protagonist was, whether the original Culhwch or the late-coming Arthur.[24] On that, compare dismissal of Arthur as having a 'disappointingly minor role', this supposed 'great king of the British' here having 'little personality' in comparison with later French and German romance.[25] No surprise, if his story has been added to Culhwch's.

On the matter of dating, evidence of the first importance was once more supplied by Simon Evans. *Culhwch* contains not a single borrowing from French (later research rules out the two listed by Evans); the *Four Branches* contain a mere handful (such as *pali* 'brocaded silk'); but in the thirteenth-century Three Romances they are common.[26] The *Four Branches* being of the later 1120s, dating of *Culhwch* to the (later) 1090s is hence confirmed by this singular absence of French influence. In a guide for beginners, Mac Cana more cautiously referred to the 'eleventh century' as possible.[27] In what remains the essential *Who's Who* of early British tradition, Rachel Bromwich pointed out another paucity or lack in *Culhwch*. Its author knew little of the Triads, one of the oral *aides-mémoire* of a medieval Welsh bard and vital to his training.[28] Implication: the writer was not a professional bard. This accords with other evidence for his being a cleric (if a rather unclerical one).

Weighty views on his language were again provided by Simon Evans, with further emphasis on its archaism (clearly predating that of the *Four Branches*), pointing to composition about the year 1100.[29] The linguistic case for 1100 tallies exactly with the historical one, as we shall see. On other matters there were grounds for revisionism. Opinion on Irish aspects of a Welsh classic, enunciated by Saunders Lewis in 1932, came under scrutiny, with the conclusion that the story shows no 'deep acquaintance with Irish geography' (or, indeed, Irish literature).[30] Wishful thinking met uncomfortable fact. Against it are careful reflections on Arthur, whose introduction to the *Culhwch* narrative 'created an impossible tension between the two heroes'. By the time it ends, Culhwch is hardly to be seen. Arthur's presence was 'overpowering'. It 'could brook no competition'.[31] Such are the artistic problems of making one tale out of two.

In 1992 appeared the standard edition of *Culhwch*. It should have been the beginning of a new enlightenment. But it now appears as a last monument of Welsh scholarship's golden age. Its introduction, the best introduction to the text, contains fundamental points. The story belongs to a 'primitive world' which is 'beyond our sympathy and comprehension'. Its author was yet at home with 'the native learning of the Welsh Church', especially Latin lives of St Cadog and St David. (The first of these, written in about 1093 when the Norman conquest of Glamorgan was threatened but not begun, is major evidence for when *Culhwch* was composed.) The editors also rightly come down for the text as hardly later than 1100 or so.[32] Similarly judicious is a verdict on the story as 'literary', and thus going beyond its oral sources, although they remain in evidence. But its cornucopia of wonders and heroism and farce in any case makes up for 'deficiencies in structure'.[33]

Now for a period of stasis and (worse) relapse, occurring when three generations of great Welsh scholars had effectively quit the stage. A bizarre statement is proof of this. It is on *Culhwch* as the 'oldest' of the eleven *Mabinogion* texts (true), usually dated to around 1100 (true), and so predating the *Four Branches*, perhaps composed as early as 1060.[34] How, one wonders, could a text of 1100 have language older than one of 1060? We have entered an Alice-in-Wonderland realm of illogic. Different views on those five stories are presented elsewhere.[35] In an essay-collection, discussion of *Culhwch* is restricted mainly to scribal division of its text.[36] Reference is made in an interesting study by a non-Celticist to the mythological origins of the boar chased by Arthur.[37] In another account, readers will discover that professional Celticists cannot explain such toponyms in the text as 'Sach and Salach' or 'Caer Brythwch' and thus dismiss them as perhaps 'created' or concocted terms.[38] (Not so. As maintained below, the forms are corrupt readings of Mediterranean place-names set out by Orosius, fifth-century historian. They are further evidence for *Culhwch* as by a cleric who possessed Latin learning.) Views of Higham and others are relayed in a comprehensive volume, stressing (correctly) how the originality of *Culhwch* is in its being the earliest narrative with Arthur and his companions as 'les véritables protagonistes'.[39]

Now for the first crack in the façade of traditional scholarship; for we have now an assertion on *Culhwch* as of 'the first half of the twelfth century'.[40] Curious, this, when the later *Four Branches* will not predate 1120, as shown by comment in the second and third branches on how Caswallon (= Henry I), 'usurper' and 'crowned king of London', ruled from Oxford (which Henry did only from that date); nor postdate 1135 or so, for they reveal no trace of Geoffrey of Monmouth's influence. In a posthumous publication, Mac Cana revisited supposed Irish symptoms of *Culhwch*.[41] Then a brief mention of the tale, still rightly placed in about 1100.[42] Count Tolstoy (to his credit) acknowledges what others say here, even if one disagrees with his view of the *Four Branches* as 'considerably earlier' than *Culhwch*, perhaps by 'at least a century' and so of the late tenth century.[43] Difficult to see why, if so, they contain loan-words from French; mention a king crowned in London, something unknown before 1066; or a king ruling from Oxford, unknown before the 1120s. Count Tolstoy's attitude is yet preferable to that of Professor Charles-Edwards, who does not dismiss Simon Rodway's case for *Culhwch* as of 'the second half of the twelfth century', or for its author as 'a poet' (the latter despite an unfamiliarity with the Triads, noted by Rachel Bromwich; obvious familiarity with ecclesiastical learning, also noted by her; and a disobliging attitude to the mores of secular rulers).[44]

For other pitfalls, we find Professor Higham's placing of *Culhwch* 'to around 1000' (where he has misread '1100' in the edition cited by him).[45] Also concerning scholarly error, there appeared at this time a correction of the text's 'Caer Se ac Asse' as representing 'Syracussa(na)' or Syracuse, Sicily; 'lotor a fotor' as the River Ot(t)orogor(r)a, east of the Ganges; and 'Sach a Salach' as Arachosia, in Afghanistan. All these will come from one short passage in Orosius's fifth-century history of the world.[46]

Different lapses are evidenced at Oxford, where we find respectful notice of Simon Rodway on *Culhwch* as of about '1150'; better, however, is what follows on Irish elements of the tale as fewer than supposed, the author lacking 'any real knowledge of Irish literature'.[47] Then location of the text to within the half-century *following* 1150.[48] Thereafter not only a failure to put *Culhwch* before the *Four Branches*, but linking of those latter tales with the monastery of Clynnog in west Gwynedd, despite their total lack of ecclesiastical symptoms (in contrast to their singular concern with married love, motherhood, wet-nursing, child-rearing: all matters for wives, not monks).[49] Finally, Dr Padel, whose ultra-conservatism saves him from the errors of others, so that he places *Culhwch* 'earlier than Geoffrey of Monmouth's *History of the Kings of Britain*' of about 1138.[50] Which must be so.

There are other approaches. Supposedly nonsense in *Culhwch* will instead be allusions (miscopied by scribes) to Byzacium, Hadrumentum, Carthage (a region and two cities in what is now Tunisia).[51] Emendation there will show further comment on such forms as unsatisfactory.[52] Count Tolstoy reminds us of pre-Christian elements in the episode of Mabon, prisoner of Gloucester.[53] Elsewhere is desultory commentary on *Culhwch* and other texts.[54] On the last we say (a) that, despite what some maintain, a date of the late 1090s for *Culhwch* is certain; (b) the *Four Branches* were written some thirty years later; and (c) the *Ynys Weir* of the Triads is not Lundy Island (in the Bristol Channel), as the Welsh came to believe, but the Orkney Archipelago, taking its name from the *Gweir* 'bend' or cape by John o' Groats, as proved by Ptolemy's *Virvedrum* 'great bend' or Duncansby Head, Caithness. Hence the early Welsh belief that the rightful sovereign of Britain would possess a threefold control of islands (Orkney, Anglesey, Wight) off its coast.

If there are gleams of progress in recent work, they still peep through darkness. Nick Higham describes *Culhwch* as of the eleventh century (good), but with 'accretions until the thirteenth'.[55] Reference to Bromwich and Evans, whom he cites here, yet shows those 'accretions' as minor. Joan Radner and Ned Sturzer are invoked for *Culhwch* as a parody which 'pokes fun' at Welsh 'native literary conventions' (which may be so) for 'courtly audiences of the twelfth and thirteenth centuries' (which cannot be so, the author being an eleventh-century cleric with a clerical audience).[56] Then observation on confusion, brought out by a remark about how *Culhwch* is for some a work of about 1100, for others of the later twelfth century or even the 'first half of the thirteenth'.[57] Contrast, however, the Three Romances, which really are of the thirteenth century and inhabit another world, courtly and refined as that of *Culhwch* is savage. It yet does not stop another from regarding *Culhwch* as perhaps of 'the second half of the twelfth century'.[58] This despite the absence of French loanwords, lack of influence from Geoffrey of Monmouth in the 1130s, and so on. This unorthodox orthodoxy amongst the Welsh appears again in description of *Culhwch* as of 'the eleventh or twelfth century'.[59] As for the most recent writers, they help little. One holds up Rhys ap Tewder (d. 1093), who dominated West Wales and in 1081 even came to terms with the Conqueror, as a man who might find the Arthur of *Culhwch* a 'prestigious predecessor and role model'.[60] Not so. Showing knowledge of what Lifris in about 1093 wrote of St Cadog, the author compiled his saga when Rhys was dead and buried. There is further darkening of counsel from another, who takes seriously views on a twelfth-century original.[61] But such a position is irreconcilable with that of the *Four Branches*, conterminous with the last years of Henry I (d. 1135), and their language devoid of the archaisms in *Culhwch*.

In short, the above is an x-ray plate of Celtic Scholarship in the last hundred years. Comparison of present-day work with that of earlier scholars (Rachel Bromwich, D. Simon Evans, Brynley F. Roberts) reveals degeneration. The remedies are obvious. They involve a return to the standards of those scholars: qualities to be recalled as we turn to *Breuddwyd Rhonabwy*, Rhonabwy's Dream.

2. The Dream of Rhonabwy

In *Culhwch and Olwen*, Arthurian narrative found itself ready-born with mockery of itself. The pattern continues in a different mode with the satirical tale of Rhonabwy, a protagonist who spends bad nights in a bad inn (the narrator setting out with relish its squalid indignities), and yet there having a wondrous dream of a visit to Arthur's court, placed on the banks of the River Severn not far from Welshpool, Powys, where Arthur is presented in a curiously dream-like way as a monarch unable to control events, such as the slaughter of his men by supernatural ravens. This odd but sophisticated narrative has, naturally, been a puzzle for critics. Not easy to know what to make of it.

More than a century ago the tale was thus placed with *Culhwch* as the 'oldest of the Arthurian group', with Arthur there 'not yet a mighty emperor', unlike the powerful sovereign of the later Three Romances (of Owain, Geraint, Peredur), and with his court still in Cornwall, and nothing on 'the dazzling splendour' of Caerleon, Wales.[62] This is misleading. True, the story ends with reference to Arthur's court in Cornwall, an archaic feature. But there are tell-tale signs in, for example, allusions to Arthur and 'Mount Badon'. Vernacular Welsh tradition had nothing on Arthur and 'Badon' until it was seduced by Geoffrey of Monmouth's fictions of the 1130s. Our text postdates Geoffrey, then.

Sir John Lloyd (d. 1947) commented on 'halcyon days' when Arthur and his knights 'spread their camp' by the River Severn close to Welshpool, Powys.[63] That (supposed) Arthurian glory is the key to interpretation. The Chadwicks helpfully noted Arthur's chagrin when he learns that Britain is guarded by Rhonabwy and his fellows, 'so puny in comparison with the men of old'. They also pointed out the author's reference to Madog ap Maredudd (d. 1160), King of Powys.[64] The text will postdate him. Themes of lost glory were seized upon by Saunders Lewis (his whole life a mission to restore Wales's greatness). Lewis not only quoted Arthur's contemptuous words on the servile wretches who now defend Britain, but underlined the contrast of the 'long house' where Rhonabwy sojourned (it was full of smoke and fleas and dung and churlish denizens) with the splendid pavilions of Arthur's vanished 'golden world'.[65] A different emphasis came from Robert Richards. Although a Welsh patriot and politician (three times Labour MP for Wrexham), he used the tale as evidence not for the penury of the time but its opulence. Riders who come to Arthur have cloaks fringed with 'golden purple', or swords with 'gleaming' hilts of gold, or helmets set with jewels and crowned by images of a leopard or a lion or a griffin.[66] This period ends with an admirable edition of the text by Melville Richards, also from the great age of Welsh scholarship.[67] Likewise belonging to that era is a masterly translation by two Aberystwyth professors, who note the author's unusual realism, whether for a bed's disgusting state, or for Powys topography.[68]

Some contributions from the 1950s remain useful. Rachel Bromwich, who saw the narrative as parodying both the 'Vision convention' and work by professional Welsh storytellers, followed Richards for it as of the 1220s.[69] Sir Thomas Parry said more. The story, of 'the middle of the thirteenth century', is planned. It is no 'folk-tale'. It also has a 'dream as framework', a form common in Irish but rare in Welsh. Remarkable too is its 'strong element of satire'. Rhonabwy lodges in no princely palace but a hovel, its floor slippery 'with cow dung and urine'; Arthur is a *roi fainéant*, playing board-games while ravens are 'tearing his men to pieces'; when bards arrive, 'nobody understood their poem'. We have an 'unheroic' Arthur in a highly 'literary' text.[70] A Powys wit was fed by the hand of Welsh tradition, and then bit it. On that inherited past, Loomis noted how the deadly ravens of Owain were recognized long ago as a 'very old' motif.[71] Yet the author's knowledge had limitations, for he added 'almost nothing indubitably native' to what occurs in earlier material.[72] Later on, with the Three Romances, we find the same thing. In a trio of French stories that happen to be written in Welsh, a few Celtic archaisms crop out (such as Peredur's slaughter of Gloucester witches), like Eozoic rocks towering above landscapes of gardens and orchards. But those things are mere survivors from a lost world.

Sir Idris Foster had various comments. Rhonabwy sleeps in squalor on 'a yellow ox-hide', surely an Irish symptom, because Irish prophets used such hides to discover the future. The Madog of the text ruled Powys from 1138 to 1160 (when he died), but the text itself may be of 1220 to 1225. Geoffrey of Monmouth's influence is shown by mention of Arthur at 'Badon' (*recte*, Braydon, near Swindon).[73] So, a blend of the archaic (couches of divination, Owain's ravens) with Geoffrey's pseudo-history and thirteenth-century Welsh decline. An interesting combination. Gwyn Jones might well speak of its 'brilliant' author's unique 'appreciation and mockery of Arthur and the great men of the past'.[74] As for dates, Simon Evans set them down as '1220-5' or so.[75] Another here agreed, also making three observations. Its satirical element makes the story unlike anything else; it was not the kind of thing to entertain 'a prince in his court'. It was yet a tribute to Powys in the time of Madog ap Maredudd, whose kingdom stretched from the sources of the Wye and Severn almost to Caerleon, on the lower Usk. But it was hardly the work of a professional storyteller or bard. Perhaps it was the ribald jest of a monk at Strata Marcella, not far from Welshpool?[76] Against that is the narrative's having no obvious sign of an ecclesiastical mentality or learning. A disenchanted court official seems likelier here. Geoffrey Ashe added another detail, on how that author styled Arthur as *amherawdyr*, emperor, in contrast to earliest British tradition, which knows of him as a bold commander, not a ruler.[77] Once more, a fantasy supplied by Geoffrey of Monmouth. The defects of Rhonabwy's 'uncomfortable lodgings' in 'an old black grange' with 'a great deal of smoke coming from it' were vividly conveyed by Kenneth Jackson.[78]

Breuddwyd Rhonabwy was then subject of a chapter by D. G. Jones, Bangor lexicographer, who related it to modern Irish comic writing (Samuel Beckett, Flann O'Brien) and (after Erich Auerbach) Old French epic.[79] But this does not get us very far. Better are a translator's comments on Arthur's court as here 'the noblest and most glorious' in Britain, and how Arthur yet plays a minor role, 'a king rather than a hero' with his achievement 'largely in the past'. Conclusion: the narrative reveals little about 'the development of Arthur in Celtic literature'.[80] Arthur's origins as a North Briton having been forgotten, no surprise; even so (as already noted after Gwyn Jones), the notion of him as warrior and defender remains.

Now something vital: the text's thirteen French loanwords. They allude to the luxurious panoply of chivalry (such as *asur* or azure, *cristal* or crystal, *ystondard* or standard). There are substantially more than in the *Four Branches* of the 1120s or so, but far fewer than in the Three Romances of the thirteenth century's middle decades.[81] That tends to confirm dating on other grounds to the 1220s. Proinsias Mac Cana then followed Parry on the 'literary' nature of the tale; thought a twelfth-century dating as likely as a thirteenth-century one; observed that the tale has 'has no "plot" worth mentioning'; saw it as 'parody rather than satire'; noted Irish parallels; and defined its essence as 'literary virtuosity'.[82] In an essential guide to Welsh lore, the tale's self-description as *ystorya* is highlighted. It was not so much a 'history' as part of a 'national inheritance' handed down on the past.[83] In a wide-ranging survey (including film and other media), the story is (with reason) styled as having 'comedy of a high order' and as exploding 'myths' of Arthur and bards and Madog (d. 1160) himself, as well as subverting 'accepted notions of interlace' and digression.[84] An intriguing remark, its author elsewhere citing discussion by J. K. Bollard and Ceri Lloyd-Morgan on how the unknown writer mocked or sent up 'the prolixity of contemporary romance' in Welsh much as Chaucer did for English equivalents with his doleful tale of Sir Thopas.[85]

Now for change and (it seems) not one for the better. It appears in a passage on when *Breuddwyd Rhonabwy* was written. Melville Richards in 1948 opted for the early thirteenth century; Mary Giffin in 1958 for about 1300; Thomas Charles-Edwards in 1970 and Eric Hamp in 1972 for the twelfth century (on the simplistic view that a text on Madog ap Maredudd will be of his time); Angela Carson in

1974 for the late fourteenth; Edgar Slotkin in 1989 for soon after
1160; Ceri Lloyd-Morgan in 1991 for much later than that. Then a
further strange opinion: that the text postdates the Three Romances
(of the thirteenth century), because it subverts the chivalric romances found therein, and the writer could not have done that
before they existed. Implication: composition in the late thirteenth
century or even early fourteenth.[86] All the more reason to grip hold
of fact. So we state plainly that, on the French linguistic element
alone, the *Dream* long postdates the *Four Branches* (of the late 1120s
or so), but predates the Three Romances (of the thirteenth century's
second or third quarter).

In a short but illuminating account, *Breuddwyd Rhonabwy* is
related to the period after the Anglo- or Cambro-Norman invasion
of Ireland in 1169, when writers such as Gerald of Wales (in the
1180s) showed first-hand knowledge of the Irish and their customs.[87]
Hence a dream as the narrative's framework, or an ox's hide as a
means of nocturnal divination. Both were features of Irish tradition.
The latter was thought to 'release omens' (in a phrase applied by
Eliot in *The Dry Salvages* to seances, horoscopes, crystal balls, tea-
leaves, playing-cards).

Later commentators say this. The tale 'may be of the thirteenth
century'. Or 'it may be a product of Madog's own lifetime' (and so
before 1160).[88] That despite the lateness of its language; and the
circumstance that Madog, Powys king (and formidable adversary),
might have been undelighted had the text circulated in his day. A
slightly better opinion is 'at the end of the twelfth century' or 'early
decades of the thirteenth'.[89] Better again is comparative dating of the
Four Branches and the *Dream*, at least mentioning Old French
evidence, although unfortunately silent on lack of influence in the
former of Geoffrey of Monmouth (putting that narrative quartet to
before the mid-1130s), so that Rhonabwy's adventures postdate
those of Pwyll or Branwen by four generations.[90] It is preferable to
another on the *Dream* as of 'between the late twelfth and the late
fourteenth century'.[91] Hence an unfortunate declaration on the text

as of 'the decades around 1300'.[92] That is three generations too late. Also unhelpful is a verdict of between the 1150s and 'beginning of the fourteenth century'.[93] Or, again, Professor McKenna, who 'cannot date the text any earlier than about 1380' (when the sole known copy was written down); it could be of the twelfth century's 'second half'; or of 'the early fourteenth century'.[94] It is time to rescue her and others from (in Jane Austen's phrase) a 'state of such insensibility'. There is not a scrap of evidence to reject composition of *The Dream of Rhonabwy* in the early 1220s, as proposed by Melville Richards and D. Simon Evans. It will predate the Three Romances (with their copious borrowings from French) by some twenty to fifty years; as can be shown by the linguistic and other analysis of those very tales, to which we now turn.

3. The Three Romances: *Geraint, Owain, Peredur*

In discussing the *Mabinogion*'s most recent tales we not only discover, as it were, the family resemblance of three literary sisters, but a further one with cousins over in France, being the poems of *Erec* and *Yvain* and *Perceval* written (in that order) by Chrétien de Troyes (who began the last one after 14 May 1181). An international aspect of Welsh literature, then. From the nineteenth century onwards has been debate on which trio is the older, and how they relate to each other. We now know that the French sisters predate their cousins. They are of the later twelfth century: their Welsh kindred of the mid-thirteenth. How these conclusions were reached (with implications for sources and transmission) is instructive.

First, a summary of plot, or plots. Geraint (historically a king of south-west Britain, grandson of the Constantine denounced in 536 by Gildas and himself perhaps mentioned in Aneirin's *Gododdin* of 603 or so) is one of Arthur's knights. At a tournament he wins the hand of Enid; they marry, he goes to his realm to act as regent for his father; the couple are at first devoted; Geraint then mistakenly thinks Enid unfaithful to him; but, through a series of tests or trials, she vindicates herself and they are reconciled. In a last adventure, Geraint defeats 'the knight of the hedge of mist' and removes its enchantment. As for Owain, he too is historical, being son to Urien, patron of Taliesin and the ruler (in the 580s or so) of Rheged, with its court near Penrith, Cumbria. Seven centuries later, we find him the protagonist of a tale also called *The Lady of the Fountain*. If Geraint won Enid by prowess in a tournament, Owain (knight of Arthur) finds a wife by defeating the Knight of the Fountain and marrying his widow (the 'Lady'). He returns to Caerleon-upon-Usk, forgets his wife, goes mad, then recovers his wits. With a lion's assistance he performs acts of valour and is again honoured as chevalier and spouse. As for Peredur, he seems to have been a North Briton, but we know little of him. In the narrative he is brought up by his mother, who tries to shield him from the dangers of knighthood (which has killed his father and brothers). It is unavailing. Peredur makes his way to Arthur's court; undergoes chivalric trials; is then trained by two uncles, during which period he witnesses a mystic procession (with a bleeding lance and a head upon a salver); receives further instruction on combat from the Witches of Gloucester; and thereafter spends fourteen years of adventure, including a period ruling Constantinople with its Empress. Returning abruptly to Arthur, he finds himself abused by a loathly lady for not making enquiries on the mysterious lance and platter, actions which would have lifted a curse upon the king and his realm. The close is dramatic. Peredur wipes out the Gloucester coven of witches, who were responsible for acts of evil on his kinsmen and others. In short, myths a-plenty (Celtic and Christian) for lands accursed, sacred springs, sovereignty goddesses, Calvary, John the Baptist, warrior witches, waste lands, ailing kings. Abundant material too for enquiry (on construction, sources, authorial purpose, textual evolution) in three narratives which are Arthurian, but with Arthur much in the background.

Before the Great War, Morrice noticed how Arthur is no longer the 'petty chieftain' of *Culhwch*. He has become a 'powerful emperor' with a court of 'unrivalled splendour' at Caerleon, and with 'knight-errantry' in abundance, all deriving from Geoffrey of Monmouth's historical fantasies.[95] Researches on the Arthurian legend by Sir John Rhŷs were then noted, with comment on how the sixth-century North British prince Owain has entered 'the realm of fable' with 'perhaps overmuch emphasis' by Rhŷs on a supposed 'mythological element' there.[96] As for the chivalry and 'knight-errantry', Sir Ifor Williams put it differently. The stories of Peredur and the like have 'spent time in Paris' and left off some of their Welsh garb, coming home wearing French fashions.[97] Modern reactions to that *dillad Ffrengig* were various. Those seeking Celtic origins passed it by, leaving merely a cursory reference to the 'nine witches of Gloucester' as a Celtic survival in *Peredur*.[98] In another camp was Saunders Lewis, a Welshman receptive to *la civilization française*, thanks in part to the Great War (where he served in the trenches, there reading patriotic and Catholic writings by Maurice Barrès). Lewis brings out the division amongst Celticists concerning the Romances. Some dismiss them as poor imitations of genuine Welsh tradition; others welcome them as a new kind of narrative. Lewis was in the second camp. If issues of dating hindered our interpretation, he yet saw all three as resembling 'springs' flowing forth when others have run dry. Behind them (he thought) were 'French metrical romances' predating Chrétien; they themselves were composed in the 'last quarter of the twelfth century', their artistry perhaps making them the 'supreme achievement' of medieval Welsh prose.[99] Wrong on some (perhaps all) of these points, Lewis yet (as always) challenged readers into thinking.

Different again was the response of Robert Richards, MP, who treated the romances as portraits of their age, with details of the visor of a knight's helmet, of his cross-bow (made of ivory) and dagger, of competitors injured at tournaments, of a castle's dangerous portcullis, of a bed with scarlet covers of silk and other expensive fabrics (all these in *Owain*), or, at a lower level (in *Geraint*) hay-harvesters working from dawn, with bread and meat and wine sent to feed them.[100] Within romance there was, then, realism of a kind. After that, a return to origins. Melville Richards noted uncertainty on dating, but still put the three to before 1200, with their material drawn from narratives in Old French that were also used by Chrétien, the Welsh texts having a French ambience but plots unlike his.[101] Once more, the attempt to make out *Mabinogion* tales as far older than they are. They surely long postdate 1200.

On that French influence, compare again the remarks of translators, finding both 'a slackening of interest' and 'vague topography' as opposed to earlier Welsh tales, with 'unfortunate' results (so that few of us will care about events depicted, whether in a lady's bower or the nearby tilt-yard).[102] As for how they came about, Rachel Bromwich gave a post-Chrétien dating as 'probable', he and the Welsh *conteurs* having access to a lost French original (in prose?) of about 1150.[103] So, too, Sir Thomas Parry, making lucid observations on themes common to the three stories: each has a clear protagonist (Geraint, Owain, Peredur), as not so in other Middle Welsh prose; each represents Arthur no more as a 'daring chieftain', but as an 'emperor' possessed of a 'refined' court at Caerleon-on-Usk; Wales beyond its walls is a 'vague and unlocalized' never-never land; and manners are now chivalric, full of 'a polite grace and courtesy'. Even in the *Four Branches of the Mabinogi* is slaughter of staghound pups; women threatened with death by burning; maiming of horses; wife-battering; rape. But no such brutality here.[104] In contrast was Loomis, diffuse as Parry was concise, barring his observation on *Owain* as 'probably no older than 1180' (for which read 'certainly no later than 1280').[105]

These tales were studied in full by Sir Idris Foster. On their relation to Chrétien, he declared that 'It is not proposed here to attempt a final answer to these questions, but rather to consider some of the findings of recent scholarship.' All the same, place-names in the text reveal the author of *Geraint* as living 'between the Severn and the Taff'. After remarks on *Owain* there comes analysis of *Peredur*, its relationship to Chrétien's *Perceval* a problem 'more complicated' than for the other narratives. Conclusions for all three of them have surprises. The sources common to them and to

Chrétien are sometimes 'preserved more accurately' in Welsh, sometimes in French. Names of people and places were retained 'much more fully and accurately' by Chrétien than by 'the Welshman [but why one author, not three?], who suppresses and substitutes with great freedom', and who did not have the (long lost) original French text before him. Many 'traditional' motifs well-reproduced by Chrétien thus appear confusedly in the Welsh redactions, being proof of authorial 'failing recollection'. As for dates, Foster came down (after Melville Richards) for *Owain* as having 'an exemplar dated about 1200' in south-east Wales; and 'it is not improbable that *Geraint* and *Peredur* are also to be traced to that region' (and presumably the same date).[106] That '1200' has remained a stumbling block for many.

Later writers take on diverse aspects. As regards literary merit, Gwyn Jones lacked the enthusiasm of Saunders Lewis. The Arthur of the three texts is 'the shadow of a shade', their heroines are 'pallid', and their chivalry and 'emotional colouring' set few 'bells ringing' today. All the same, as romances they display the 'skill and tact of their authors' (Jones did not attribute them to one man).[107] Kenneth Jackson provided insight on an episode in *Peredur*. A duck has been killed in mid-winter; a raven feeds upon it; Peredur, seeing black raven, white snow, red blood, compares them severally to the hair, flesh, and cheeks of the woman he adores. The same motif occurs in the early Irish story of Deirdre, as well as modern Irish and Scottish Gaelic folktales. But there is no reason to regard it as especially Celtic (as once thought). It occurs in 'several international popular tales' (those of Snow White and Cinderella amongst them).[108] An interesting point. We return to it at this chapter's close in criticizing a study of 2024.

Great linguist though Simon Evans was, he still located *Geraint* and its fellows to about 1200.[109] R. L. Thomson went further. His edition of *Owain* is admirable in its completeness, but not in all its conclusions, especially (after Sir Ifor Williams) on the *Four Branches of the Mabinogi* as being of 'before 1100' (*recte*, of about 1128), so that *Owain* 'had a written form' almost certainly by 1150 and 'perhaps by the beginning of the twelfth century'.[110] It would long predate Chrétien. A startling claim. Yet it cannot be right. Nevertheless, it is a credit to Thomson's memory that he discussed medieval culture and French loanwords in ways that put this tale and others within the decades about 1250. Looking back far beyond those years, Nora Chadwick again took up *Peredur*'s Nine Witches of Gloucester, noting parallels to this school of women-warriors in Irish tradition, where wise women also train men in violence.[111] Mac Cana noted another curious archaism, interpreting *Owain*'s 'monstrous but benign keeper of the forest' as deriving from horned Cernunnos, Celtic herdsman-god. That is why he can summon beasts of the wood (snakes amongst them) 'through the belling of a stag'.[112] Under the French or Parisian fashions of these stories, then, some ancient mysteries. Further aspects (of an eye for wonders and detail) are made clear by Jackson's translations: Peredur recovering a gaming-board from a castle perilous; Peredur witnessing a riverside tree, one half 'blazing up to its very top' and the other in green leaf; Enid admiring the 'marvellous beauty' of Geraint, asleep with 'the sun shining on the bed'; also in early morning, a lad taking 'bread and meat and wine' to mowers in the field, and offering some of what he has to Geraint (famished after a night in the forest). Jackson dated all these passages to the twelfth century.[113]

In an outstanding contribution, Rachel Bromwich dealt with diverse aspects of the tales. Although quoting Ifor Williams's later (and brilliant) remark of 1946 on how these Welsh legends 'had spent time on the Continent and come back to Wales dressed in Paris fashions (*ffasiwn Paris*)', she also undermined it. It implied that the Welsh authors worked from French texts, which she thought hardly so. She stressed their native features (such as political sovereignty bestowed by a goddess), which she thought settled dispute on links with Chrétien de Troyes (he and the Welsh alike having access to the same original material, as opposed to Welsh writers using Chrétien). Her knowledge of Celtic tradition naturally gave her an authority not possessed by most other commentators. Her study should be better known than it is. It guides us to research on differences in spelling and so on as indicating that the three texts are not by the same hand. The sole flaw in her arguments was on dating. She was sure that the Welsh stories were older than Chrétien's, in part because they show no awareness of later French literature. French loanwords for garments or fabrics or weapons and the like were merely due to composition in the bilingual society of south-east Wales 'during the twelfth century' (*yn ystod y ddeuddegfed ganrif*).[114] Expert on literature, she was not expert on medieval technology, which will direct us to the thirteenth century's middle decades.

A contrary slant on French influence underlines the difficulties. R. L. Thomson was cited on how *Owain* and its associates go back to Welsh stories that were used by French writers and then returned in French guise to Wales, where storytellers turned them back into Welsh. They 'derive from French reworkings of Celtic originals', this explanation (if 'a trifle artificial') accounting for the French elements therein.[115] Quite the opposite of Rachel Bromwich's view of them as old and owing nothing to France except a veneer of words and manners. Closer to her are statements on the stories as of the twelfth century, their matter then passing over to France and becoming known to Chrétien and others. Back in Wales, the stories remained in circulation, attempts eventually being made to adapt them to what had developed in French (*datblygiadau Ffrengig*).[116]

Then came a weighty account of linguistic chronology. Together with evidence (discussed below) on windmills and spurs, it upturns notions both on the tales as predating Chrétien (which is simplistic), and on Celtic narratives entering French literature and coming back to Wales (which is over-complex). It is this. *Peredur* and the like swarm with French loanwords. They include even daily terms, like *costrel* 'bottle', *ffiol* 'bowl', *forest* 'great wood', *twel* 'towel', *ystabyl* 'stable'. We have moved on from mere imported luxury items like *pali* 'brocaded silk'.[117] That puts *Peredur* and the like long after the floruit of Chrétien de Troyes.

Naturally, implications of that took time to sink in. Yet there were signs of progress. Allusions in Welsh bardic poetry to the *matière de France* (Charlemagne, Roland, Oliver) appear in the thirteenth century only (and not early in that century).[118] Conclusion: to twelfth-century Welsh writers, French literary culture was effectively unknown. No surprise, then, if Mac Cana dismissed notions of the Welsh Arthurian trio as deriving from Chrétien; or of British tales carried to France and then coming back to Wales (their originals having mysteriously 'died out on their home ground'). Preferable is the hypothesis (after Bobi Jones and Rachel Bromwich) of narratives which 'evolved in a bilingual environment in Wales' and surely its south-east (ever open to change from beyond). While they used the same source as Chrétien did, he often retained native symptoms (names of people or places) which they discarded. Mac Cana also ruled out a common author for them. There were at least two, *Geraint* not being by whoever wrote the others. But he stumbled on placing them between '1100 and 1200'.[119]

Besides a wealth of information on the origins (historical or not) of men and women in the three stories, Rachel Bromwich accepted Myrddin Lloyd's observation on how Welsh bards of the twelfth century never mention Continental romance or the fictions of Geoffrey of Monmouth (which undermines her aside here on *Geraint* as 'based' on a French source).[120] Why, we might ask, should our trio of tales (with French language and culture there so apparent) belong to that same twelfth century? Will they not be of the thirteenth century, when knowledge of France was more widespread in Wales?

In the 1980s came a new (and even entertaining) approach (in the names of structuralism and post-structuralism) from Bill McCann. He pointed out that, while French critics regard the Welsh Arthurian romances as primitive and 'ansoffistigedig', the Welsh think more highly of them. He quoted T. Gwynn Jones (in a 1926 paper) on Chrétien's poems as 'long and tortuous', with the French poet's Welsh *confrères* left as 'incomparably the best story-tellers'. (Although a great poet, Gwynn Jones was clearly at a loss with Chrétien's delight in *entrelacement*.) McCann's article is useful for reference to Lévi-Strauss and other Continental theorists, as also to research (some of it unpublished) by British Celticists.[121] Then for the 1990s and a jolt from an American reference book. In a series of entries, our three Welsh texts are stated as 'probably' of 'the thirteenth century'.[122] A victory has been won. By the same author is more revisionism, transforming our understanding of these texts. Acknowledgement is made to *Geraint* as displaying interlacement, a narrative technique pioneered by Chrétien; and to the Three Romances as postdating their French equivalents. Those Welsh texts, treated throughout with a praiseworthy sensitivity and fairness and perception, here find their ablest interpreter in essays to be read and read again; not least for his observation that the years before the final collapse of Welsh independence in 1282 were not ones of 'decline'; instead, they display 'a flowering of native culture at a time of overwhelming political and social change'.[123] Certainly more helpful than 'probably (*mae'n debyg*) some time in the twelfth or thirteenth century'.[124] Also to be jettisoned is '1150-1250' and perhaps 'later rather than earlier' given thirty years ago by the present writer.[125] Research on material culture rules out anything before 1220 or even 1230. It perhaps tells us more than comments on these stories as 'tales to be performed'.[126]

In 2003 the writer discussed a passage in *Peredur* on a valley full of windmills, complete with head miller, a 'big' confident man with 'the look of a craftsman about him'. Windmills came to medieval Europe from the Arab world (its parched landscapes no place for water-mills). The oldest known windmill in Britain is one mentioned in 1170, at Swineshead, near Boston, Lincolnshire. That shifts *Peredur* forwards to 1200 or (better) after that. The Welsh author mentioned the new technology of his day, and time was needed for that to become known in Wales.[127] Windmills thus confirm the thirteenth-century date implicit in Simon Evans's catalogues of loanwords, so abundant with the Three Romances.

Despite that, one translator in Wales said no more on the question than that the oldest surviving manuscript here (it is of *Peredur*) was copied in the decades around 1300.[128] Equally vague is a statement on how these three legends of Arthur 'evolved during the twelfth century in a shared cultural environment' of Welsh and French cheek-by-jowl in Glamorgan and Gwent.[129] Against that is 'by the first half, probably by the first quarter of the thirteenth century' (where 'by' is a slip for 'in') for composition of *Peredur, Owain, Geraint*.[130] A move in the right direction. Then some curious statements from the same writer. *Peredur* and its partners are said to 'derive' from Chrétien (not from a source common to both). They are not by 'the same redactor or author'. (One agrees.) Although often placed in 'a single milieu', this is dismissed as 'highly unlikely'; while *Geraint* may be from south-east Wales, the first written copies of *Peredur* are from the north-west. Despite that, the two share more vocabulary (134 items) with each other than they do with *Owain*. (A fundamental insight if so, perhaps showing that the author of *Geraint* travelled from Gwent to Gwynedd.) It is asserted that there is 'insufficient evidence' to establish dates with precision. On the basis of supposed French sources other than Chrétien, *Peredur* might yet be of 1225-50 or so; *Geraint* and *Owain* may be 'slightly earlier', with 1210 to 1230 'a reasonable guess'. At this point, however, all confidence is destroyed by association of the *Four Branches of the Mabinogi* with the court of Llywelyn the Great (d. 1240) as a 'centre for literary production'.[131] Not so.

After that, recalling that dry-as-dust chronology matters less (in the end) than wonder-tales and literary art, one turns with some relief to analysis of the tree seen by Peredur, one half of it in green leaf, the other all ablaze. Thanks to Matthew Arnold (eminent Victorian), it has become a 'celebrated example of Celtic magic', that 'magic' being in no way mystical or esoteric, but (in Kenneth Jackson's words) merely due to a 'vastly greater power of inventiveness and imagination' amongst Welsh and Irish writers; where they were aided by images of a tree on fire in bardic language.[132] *Peredur*'s author did not create the episode from nothing.

The present writer then discussed spurs. In *Owain* is mention of a rowel-spur, equipped with a tiny wheel. The oldest evidence for these in Britain is on a royal seal of 1218; they were a sophistication of Henry III's reign. That puts *Owain* after 1220 and presumably after 1230.[133] After that one reads with interest a view on the narrative trio as probably not 'composed before the thirteenth century' and, for *Geraint* and *Peredur*, no later than late-thirteenth-century copies of them.[134] But that tell-tale spur indicates a narrower scope, of the thirteenth century's middle decades. We can thus modify one writer's 'early thirteenth century' for them, while reserving judgement on how they 'pointedly avoid or revise the colonialist tropes of Chrétien' and a confidence in them (after Dr Lloyd-Morgan) as 'indeed translations of Chrétien' (not mere versions of his sources).[135] Just as in the 1980s a forward-looking critic might speak of Lévi-Strauss and post-structuralism, so with the above in the 2010s we hear of Homi Bhabha and Edward Said and post-colonialism. This is welcome. French culture in Britain reaching its zenith under Henry III (also the age of Llywelyn the Great and Llywelyn the Last), the more reason to scrutinize, on lines indicated by this last critic, French symptoms *vis-à-vis* colonialism (cultural and otherwise) as reflected in *Geraint, Owain, Peredur*.

It also brings us to their orientalism: a neglected subject. There is much on it (especially for Constantinople) in an original monograph. That aside, one yet notices that (a) dating is there still thought 'uncertain' (late twelfth century? 1250 x 1284?), as is (b) their relation to Chrétien ('derivations from French'? with pre-French 'elements'?).[136] Another scholar makes the interesting proposal that native Welsh law casts light on 'conventions regarding etiquette' in *Geraint* and *Peredur*.[137] After that, some confusion on *Peredur*. It is 'an adaptation' of Chrétien's *Perceval*; it yet draws on 'the French cultural resources' of Wales's 'twelfth-century' Anglo-Norman colonizers in order to 'subvert that material', with Arthur's court becoming that of a 'foreign power'; and despair on the (supposed) lack of a 'definite context in which to interpret the texts'.[138] This does not add up. If *Peredur* derives from *Perceval*, it belongs to the thirteenth century, not the twelfth. Hard also to see why Arthur should there be an alien oppressor, when he was taken as Welsh. As for 'context', it is more 'definite' than assumed. *Peredur* and the like relate to Wales in the middle or later years of Henry III's reign (1216-72). Wherever our authors wrote, they could not ignore the Marcher lordships, the result of military aggression and occupation. The fact might well linger in a writer's mind when representing Arthur, whether he knew it or not.

A complete volume for the subject yet has too much of the inconclusive and unsatisfactory. Take, for example, its offering on *Owain*. Ceri Lloyd-Morgan is quoted in it for a dating to 'the second or third decade of the thirteenth century' (too early); the relation to Chrétien's *Ywain* is said to be 'difficult to define', because the Welsh text provides little on its 'degree of dependence'; 'irrefutable proof' on the question is therefore 'unlikely'; yet few (we are told) now think that any parallels are due to a 'common source'. Instead, Chrétien's text went through wholesale 'adaptation' within Wales. (Even if these stories reached Wales in the latest 'Paris fashions', then, they soon shed their expensive new garments and became thoroughly Welsh.) No wonder, therefore, that imperial Arthur is encountered 'seated on a pile of fresh rushes' (if with a cushion). All that despite supposed influence from 'twelfth-century' discourses of 'courtly love and chivalry'.[139] There are three problems in the above: (a) we shall never have proper focus on our material if we cannot date it; (b) hesitant derivation of *Owain* from *Ywain* does not face up to how Chrétien knew of this British hero in the first place, so that the French poet's source remains elusive; (c) no progress can in any case be made if one ignores fundamental research, such as that by R. L. Thomson on rowel spurs.[140] So we say again that *Owain* hardly predates 1230. We should relate everything in the Three Romances to the reign of Henry III, when (English civil wars notwithstanding)

French culture reached a high-water mark in Britain.

Finally, two recent books. In the first, barring a reference to windmills, regarded by the author as 'superficially' (*sic*) indicating composition after about 1200, one searches with difficulty for rulings on when the author of *Peredur* wrote.[141] In the second, remarks on what Deirdre said after witnessing red blood and raven black in white snow (it prompted thoughts of her wished-for lover) do not compare well with Jackson's 1961 treatment of the theme. Jackson proved something (that the theme is international, not especially Welsh or Irish). The later critic (who never mentions Jackson) comments merely on (for instance) how Deirdre was changed by what she saw.[142] But any reader could work that out. Conclusion from these recent studies: standards amongst Celticists have declined. Yet resolute enquirers may take courage. Admirable editions of *Culhwch and Olwen* and *The Dream of Rhonabwy* have settled most of the questions on them. There is no such agreement for *Geraint, Owain, Peredur*. So we end with an objective. Factual assessment of those texts is still to seek; there are tasks to be done.

Notes

1. John Rhŷs, *Celtic Britain*, 3rd edn (London, 1904), 307-8.

2. *The Mabinogion*, tr. Charlotte Guest (London, 1906), 8.

3. J. C. Morrice, *A Manual of Welsh Literature* (Bangor, 1908), 29, 30.

4. E. K. Chambers, *Arthur of Britain* (London, 1927), 70, 71.

5. W. J. Gruffydd, *Math vab Mathonwy* (Cardiff, 1928), 251-2.

6. H. M. Chadwick and N. K. Chadwick, *The Growth of Literature: The Ancient Literatures of Europe* (Cambridge, 1932), 45.

7. Saunders Lewis, *Braslun o Hanes Llenyddiaeth Gymraeg* (Caerdydd, 1932), 38-9.

8. Robert Richards, *Cymru'r Oesau Canol* (Wrecsam, 1933), 420.

9. *Canu Aneirin*, ed. Ifor Williams (Caerdydd, 1938), 363.

10. *The Mabinogion*, tr. Gwyn Jones and Thomas Jones (London, 1949), xxi-xxvii.

11. Rachel Bromwich, 'The Character of the Early Welsh Tradition', in *Studies in Early British History*, ed. N. K. Chadwick (Cambridge, 1954), 83-136.

12. Thomas Parry, *A History of Welsh Literature* (Oxford, 1955), 75-80.

13. R. S. Loomis, *Wales and the Arthurian Legend* (Cardiff, 1956), 192.

14. Geoffrey Ashe, *King Arthur's Avalon: The Story of Glastonbury* (London, 1957), 88.

15. I. Ll. Foster, '*Culhwch and Olwen* and *Rhonabwy's Dream*', in *Arthurian Literature in the Middle Ages*, ed. R. S. Loomis (Oxford, 1959), 31-43.

16. Gwyn Jones, 'The Prose Romances of Medieval Wales', in *Wales Through the Ages: From the Earliest Times to 1485*, ed. A. J. Roderick (Swansea, 1959), 138-44.

17. K. H. Jackson, *The International Popular Tale and Early Welsh Tradition* (Cardiff, 1961), 71-81.

18. Alwyn Rees and Brynley Rees, *Celtic Heritage* (London, 1961), 262-4.

19. D. Simon Evans, *A Grammar of Middle Welsh* (Dublin, 1964), xxx.

20. Geoffrey Ashe, 'The Arthurian Fact', in *The Quest for Arthur's Britain*, ed. Geoffrey Ashe (London, 1968), 27-57.

21. K. H. Jackson, *The Gododdin: The Oldest Scottish Poem* (Edinburgh, 1969), 112, 155.

22. Proinsias Mac Cana, *Celtic Mythology* (London, 1970), 33.

23. K. H. Jackson, *A Celtic Miscellany*, 2nd edn (Harmondsworth, 1971), 182-3, 197-8, 201-4.

24. Idris Foster, 'Culhwch ac Olwen', in *Y Traddodiad Rhyddiaith yn yr Oesau Canol*, ed. Geraint Bowen (Llandysul, 1974), 65-82.

25. *The Mabinogion*, tr. Jeffrey Gantz (Harmondsworth, 1976), 134-5.

26. *Historia Gruffudd ap Cynan*, ed. D. Simon Evans (Caerdydd, 1977), ccciv.

27. Proinsias Mac Cana, *Writers of Wales: The Mabinogi* (Cardiff, 1977), 62.

28. Rachel Bromwich, *Trioedd Ynys Prydein*, 2nd edn (Cardiff, 1978), xci-iii.

29. D. Simon Evans, 'Culhwch ac Olwen', *Ysgrifau Beirniadol*, xiii (1985), 101-13.

30. Patrick Sims-Williams, 'The Irish Geography of *Culhwch and Olwen*', in *Sages, Saints, and Storytellers*, ed. Donnchadh Ó Corráin, Liam Breatnach, Kim McCone (Maynooth, 1989), 412-26.

31. B. F. Roberts, '*Culhwch ac Olwen*, The Triads, Saints' Lives', in *The Arthur of the Welsh*, ed. Rachel Bromwich, A. O. H. Jarman, B. F. Roberts (Cardiff, 1991), 73-95.

32. *Culhwch and Olwen*, ed. Rachel Bromwich and D. Simon Evans (Cardiff, 1992), lxxviii, lxxix, lxxxi.

33. B. F. Roberts, *Studies on Middle Welsh Literature* (Lewiston, 1992), 55-6.

34. Sioned Davies, *Crefft y Cyfarwydd* (Caerdydd, 1995), 7.

35. A. Breeze, *Medieval Welsh Literature* (Dublin, 1997), 68-82.

36. Sioned Davies, 'Written Text as Performance', in *Literacy in Medieval Celtic Societies*, ed. Huw Pryce (Cambridge, 1998), 133-48.

37. N. J. Higham, *King Arthur: Myth-Making and History* (London, 2002), 88.

38. Sioned Davies, 'Performing *Culhwch ac Olwen*', in *Arthurian Literature xxi: Celtic Arthurian Material*, ed. Ceridwen Lloyd-Morgan (Cambridge, 2004), 29-51.

39. Martin Aurell, *La Légende du roi Arthur* (Paris, 2007), 55.

40. *The Mabinogion*, tr. Sioned Davies (Oxford, 2007), xxii.

41. Proinsias Mac Cana, 'Ireland and Wales in the Middle Ages: An Overview', in *Ireland and Wales in the Middle Ages*, ed. Karen Jankulak and J. M. Wooding (Dublin, 2007), 17-45.

42. Anon., 'Mabinogion, The', in *The Welsh Academy Encyclopaedia of Wales*, ed. John Davies, Nigel Jenkins, Menna Baines, P. I. Lynch (Cardiff, 2008), 525-6.

43. Nikolai Tolstoy, *The Oldest British Prose Literature* (Lewiston, 2009), vi-vii.

44. Thomas Charles-Edwards, 'The Date of *Culhwch ac Olwen*', in *Bile ós Chrannaibh*, ed. Wilson McLeod, Abigail Burnyeat, D. U. Stiùbhart, T. O. Clancy, Roibeard Ó Maolalaigh (Ceann Drochaid, 2010), 45-56.

45. Nick Higham, 'The Chroniclers of Early Britain', in *The Arthur of Medieval Latin Learning*, ed. Siân Echard (Cardiff, 2010), 9-25.

46. Mark Williams, *Fiery Shapes* (Oxford, 2010), 67 n. 1.

47. A. Breeze, 'Orosius, the Book of Taliesin, and *Culhwch and Olwen*', *Studia Celtica* 45 (2011), 203-9.

48. Patrick Sims-Williams, *Irish Influence on Medieval Welsh Literature* (Oxford, 2011), 39 n. 60, 187.

49. Thomas Charles-Edwards, *Wales and the Britons: 350-1064* (Oxford, 2013), 654-5.

50. Oliver Padel, *Writers of Wales: Medieval Arthurian Literature*, rev. edn (Cardiff, 2013), 12.

51. A. Breeze, 'Caer Brythwch and Brythach and Nerthach in *Culhwch and Olwen*', *The Journal of Literary Onomastics* 3 (2013-14), 1-4.

52. Natalia I. Petrovskaia, *Medieval Welsh Perceptions of the Orient* (Turnhout, 2015), 148-9.

53. Nikolai Tolstoy, *The Mysteries of Stonehenge* (Stroud, 2016), 486-90.

54. Krista Kapphahn, 'There and Back Again', in *Arthur, la mer et la guerre*, ed. Alban Gautier, Marc Rolland, Michelle Szkilnik (Paris, 2017), 67-81.

55. N. J. Higham, *King Arthur: The Making of the Legend* (New Haven, 2018), 237.

56. Robin Chapman Stacey, *Law and the Imagination in Medieval Wales* (Philadelphia, 2018), 146.

57. Diana Luft, 'Commemorating the Past After 1066', in *The Cambridge History of Welsh Literature*, ed. Geraint Evans and Helen Fulton (Cambridge, 2019), 73-92.

58. Simon Rodway, '*Culhwch ac Olwen*', in *Arthur in the Celtic Languages*, ed. Ceridwen Lloyd-Morgan and Erich Poppe (Cardiff, 2019), 67-79.

59. Rebecca Thomas, *History and Identity in Early Medieval Wales* (Cardiff, 2022), 37.

60. Helen Fulton, 'The Invention of Arthurian Britain', in *The Arthurian World*, ed. Victoria Coldham-Fussell, Miriam Edlich-Mutt, Renée Ward (London, 2022), 35–48.

61. Melissa Ridley Elmes, 'Arthurian Ethics Before the Pentecostal Oath', in *Ethics in the Arthurian Legend*, ed. Melissa Ridley Elmes and Evelyn Meyer (London, 2023), 8-34.

62. J. C. Morrice, *A Manual of Welsh Literature* (Bangor, 1908), 30.

63. J. E. Lloyd, *A History of Wales* (London, 1911), 248.

64. H. M. Chadwick and N. K. Chadwick, *The Growth of Literature: The Ancient Literatures of Europe* (Cambridge, 1932), 15, 45.

65. Saunders Lewis, *Braslun o Hanes Llenyddiaeth Gymraeg* (Caerdydd, 1932), 41-2.

66. Robert Richards, *Cymru'r Oesau Canol* (Wrecsam, 1933), 420.

67. *Breudwyt Ronabwy*, ed. Melville Richards (Caerdydd, 1948).

68. *The Mabinogion*, tr. Gwyn Jones and Thomas Jones (London, 1949), xxvii.

69. Rachel Bromwich, 'The Character of the Early Welsh Tradition', in *Studies in Early British History*, ed. N. K. Chadwick (Cambridge, 1954), 83-136.

70. Thomas Parry, *A History of Welsh Literature* (Oxford, 1955), 81-4.

71. R. S. Loomis, *Wales and the Arthurian Legend* (Cardiff, 1956), 97-8.

72. Geoffrey Ashe, *King Arthur's Avalon: The Story of Glastonbury* (London, 1957), 89.

73. I. Ll. Foster, '*Culhwch and Olwen* and *Rhonabwy's Dream*', in *Arthurian Literature in the Middle Ages*, ed. R. S. Loomis (Oxford, 1959), 31-43.

74. Gwyn Jones, 'The Prose Romances of Medieval Wales', in *Wales Through the Ages: From the Earliest Times to 1485*, ed. A. J. Roderick (Swansea, 1959), 138-44.

75. D. Simon Evans, *A Grammar of Middle Welsh* (Dublin, 1964), xxx.

76. Enid Roberts, *Braslun o Hanes Llên Powys* (Dinbych, 1965), 37-42.

77. Geoffrey Ashe, 'The Arthurian Fact', in *The Quest for Arthur's Britain*, ed. Geoffrey Ashe (London, 1968), 27-57.

78. K. H. Jackson, *A Celtic Miscellany*, 2nd edn (Harmondsworth, 1971), 179.

79. Dafydd Glyn Jones, 'Breuddwyd Rhonabwy', in *Y Traddodiad Rhyddiaith yn yr Oesau Canol*, ed. Geraint Bowen (Llandysul, 1974), 176-95.

80. *The Mabinogion*, tr. Jeffrey Gantz (Harmondsworth, 1976), 20.

81. *Historia Gruffudd ap Cynan*, ed. D. Simon Evans (Caerdydd, 1977), ccciv.

82. Proinsias Mac Cana, *Writers of Wales: The Mabinogi* (Cardiff, 1977), 87-97.

83. Rachel Bromwich, *Trioedd Ynys Prydein*, 2nd edn (Cardiff, 1978), lxxi n. 4.

84. B. F. Roberts, '*Dream of Rhonabwy, The*', in *The New Arthurian Encyclopedia*, ed. Norris J. Lacy (Chicago, 1991), 120-1.

85. B. F. Roberts, *Studies on Middle Welsh Literature* (Lewiston, 1992), 71.

86. Sioned Davies, *Crefft y Cyfarwydd* (Caerdydd, 1995), 14-15.

87. A. Breeze, *Medieval Welsh Literature* (Dublin, 1997), 85-7.

88. *The Mabinogion*, tr. Sioned Davies (Oxford, 2007), xxi.

89. Anon., '*Mabinogion, The*', in *The Welsh Academy Encyclopaedia of Wales*, ed. John Davies, Nigel Jenkins, Menna Baines, P. I. Lynch (Cardiff, 2008), 525-6.

90. Patrick Sims-Williams, *Irish Influence on Medieval Welsh Literature* (Oxford, 2011), 190.

91. Oliver Padel, *Writers of Wales: Medieval Arthurian Literature*, rev. edn (Cardiff, 2013), 72.

92. N. J. Higham, *King Arthur: The Making of the Legend* (New Haven, 2018), 268.

93. Diana Luft, 'Commemorating the Past After 1066', in *The Cambridge History of Welsh Literature*, ed. Geraint Evans and Helen Fulton (Cambridge, 2019), 73-92.

94. Catherine McKenna, '*Breuddwyd Rhonabwy*', in *Arthur in the Celtic Languages*, ed. Ceridwen Lloyd-Morgan and Erich Poppe (Cardiff, 2019), 80-91.

95. J. C. Morrice, *A Manual of Welsh Literature* (Bangor, 1908), 30-1.

96. J. E. Lloyd, *A History of Wales* (London, 1911), 165.

97. *Pedeir Keinc y Mabinogi*, ed. Ifor Williams (Caerdydd, 1930), li.

98. H. M. Chadwick and N. K. Chadwick, *The Growth of Literature: The Ancient Literatures of Europe* (Cambridge, 1932), 214, 647.

99. Saunders Lewis, *Braslun o Hanes Llenyddiaeth Gymraeg* (Caerdydd, 1932), 43-5.

100. Robert Richards, *Cymru'r Oesau Canol* (Wrecsam, 1933), 421, 423.

101. *Breudwyt Ronabwy*, ed. Melville Richards (Caerdydd, 1948), xl.

102. *The Mabinogion*, tr. Gwyn Jones and Thomas Jones (London, 1949), xxvii–xxx.

103. Rachel Bromwich, 'The Character of the Early Welsh Tradition', in *Studies in Early British History*, ed. N. K. Chadwick (Cambridge, 1954), 83–136.

104. Thomas Parry, *A History of Welsh Literature* (Oxford, 1955), 86–8.

105. R. S. Loomis, *Wales and the Arthurian Legend* (Cardiff, 1956), 159.

106. I. Ll. Foster, '*Gereint, Owein*, and *Peredur*', in *Arthurian Literature in the Middle Ages*, ed. R. S. Loomis (Oxford, 1959), 192–205.

107. Gwyn Jones, 'The Prose Romances of Medieval Wales', in *Wales Through the Ages: From the Earliest Times to 1485*, ed. A. J. Roderick (Swansea, 1959), 138–44.

108. K. H. Jackson, *The International Popular Tale and Early Welsh Tradition* (Cardiff, 1961), 114–15.

109. D. Simon Evans, *A Grammar of Middle Welsh* (Dublin, 1964), xxx.

110. *Owein, or Chwedyl Iarlles y Ffynnawn*, ed. R. L. Thomson (Dublin, 1968), xxi.

111. N. K. Chadwick, *The Celts* (Harmondsworth, 1970), 134–6.

112. Proinsias Mac Cana, *Celtic Mythology* (London, 1970), 47.

113. K. H. Jackson, *A Celtic Miscellany*, 2nd edn (Harmondsworth, 1971), 152, 160, 177–8.

114. Rachel Bromwich, 'Dwy Chwedl a Thair Rhamant', in *Y Traddodiad Rhyddiaith yn yr Oesau Canol*, ed. Geraint Bowen (Llandysul, 1974), 143–75.

115. *The Mabinogion*, tr. Jeffrey Gantz (Harmondsworth, 1976), 25.

116. *Historia Peredur vab Efrawc*, ed. Glenys Witchard Goetinck (Caerdydd, 1976), xxiii.

117. *Historia Gruffudd ap Cynan*, ed. D. Simon Evans (Caerdydd, 1977), ccciv.

118. D. Myrddin Lloyd, *Rhai Agweddau ar Ddysg y Gogynfeirdd* (Caerdydd, 1977), 14.

119. Proinsias Mac Cana, *Writers of Wales: The Mabinogi* (Cardiff, 1977), 99–101.

120. Rachel Bromwich, *Trioedd Ynys Prydein*, 2nd edn (Cardiff, 1978), lxxix.

121. W. J. McCann, 'Adeiledd y Tair Rhamant', *Ysgrifau Beirniadol* 13 (1985),

123-33.

122. B. F. Roberts, '*Geraint and Enid*', '*Owain*', '*Peredur*', in *The New Arthurian Encyclopedia*, ed. Norris J. Lacy (Chicago, 1991), 182, 348, 357-8.

123. B. F. Roberts, *Studies on Middle Welsh Literature* (Lewiston, 1992), 144.

124. Sioned Davies, *Crefft y Cyfarwydd* (Caerdydd, 1995), 12.

125. A. Breeze, *Medieval Welsh Literature* (Dublin, 1997), 89.

126. Sioned Davies, 'Written Text as Performance', in *Literacy in Medieval Celtic Societies*, ed. Hugh Pryce (Cambridge, 1998), 133-48.

127. A. Breeze, '*Peredur Son of Efrawg* and Windmills', *Celtica* 24 (2003), 58-64.

128. *The Mabinogion*, tr. Sioned Davies (Oxford, 2007), xxiv-xxv.

129. Anon., '*Mabinogion, The*', in *The Welsh Academy Encyclopaedia of Wales*, ed. John Davies, Nigel Jenkins, Menna Baines, P. I. Lynch (Cardiff, 2008), 525-6.

130. Ceri Lloyd-Morgan, 'Literary Borrowing in Medieval Wales and England', in *Authority and Subjugation in Writing of Medieval Wales*, ed. Ruth Kennedy and Simon Meecham-Jones (Basingstoke, 2008), 159-73.

131. Ceridwen Lloyd-Morgan, 'Migrating Narratives', in *A Companion to Arthurian Literature*, ed. Helen Fulton (Basingstoke, 2009), 128–41.

132. Patrick Sims-Williams, *Irish Influence on Medieval Welsh Literature* (Oxford, 2011), 131.

133. A. Breeze, 'Spurs, Horse-Armour, and the Date of *Owein*', in *Lochlann*, ed. Cathinka Hambro and L. I. Widerøe (Oslo, 2013), 105-10.

134. Oliver Padel, *Writers of Wales: Medieval Arthurian Literature*, rev. edn (Cardiff, 2013), 61.

135. Michael A. Faletra, *Wales and the Medieval Colonial Imagination* (New York, 2014), 130-1, 211.

136. Natalia I. Petrovskaia, *Medieval Welsh Perceptions of the Orient* (Turnhout, 2015), 172.

137. Robin Chapman Stacey, *Law and the Imagination in Medieval Wales* (Philadelphia, 2018), 21.

138. Diana Luft, 'Commemorating the Past After 1066', in *The Cambridge History of Welsh Literature*, ed. Geraint Evans and Helen Fulton (Cambridge, 2019), 73-92.

139. Regine Reck, '*Owain* or *Chwedyl Iarlles y Ffynnawn*', in *Arthur in the Celtic Languages*, ed. Ceridwen Lloyd-Morgan and Erich Poppe (Cardiff, 2019), 117-31.

140. A. Breeze, 'Epic and Romance in Welsh and Irish', in *Epic and Romance: A Guide to Medieval European Literature*, ed. Leonard Neidorf and Liu Yang (Nanjing, 2021), 44-66.

141. Natalia I. Petrovskaia, *This Is Not a Grail Romance: Understanding 'Historia Peredur vab Efrawc'* (Cardiff, 2023), 70-1.

142. Joanne Findon, *Bound and Free: Voices of Mortal and Otherworld Women in Medieval Irish Literature* (Toronto, 2024), 55-6.

CHAPTER FIVE

GEOFFREY OF MONMOUTH

In the literatures of Britain, Geoffrey of Monmouth (d. 1155) has during ten centuries been a joker in the pack. His *Historia Regum Britanniae* or 'History of the Kings of Britain' is an imposture or hoax or fake that has enjoyed a stupefying success. It launched the legend of Arthur upon a Europe eager for it; its fictions accelerated British political unity; without it we should not have Shakespeare's Lear or Cymbeline; and its placing of Arthur's birth at Tintagel still puts millions of dollars into Cornish tourism. Everywhere spoken against, Geoffrey cannot be ignored.

His life and cavalier treatment of antiquity are the themes of this chapter, so that for the latter we deal with how he used sources; his presentation of Arthur; and the reception of his work. The last provides an interesting lesson, offering the spectacle of kings and their ministers appropriating pseudo-history for affairs of state, and of gifted scholars defending the indefensible. These aspects in mind, we begin our survey with Sir John Rhŷs (d. 1915) of Oxford.

He put his finger upon a paradox. Although Geoffrey was devoid of scholarly principle, he was still a blessing for poets, as with his blithe explanations of *Cymru* (Wales) from 'an eponymous hero called Kamber' or *Lloegr* (Welsh for England south of the Humber) from Locrinus, as imaginary as Kamber. On the latter, Rhŷs (to his credit) directed readers to Milton's *Comus*.[1] Locrinus is there styled father to the River Severn's tutelary nymph:

> Sabrina is her name, a virgin pure:
>
> Whilom she was the daughter of Locrine

-- Milton having taken the story from the 'chronicle of Briton kings' in Spenser's *Faerie Queene* (book two), where Sabrina ('sad virgin innocent of all') ends tragically. Bad history made good poetry. Imagination defeated truth; for a while.

A popular historian (even if swallowing some eighteenth-century fabrications) then noted four facts. Geoffrey's major work was a 'treasure-house' for poets and romancers; it is dedicated to Robert, Earl of Gloucester (d. 1147); Geoffrey claimed that he translated it from a book belonging to Walter, Archdeacon of Oxford; but its 'fabulous character' was soon recognized, so that Gerald of Wales (d. 1223) had a malicious story on how the mere presence of a copy attracted demons.[2] Gerald, a medieval writer, was more astute than many Renaissance scholars (as we shall see). Weighty comment came thereafter from Sir John Lloyd (d. 1947). For him, Geoffrey was a man who 'nourished the pride of the Welsh race' (really a comment on Lloyd's own patriotism, for that was scarcely Geoffrey's purpose). He was surely 'a native of Monmouth' and one of the 'foreign settlement' there, with his father apparently a Breton called Arthur. Dismissing early modern forgeries, Lloyd cited the first evidence for Geoffrey's career as an Oxford charter of 1129; *Historia Regum Britanniae* was in circulation by 1139, when we hear of a manuscript at Bec, Normandy; another manuscript (now in Bern, Switzerland) has a dedication to both Robert of Gloucester and King Stephen, suggesting initial publication in 1136-8. Geoffrey in 1152 became Bishop of St Asaph; he died in 1155, never (it seems) having visited his see, then under Welsh control. On his merits as a chronicler, Lloyd was blunt. Geoffrey's main feature is 'irresponsible gaiety'. To seek veracity from him is 'idle'.[3]

After Lloyd, a minor historian who (while repeating untruths on Geoffrey's supposed links with Glamorgan) commented on the 'extraordinary popularity' of his writings (which is true) and how they 'did much to soften and mitigate' bitterness of Welsh, English, and Norman (which is debatable).[4] More important was analysis by Hugh Williams (d. 1911). A distinguished editor of Gildas (493-570), Williams dismissed Geoffrey's work as a 'travesty of history'; 'no conclusion can safely be based upon any statement' in it which is not confirmed by Gildas, Bede, or the ninth-century *Historia Brittonum*; and six pages follow in which Williams anatomizes Geoffrey's 'methods' on (say) St Helen (d. 330?), mother of Constantine the Great, as a 'British princess' (compare Evelyn Waugh's novel *Helena*), or on Maelgwn Gwynedd and other kings savaged in 536 by Gildas, who now appear not as contemporaries but 'five *successive* Welsh princes!' While admitting Geoffrey's talents as a skilful and entertaining author, Williams yet closed by noting wrath to come, in the form of Polydore Vergil's *Anglica Historia* (1534), wherein Geoffrey was 'ruthlessly' condemned; after which Polydore was himself 'bitterly assailed' by Welsh and other humanists including John Leland (d. 1552), Sir John Price (d. 1555), Humphrey Lhuyd (d. 1568), David Powell (d. 1598).[5] Change was slow to come.

An anthology of verse and prose lets us appreciate Geoffrey's flashy talents in two passages. First is one on Arthur's coronation. It is an exercise in pomp and ostentation. In the procession to Caerleon Cathedral, four kings (of Scotland, Cornwall, Dyfed, Gwynedd) advance ('as was their right'), their dignity indicated by attendants bearing swords of gold; from another direction and preceding Arthur's queen come their four consorts, carrying white doves as (in a later poet's phrase) emblems of their 'softer power'. Quite different is a second passage, full of violence and cruelty. Arthur fights a revolting lustful giant, who (amongst other bestial crimes) had kidnapped the maiden Helena, of noble blood, who yet frustrated his intentions when she died of shock in his arms. After a titanic struggle, Arthur drives his sword into the creature's skull and kills him.

This cleansing triumph took place at Mont-Saint-Michel (off the French coast), where Helena's grieving uncle, Duke Hoel, had a chapel built over her grave, so that the peak, *nomen ex tumulo puellae nactus*, is to this day called 'Helena's Tomb'.[6] Each of these episodes brings out Geoffrey's talent for the sensational. He was a clever writer, whether with the opulence of a coronation or the blood and gore of combat, the latter ending with details of a virgin's shrine: a touch of plausible pathos. His concept of Arthur is interesting. If the paraphernalia of feudal monarchy is a false addition, Arthur is still a man of war, who defends his people (which is historical); there are also Welsh legends of him as a savage fighting-man who rids his people of monsters; curiously at odds with the imperial ruler of Caerleon, who attends high mass and is surrounded by noblemen in ermine.

This in mind, we turn to Sir Edmund Chambers (d. 1954), expert on Shakespeare and the medieval stage, who provided an admirable survey (citation of post-medieval forgeries notwithstanding) of Geoffrey's literary techniques, sources, ethics ('some of Geoffrey's contemporaries thought him a liar'), critics, and reputation.[7] After this, Saunders Lewis provided comment at a differing angle, at once Welsh and European. For Lewis, 1136 marked an end and a beginning. Welsh narrative prose passed from its first period to its second. In *Historia Regum Britanniae*, Geoffrey purported to tell how the Britons came from Troy to Britain; how they named the island after their leader Brutus (ancestor of Milton's 'Locrine' and Sabrina); and how they achieved imperial greatness under Arthur, after whom they declined, being left with nothing but the part called *Cymru*, Wales. Lewis added that the text was turned into Welsh under the title of *Brut*, after Brutus (there are now thought to be six separate medieval Welsh versions, not just one); and cited Edmond Faral (d. 1958) of the Collège de France for it as 'central to medieval Latin literature', naturally showing the influence of Ovid, Lucan, Statius, and (above all) Vergil's *Aeneid* and St Jerome's Vulgate Bible. For Lewis, 1136 was a year of revolution: swift, in the manner of revolutions. With it, the old Celtic-Irish culture of Welsh narrative prose was 'destroyed'. He said (rightly) that *Culhwch* and the *Four Branches of the Mabinogi* belong to the age before Geoffrey and thus display symptoms Irish or pagan or pan-Celtic. After 1136, the eyes of Welsh storytellers turned from West to South, from Ireland to the European Continent, from Irish Sea to English Channel. *Trowyd o'r byd Celtaidd i'r byd Rhufeinig*; there was a shift from Celtic world to Roman world.[8] Lewis having a wizard's potent charm and gift of prophecy, one forces oneself to qualify that, recalling that *Culhwch* shows little direct knowledge of Ireland; that the *Four Branches* do not present the Irish positively; that *Rhonabwy's Dream* has Irish aspects (sardonic mockery, an ox-hide as oneiromantic couch), despite post-dating Geoffrey; that, after the Anglo-Cambro-Norman invasion of 1169, Ireland became better known to the Welsh, not less; and that the Welsh and Irish had no real idea of linguistic kinship until the nineteenth century, when J. K. Zeuss (d. 1856) demonstrated the precise inter-relationship of their languages.

If Saunders Lewis wrote with an awareness of tradition Celtic and Latin and French, Robert Richards wrote as a lecturer in economics and a socialist politician, observing that Robert of Gloucester (one of Henry I's 24 or so illegitimate children) was Lord of Glamorgan, and used wealth from his domains to support not only Geoffrey but also William of Malmesbury (d. 1143?), historian of another stamp.[9] Money in both cases well spent, whether for fact or fiction. An account written mainly after Sir John Lloyd gives biographical facts and speculation on the 'very ancient volume in the British tongue', which Geoffrey claimed as belonging to his friend Walter, Archdeacon of Oxford, who let him 'translate' it to produce *Historia Regum Britanniae*. The scholar-poet W. J. Gruffydd (d. 1954) thought the manuscript likely to exist; Henry Lewis (philologist) and Stuart Piggott (archaeologist) were more negative. What is not in doubt is that Geoffrey's 'very meagre and bare' sources included Gildas, Bede, Welsh genealogies, and *Historia Brittonum*, plus a supposed list of Britain's Twenty-Eight Roman Cities (most of them no such thing, but forts on the Cornish coast or Antonine Wall, or Celtic monasteries in south-east Wales). To that historical medley was added material from Vergil, Lucan, Juvenal, the Latin Bible, the Church Fathers, local folklore.[10] Similar words on Walter's alleged *liber vetustissimus* written in *Britannicus sermo* were then given by Henry Lewis (who left open whether it ever existed), as were particulars on Geoffrey's sources.[11]

That mysterious manuscript, bad penny of British historiography, appears yet again in French guise. The *répercussion troublante* of its consequences (paralleling the eighteenth-century craze for Ossian) can be dismissed as *un ensemble fantaisiste* or (in Gerald of Wales's phrase) a *fabulosa historia*.[12] 'Invented story' or not, its fictions were long in the dying. (For visitors to Cornwall's Tintagel as Arthur's 'birthplace', or nearby Camelford as site of his 'last battle', they live even now.) Those inventions meant centuries of scholarly confrontation, ably chronicled by Sir Thomas Kendrick, who (besides a judicious account of the *History* and its influence, so that it even supplied precedents 'quoted in parliament') set out arguments of John Leland and other humanists versus Polydore Vergil; explored the 'extraordinary complexity and ingenuity' with which its pseudo-history was treated in that dubious masterpiece, Spenser's *Fairie Queene*; and remarked astutely on how Shakespeare would have 'nothing to do' with the notion of Tudor England's deriving glory from Trojan Britain.[13] Spenser's soul fed upon bogus history and bogus ideology and bogus language. Shakespeare, a greater artist, had no time for them.

After such uncritical praise or curt dismissal, we come to Geoffrey as (at times) a truth-teller, shown in a response by Rachel Bromwich (1915-2010), profoundly learned on British lore. She observed that Geoffrey did not invent the kings and heroes and sages and *femmes fatales* who inhabit his pages. Celtic stories of them can be shown to predate him, as proved by reference to Merlin the magician in the poem *Armes Prydein* ('The Prophecy of Britain'), composed in 940 after the West Saxons capitulated to Vikings at Leicester (thereby boosting the revanchism of militants in West Wales. For them, Merlin was amongst ancestral voices prophesying war). Nor did Geoffrey invent stories of Arthur, Vortigern, Cadwallon. He borrowed from what had long been known in Wales. The unexpected outcome is that he 'undoubtedly perpetuates many fragments of stories' from the British past. If to seek history in him is to chase a will-o'-the wisp, he is yet a 'field of study' on traditions otherwise lost.[14] There is more below on that exacting task. After what Wales gave Geoffrey, what Geoffrey gave Wales, in the form of translations of his *Historia* by different Welshmen, each unaware of the others, but all striving (with limited success) to turn their author's 'cumbrous sentences' into natural Welsh.[15] In a volume of interest, but requiring caution, one reads how J. S. P. Tatlock (of California) was convinced of there being no 'developed Arthur-saga' previous to Geoffrey.[16] Clarification is needed. *Culhwch* predates *Historia Regum Britanniae* by some forty years; on the other hand, it was Geoffrey who created Arthur's biography as we now have it.

As for that Arthur, there is analysis on what Geoffrey made of him. He is now 'a compound of the historical military leader and the enigmatic fairy prince' and comes with 'amazing embellishments'. If there is no Round Table or Holy Grail, there is still Arthur's conception by Igerne, whose husband is impersonated by Uther with the aid of Merlin. Arthur comes to power; conquers Ireland, Iceland, Norway, Denmark, Gaul; holds a magnificent court at Caerleon; is eventually provoked into war with Rome; when about to achieve final victory, hears of treachery back in Britain; he returns to defeat the usurper Modred at battle in Cornwall, but is gravely wounded and is carried away to the mysterious 'Isle of Avalon' (its whereabouts left deliberately vague). Once we remove the sensational episodes of campaigning and sexual deceit and Caerleon's gallant knights and lovely ladies and Arthur's mysterious future return, there can still be traced Arthur the hero-warrior, defender of his people, and meeting his doom at *Camlan* (now moved from Cumbria to Cornwall), Geoffrey also placing that conflict in 542 (near the real date of 537). What is new, however, is Arthur as emperor, 'a kind of Charlemagne, rebuilder of the Western Empire'.[17] A powerful if fallacious theme, with a surprising modern equivalent in the Arthur of John Morris's *The Age of Arthur* (1973) or *Londinium* (1982), where we find again Geoffrey's fantasy ruler, still in borrowed imperial robes. After a fake ruler, a fake prelate, namely Arthur's Archbishop of Caerleon, *de facto* his supreme royal chaplain, and subject of a study using Tatlock and Rachel Bromwich for the Welsh sources, with genuine British saints (like Dyfrig) promoted by Geoffrey's deft imagination to offices that would have astounded them.[18] Again, fact and plausible fiction, cleverly blended.

The year 1959 provided studies of Geoffrey by two Welshmen and two Americans. All offer insights. The first is informative on book culture: the four 'editions' of Geoffrey's *Historia* between 1136 and 1148; Sallust and Ovid as authors quoted therein; the hundreds of medieval manuscripts, their variants needing Herculean resolution to disentangle them; an *editio princeps* at Paris in 1508, with another edition in 1517 and a third (at Heidelberg) in 1587.[19] All attest Geoffrey's (and Arthur's) continental fame. The second study ranges farther: on the paradox of how twelfth- and thirteenth-century Wales, threatened gravely by 'Norman and English aggression', yet 'suddenly found herself wielding an immense influence' in the sphere of 'imaginative literature'; on Geoffrey's life, sources, and motives for writing, which were pro-Norman and certainly not pro-Welsh; on how his work was yet 'well-received' in Wales, where its picture of a 'resplendent' British past helped compensate for 'national degradation' after conquest in 1282 (so that bards used it to extol ancient British grandeur and heroism); on Welsh scholars of the Renaissance (Sir John Price, Humphrey Llwyd), who laboured to defend its veracity; and their eighteenth-century successors, who still took it *au pied de la lettre*, above all in the bizarre and irascible writings of Theophilus Evans and Lewis Morris. Their touching faith in Geoffrey contrasts with the scepticism of William of Newburgh (d. 1198?), who denounced his book as 'a collection of fairy-tales', or Gerald of Wales (d. 1223?), who thought a copy useful for summoning up devils. It was all deplorable; and yet Geoffrey's Arthur, 'a mighty emperor whose court was the centre of the world', had the potency and indestructability of myth.[20]

As for the US critics, they gave further perspectives, as on the Church. Although nothing shows Geoffrey to have been 'irreligious', he probably took orders because the Church alone offered a career for a man with his interests (those of a best-selling writer). The Church as an institution thus has little place in his *Historia*; the clerics in it are few and (St Dubricius excepted) not conspicuous for fervour; as for laymen, they are praised for secular qualities: 'brutal and ruthless' efficiency, conquest, largess. Hence in part the success of Geoffrey, a literary professional who wrote 'with an unerring eye for what would prove acceptable', his work being vivid, concrete, practical, sophisticated, and without too much of the marvellous.[21] A judicious summing-up. Thereafter came the 1960s and an essential translation, also providing judiciousness on sources. Careful scholars reject the idea that Geoffrey 'simply made up his material'. Instead, he would steal it (as Rachel Bromwich noted in 1954), an instance being the 'Nennian list of the Cities of Britain' (some twenty-eight of them).[22] The text, obscure until 2016 (for most items in it are not Roman cities at all), was cheerfully exploited to create a pseudo-history's pseudo-geography. Understanding of the places really designated in the list hence casts light on Geoffrey's topographical trickery. Also in the 1960s is a diverse volume of essays with some permanent insights, including comments on Tennyson's *Idylls of the King* as a tract for the times. In the 1870s, when the poem was going through final revisions, the French Third Republic was a fact; there had been the atrocities of the Commune; the Queen, in 'morose retirement', was unpopular; and 'English republicanism was a rising force.' Perturbed by this, Tennyson made Arthur's court 'respectable' (for the Laureate 'circled round' its dubious or inconvenient aspects), thereby giving support to constitutional royalists. Geoffrey's protean narrative was used by conservatives against the radicalism of Joseph Chamberlain or Sir Charles Dilke.[23] An unexpected outcome. Not the least surprising thing about his work.

The 1970s brought a small harvest of Galfridian Studies. In a multi-volume history of Glamorgan came an account of Geoffrey and of the stateliness bestowed on Caerleon, converting a minor garrison town into an imperial metropolis. True, Geoffrey was not from Glamorgan and Caerleon is not in Glamorgan. But Geoffrey's fictions were popular there (as elsewhere), and his vision of Caerleon, *aureis tectorum fastigiis Romam imitaretur* ('with the gold that glittered from its roof-tops, it was a match for Rome'), gave a lasting glamour to South Wales. Arthur's capital, flanked by groves and meadows, adorned by 'royal palaces' and on a 'noble river' that bore the ships of visiting 'kings and princes', was dignified too by 'a school of two hundred philosophers' expert on astronomy and other arts, as well as by churches dedicated to Julius and Aaron, martyred long before in its Roman amphitheatre.[24] Geoffrey's ideal Arthurian city lacked nothing; although he was misled by Gildas on a point which still misleads historians and archaeologists; for Julius and Aaron had nothing to do with Caerleon, being executed not at that *urbs Legionum* ('city of legions'), but at *civitas Legorum* ('city of the River Leire people') or Leicester, in the English Midlands (as proved by Gildas's statement on how their tombs were now in English territory).

If Geoffrey provided Wales with magnificence in Caerleon as Arthur's royal seat, he also provided headaches for Welsh historians, resisting attempts by others to dismiss his fabrications, where the case of Humphrey Llwyd (1527–68) is instructive. He rightly understood how accounts of Roman Britain would be 'dark' for anyone devoid of 'skill in the old *British* language' or Welsh. But he did not always practice what he preached. Unfortunately, 'his critical sense deserted him when he came to consider Brutus, Arthur, and the rest', where he was yet another to be gulled by Geoffrey's deceptions.[25] Earlier and later victims of those subterfuges were presented by Brynley Roberts. He also offered guidance on variant versions of

Historia Regum Britanniae and outlined its sources (with Geoffrey himself again deceived, this time by *Historia Brittonum*, and so placing Arthur's battles on the River Douglas in 'Linnuis' or Lincolnshire, when the stream concerned will instead be the Douglas of the *Cluduis* or Strathclyders). Roberts went on to stress, after Tatlock, that the Arthurian section of the text was 'carefully planned', being 'a microcosm of the whole work' as an ascent to greatness followed by 'tragedy and fall'; he also updated accounts of its reception in Wales, there still being 'some sixty manuscripts' of Welsh translations, in copies dating from the thirteenth to the eighteenth century.[26] To his word 'tragedy' came a useful corrective from Vinaver. If Geoffrey gave the earliest account of how Arthur's kingdom fell with a 'long and savage battle' on the banks of the River Camel, Cornwall, he yet treated events with 'epic detachment'. It was a 'military disaster for which the chances of war were alone to blame'.[27] Geoffrey was not the man to see character as destiny, or lay his finger upon moral failure, or portray men and women as reaping what they sow. Those perceptions belonged, rather, to Malory and others, endowed with an artistry that Geoffrey did not possess.

There are observations too in a Sources of History volume. The very abundance of medieval manuscripts ('some two hundred') creates difficulties for interpretation of Geoffrey's *Historia*, because he revised its text, each time modifying the dedication. A complete investigation of those matters was needed. As regards Wales, his book had three consequences. It spawned a 'romantic curiosity' about the country. Hence the wonder-tales told about Wales by medieval Flemish soldiers when they returned home. Second was its enthusiastic acceptance by the Welsh; third, their long-drawn-out and angry defence of it against sceptics. Geoffrey has had over-loyal friends even recently, including Sir Richard Southern, affirming that that contentious 'very ancient book' in Old Welsh or Old Breton really existed.[27] Despite that, Southern offered informed discourse on Geoffrey's conceptions of 'the destiny of nations', seen as their task by many twelfth-century historians.[28]

Besides those serious professionals (William of Malmesbury, Henry of Huntingdon) were less serious ones, such as twelfth century storytellers (like the celebrated Bleddri) whose art was unwritten.[29] Their importance as Geoffrey's potential sources is brought out by analysis of lore preserved in bardic mnemonics and the like.[30] It is always worth checking up there on names of individuals (emperors, kings, warriors, saints, heroines, wizards, prophets) to see what Geoffrey might learn from Wales or elsewhere and then put his own twist on it. Henry of Huntingdon 'seized with delight' the consequence of that in January 1139, when he discovered a copy of Geoffrey's *Historia* newly arrived at the monastery of Bec, Normandy. As a historian, he rejoiced in its chronological and genealogical data, just as 'the general reader' rejoiced in its 'brief and clear' and endless 'simple dramas' (campaigns, battles, conquests, youthful heroism, royal wisdom, womanly nobility, intimidating prophecies, more battles), so that there was something for everyone. Hence its 'immediate and sustained popularity'.[31]

As a change from what Wales gave Geoffrey is the contribution of Cornwall, including the names of Tintagel and the nearby River Camel.[32] Sir Rees Davies added how, giving with one hand and taking away with the other, Geoffrey in borrowing characters from the British past (such as Merlin or Medrawd) often 'mangled their reputation in the process'; even if Geoffrey also transformed Caerleon into 'Arthur's plenary court for the whole of Europe': a 'tribute to the captivating power of the Welsh borderlands' for the imagination (with equivalents in later writings, such as Housman's *A Shropshire Lad*). In a spirit not lyrical but tragic (being written on the eve of Edward I's conquest) is mention of how Llywelyn II maintained his rights, an inalienable possession inherited from Camber, son of Brutus.[33] That, too, was Geoffrey's unpredicted contribution to a struggle for national freedom, and we shall come back to it.

Discussion of historical theory likewise came to the fore, with one writer here seeing a debt to Boethian themes of rise and fall (even if Geoffrey never mentions Boethius, whose meditations upon time and destiny might have bored him).[34] More helpful in any case is a summary of Geoffrey's life, writings, sources, and purpose in a useful handbook.[35] A similar study yet offers acute analysis of his representation of Arthur, at once a *'chanson de geste* hero who engages in single combat'; a 'Norman king ambitious to extend his realms', rewarding his knights with dukedoms or asserting authority at 'crown-wearing ceremonies'; and (an archaic slip?) the slayer of the Mont-Saint-Michel giant, which takes us back to the Welsh folk-champion capable of 'freeing the land' from monsters.[36] Below Geoffrey's ready acceptance of the regalia and ceremonies of Angevin kingship might lurk the primitive. Further insights from this critic appear in comments on how *Historia Regum Britanniae*, a 'light-hearted fraud by a clever writer of few principles', yet mirrors the thought of its age on the way that 'fate or Providence' move the levers of causality, so that this 'entertaining chronicle' is raised (to some extent) by 'an eschatological view of history' deriving from the Bible and St Augustine and Orosius (and having a descendant in the *Heilsgeschichte* of modern German theologians, whom the Third Reich's distortions of the past compelled into restating the 'history of salvation').[37] Even for Geoffrey, then, there was perhaps more to history than a 'glorious past' (perceived by one writer) for 'Geoffrey's Norman masters' to appropriate, it being admirably 'free from the encumbrance' of links with the Angles and Saxons under the Norman yoke.[38] From the other side of the border, those views found a response from Master John of St Davids, learned cleric and author of Welsh lyrics in the twelfth century's third quarter. One of his poems is a brave and celebrated prophecy on how the Welsh kept their faith and language, but lost their lands 'save Wild Wales (*Gwalia*)'; they will yet one day regain sovereignty over their ancient domains, 'And the foreign people / Shall disappear'.[39] Which shows a sturdy Welsh patriot resisting Geoffrey's hegemonic colonialism.

After a cleric at St Davids, another at Kraków, in the form of Bishop Vincent Kadłubek (d. 1223), whose *Chronica Polanorum* (up to 1202) is an essential tool for historians of medieval Europe.

Vincent quoted Geoffrey, as also John of Salisbury (d. 1180), Gerald of Wales (d. 1223), Walter Map (d. 1209?), and Alexander Neckham (d. 1217). They were all sophisticated authors, the last of them a Paris-educated Abbot of Cirencester.[40] So Arthur's fame reached not only the Seine and Rhine and Danube, but the Vistula too. After Poland is Scotland, where *Scotichronicon* by Walter Bower (d. 1449), writing on Inchcolm (an island off the Fife coast), is 'a belated counterpart' to Geoffrey's work, with powerful claims (dear to the hearts of Scottish royalists) on how Arthur and those after him had no right to British dominion, because he 'was conceived out of wedlock'.[41]

Rees Davies then once more brought out Geoffrey's unsettling influence. *Historia Regum Britanniae* was more than a 'great literary hoax'. It presented 'at least four challenges', all political. First was Arthur, paradigm of 'truly great kingship', so that Edward I and his queen might in 1278 come to view his (supposed) grave at Glastonbury. Second was the dangerous notion of British *reconquista*, met with above in the poem *Armes Prydein* ('The Prophecy of Britain') of 940 and Master John of St Davids in the later twelfth century. Referred to in the *Historia*'s original text, that subversive idea was replaced in the first variant version by assurances on 'the crown of the kingdom' as for ever lost to the Britons (important evidence for its not being the original text, despite proposals of 2024 on that). Third and related to it was the concept of united British sovereignty. The island of Britain should have one ruler: something as acceptable to governments in London as Celtic military revival was not (the proof being the head of Llywelyn II, stuck on a pole and 'with a crown of ivy' after his failed insurrection of 1282). As for 'the fourth gauntlet' flung down by Geoffrey, it was the 'galaxy of kings stretching back to Brutus' a thousand years before Julius Caesar, an electrifying 'demonstration' of the British state as so long-established that, when Brutus founded it, old men could recall the fall of Troy.[42] Like other books (More's *Utopia*, Marx's *Das Kapital*), Geoffrey's historical *jeu d'esprit* had implications quite unforeseen by its author. This is especially so for its hypnotic creation of Arthur, imperial overlord.

He is with us still. So, too, are debates on Britain's political unity, and (as we shall see) British authority in Ireland.

Geoffrey's ideological legacy is therefore massive, as is his literary one. As we advance from the twentieth century to the twenty-first, we find that politics and poets are sometimes seen to be more closely aligned than one might expect. An obvious instance is Spenser. While Arthur posed artistic problems for him, the king's foreign conquests were not amongst them. The poet, an apologist for Elizabethan imperialism, readily accepted Arthur's subduing of the native Irish. Geoffrey's flippant attitude to Arthur thus goes through a distorting mirror in Spenser's grim *A View of the State of Ireland*, where Irenius justifies English rule of Ireland on the grounds that 'by good record' we know how Arthur 'had all that iland' under 'allegiance and subjection', with names of Irish places and people likewise 'proving' Arthurian conquest.[43] An Oxford spoof became a vindication for massacre and famine. Its strange and troubling effect on generations unborn is underlined elsewhere. Geoffrey's *Historia* was so widely accepted that it entered the heart even of 'Latin textual culture in England'; while English kings used it as an undoubted precedent for their 'status and political actions', above all for claims to 'rule over Wales and Scotland'.[44] A skewed and fantastic vision of the past (as often) put reason to sleep. Thanks to Geoffrey's pen, troops marched off to battles not on paper, where real blood was shed.

That sombre realization lies behind much written by others. *Historia Regum Britanniae* displays careful use of its sources (Gildas, Bede, pseudo-Nennius), making it 'acceptable' to non-experts, and providing Anglo-Norman kings with 'a precedent of heroic size' that boosted their claims to dominion over Welsh and Scots and Irish.[45] Saga fueled history. We need yet not accept one commentator, proposing that Geoffrey really believed what he made up, so that the lives of those whom he described were somehow 'more real than the lives they might have lived in actuality'.[46] Not all medieval people were so stupid, as Bede shows; even if splendid illusions are always at the service of authority, with Geoffrey propagating 'a powerful myth of origin' that after four centuries acquired 'new force from the nationalist agendas of the Elizabethans'.[47] Or, to put it another way, his 'teleological account of history feeds a nostalgia for an original wholeness', from which his patrons 'could legitimate their own rule' and 'counter the fragmentation and decentralization that marked feudalism in France'; which at least brings us face to face with real events.[48] Within this context may be mentioned a detail on Merlin. His northern aspects never appear in the *Historia*, but are made much of in Geoffrey's later *Vita Merlini*, written when he was angling for preferment (achieved in 1152 on his becoming Bishop of St Asaph).[49] Geoffrey wrote with personal advantage kept in mind. There was personal advantage for others, for Geoffrey's chronicle legitimized conquest, as again emphasized, with Arthur carrying his sway to Snowdonia and the Scottish Highlands (as English kings were to do). The *pax et iusticia* which Arthur brought them by subjugation was 'its own justification'; compare his affirming on later conquests that he had '"liberated" these territories from Roman subjection'.[50] Compare, too, a chapter on 'le monde de Geoffroi de Monmouth' and its verdict on l'*Histoire des rois de Bretagne* as 'fille de son temps', part of the twelfth century's 'Renaissance savante' with 'découvertes rhétoriques' and 'explications scientifiques' (but not, of course, 'la méthode critique des sources'), related to the 'progrès des écoles' of pre–university Oxford.[51]

After these imperial and intellectual echoes, a return to Wales and how Welshmen saw Henry VII's victory in 1485 at Bosworth Field as 'fulfilling the prophecy' in Geoffrey's great work that Britain would 'be restored to the British'.[52] Such seditious language, we re-call, vanished from later recensions of Geoffrey's text (something pointed out by Rees Davies in 2000). In a paper on the 'erasure of Wales in medieval English culture' (a surprising remark, given the way that that country was rescued from oblivion by *Historia Regum Britanniae*), we hear of varying 'discourse' (on Britishness, authority, peripherality, unequal value) which is 'central' to myths propagated by Gildas, Bede, and Geoffrey.[53] In a chapter on our author, Helen Fulton writes in similar general terms on how 'a plurality of connotative and symbolic meanings surrounds the figure of Arthur' in Geoffrey's work.[54]

Now, a surprise. Reminding us how forgeries can mislead scholars is a statement on the 'sixteenth-century Welsh Gwentian Brut', according to which Geoffrey was archdeacon at Llandaff, Glamorgan, a notion dismissed by 'most scholars'.[55] Those links with Glamorgan were rejected as early as 1911 by Sir John Lloyd. Yet there is failure to realize here that the 'Gwentian Brut' is not a Tudor document, but an eighteenth-century one. What happened was this. At the close of the Bern and Harlech manuscripts of his history is a passage by Geoffrey on Caradog of Llancarfan as a man equipped to write about Wales's later rulers. Caradog really existed. He was active in the 1130s and wrote a Latin life (still extant) of St Cadog, founder of his own Glamorgan monastery. Yet he produced nothing on secular history. The 'Gwentian Brut' attributed to him is instead a creation of the master-forger Edward Williams (d. 1826) or 'Iolo Morganwg', lavish in bestowing fool's gold on Glamorgan's past, and taking a hint from this very addition of Geoffrey to produce a chronicle of Wales from 660 to 1196. Solemnly printed as authentic in 1801-7 (and again in 1870), it was revealed as spurious by Lloyd in 1928, a proof acknowledged by Ceri Lewis and Ian Jack (in publications of 1971 and 1972 cited above). Despite them, in 2010 it still deceived scholars, confounded by dust which Geoffrey threw about almost nine centuries previous.

Confusion of another kind appears on that book (in a 'British' language) borrowed from Archdeacon Walter, whereby Geoffrey allegedly 'thematizes the current twelfth-century Gothic dynamics of textual production and reproduction'.[56] Nothing on how Celticists think such a volume non-existent. Also relating to questions of actuality is the Galfridian apologist Sir John Price (d. 1555), whose criticisms of Polydore Vergil are termed both a defence of the *Historia*'s 'credibility' and 'the identity and dignity of the Welsh'.

Geoffrey had become a 'cornerstone' of Welsh awareness.[57] Still (as Dr Johnson noted on the *Ossian* affair), one should not love one's country more than one loves the truth. Better, then, is Siân Echard, classifying Geoffrey's self-admitted use of 'oral traditions' concerning kings of the Britons as 'a stunning move from a writer of Latin history'.[58]

A complete book on our author has a chapter on the *Historia*'s Arthurian section, rightly describing the hero's eventual return to be lore which pre-dated Geoffrey. He did not invent it. This we know because in 1113 some canons from Laon (in north-east France) almost caused a riot at Bodmin when one of them doubted a Cornishman's insistence that 'Arthur was not dead'. On the same matter we can also say why Arthur's grave was 'the world's wonder' (phrase of an unknown Welsh bard) because it was 'difficult to find'.[59] Indeed. It was (and is) in North Britain, probably near the fort of Castlesteads (= *Camlan*) on Hadrian's Wall, and a long way from Wales. Welsh bards would thus naturally be evasive on its whereabouts. A further reminder that not everything stated by Geoffrey is fabricated comes from his description of an Irish army 'miserably cut to pieces' by Arthur. Its warriors are termed *gens nuda et inermis*, a people 'naked and unarmed' because they wore little and were lightly-armed: a custom known from other sources of this date (such as the slightly earlier *Four Branches of the Mabinogi*).[60]

Just as Martin Aurell in 2007 summed *Historia Regum Britanniae* up as *fille de son temps*, so too are many recent books, and none more so than one by the late Fiona Tolhurst, who maintained that Geoffrey of Monmouth was a proto-feminist, the Arthurian section of his history being a 'feminist legend'. An arresting contention. For Edward I's lawyers, those chapters vindicated English jurisdiction over Scotland; for Spenser, they justified an English dirty war in Ireland; for Fiona Tolhurst, they made Geoffrey a feminist icon. How so? Because the women there participate in 'heroism as a form of greatness' and 'consistently challenge traditional gender roles and the gender hierarchy that such roles generally produce'.[61] However one regards such views, her book deserves close reading, the contribution of women to literature ever being downplayed, so that it always merits revaluation.

Which leads us to a volume from University of Wales Press, its author rightly noting how Galfridian celebration of 'Britain as a unified kingdom' is shared by the classic *Four Branches of the Mabinogi*. That, together with exaltation of Ancient Britons as a free and noble people, 'added to the appeal of Geoffrey's work for the Welsh', for all his disobliging remarks on their degeneracy. But he also broke new ground, being the first to present 'a complete life history for Arthur, from birth to death' which was 'fully involved' in that long-standing Welsh 'concept of a unified Britain'.[62] Arthur the war-hero, Arthur the ruler of all Britain: it was a thrilling combination. The literary and political results were spectacular and (sometimes) bloody. If the sword was mightier than the pen, the sword still took hints from the pen.

Geoffrey was, then, strong on ideology. There was more to him than romances and battles and other far-off things. So much is found in another book's analysis of how Geoffrey saw the Welsh, his views on history, and his popularity, the last extending to translations of his work (into French and English, and then repeatedly into Welsh). A curious outcome for an author embedded within the 'intelligentsia of Oxford and the English royal service'.[63] This, even if one thinks that Geoffrey (like Swift in a later age) did not receive an official reward in any way proportionate to his work for the government.

Thanks to modern catalogues and editions of his writings, Geoffrey's *Nachleben* is today understood in detail, so that (for example) revisionist interpretation of work by Richard of Devizes led some to regard this latter as an ironist of the 1190s, 'whose ideas on King Arthur' were 'too absurd and too clever' for influential medieval and modern readers 'to stomach'.[64] Richard was one of the few who did not take Geoffrey at face value. In a collection of studies on Geoffrey's reception, the further point is made that, while Julia Crick in 1989 listed 215 known medieval manuscripts of his *Historia*, others have turned up since, the total given in 2007 by M. D. Reeve and Neil Wright being 219. It lets one 'déterminer l'ampleur' of his popularity with precision.[65] This especially so when one reflects upon the thousands of manuscripts that have perished. Small wonder, then, that a Galfridian tide engulfed England, France, Germany, and (by 1200) even reached Poland (see above). For Wales there are yet further indications. Not only was the earliest of the Middle Welsh translations of his history 'made probably by the end of the twelfth century', but they together were 'copied more widely than any other Welsh narrative text'.[66] Small wonder, too, if the Welsh were stout Galfridians into the eighteenth century.

The debris left behind as that inundation receded offers work even now, with diverse results. Some things have become clearer as concerns names of the mysterious 'Twenty-Eight Cities of Britain' set out in later copies of *Historia Brittonum*. Like Arthur's Twelve Battles, they have prompted confusion and misplaced confidence, augmented by Geoffrey's unscrupulous use of both. Yet muddle and error are dispelled by comparison with the Celtic languages and readiness to emend forms corrupted by scribes. The results for those 'cities' are unexpected. Some really are Roman places (Canterbury, Carlisle, London, Winchester, York). But others are former monastic or secular sites by Wales's southern border, such as *Cair Caratauc* or Caradog and *Cair Douarth* or Doward, each now in Herefordshire; while *Cair Draithou* ('fortress of beaches') is Trevelgue, a cliff-fort perched above the Atlantic north of Newquay, Cornwall.[67] Clarity on these forms will help unmask what Geoffrey did with them.

It aids us when we come to a well-illustrated and attractively-produced study of Arthurian toponymy, displaying extensive use of Geoffrey's history.[68] The same is true of another volume, containing up-to-date suggestions on his familiarity with Welsh tradition.[69] They are today's responses to a turmoil unleashed by him, which in medieval and Tudor times (compare a study of *The Mirror for Magistrates*) spawned a 'monstrous proliferation of romance stories'; a 'desperately fraught' problem of how Elizabethans should relate to ancient Britons robbed of sovereignty by English invaders; and the unnerving circumstance on whether Arthur, Christian monarch, was a Papist invention fit merely for the diatribes of 'reforming humanists' like Roger Ascham (d. 1568).[70] Geoffrey had become a sort of literary Kensitite, causing friction and disturbance wherever he went. It was the price for the 'explosive rise in popularity of stories set in the ancient British past' which left its mark throughout Europe.[71] Relating again to place, the voyages of his characters are shown to have had little interest for him, any more than battles: what really concerned Geoffrey was 'the greatness of the British people and the futility of civil warfare', so that readers would learn from past error and make Britain a kingdom once more 'united, powerful, prosperous'.[72] Except in his literary life, Geoffrey was a man of peace. Further instances of how he destabilized actuality are terms for Salisbury, which perplexed members of the English Place-Name Society in their 1939 volume for Wiltshire. This was because Geoffrey had cheerfully appropriated one of them (rightly denoting Caradog, near Ross-on-Wye, Herefordshire); the other is due to scribal misunderstanding of his text.[73] His misinformation, with consequences direct and indirect for twentieth-century toponymics, shows how an untruth once started has (in a phrase of Clough the poet) time on its own wings to fly.

In the same year appeared two books with abundant observations on Geoffrey. In the first, to be commended for an extensive bibliography, including work by researchers with whom the author does not agree, there is still a misplaced verdict on how Geoffrey's 'certain very old book' is 'likely to have existed in some form'.[74] Alas, this nine-century-old canard will not die. No matter how many times Celticists affirm that there is no evidence for such a text in Welsh or Breton, another fiction of Geoffrey remains *in situ*. In contrast is thinking of the first importance on publication of his *History*. Of the eighty or so manuscripts of before about 1210, some forty are from the Continent, where it was read 'just as swiftly' by scholars as in Britain. Hence the proposition that it was first made public there, and in late 1137 or in 1138 (not earlier). That is why Henry of Huntingdon came across it as a startling novelty not at an English monastery, but the Norman one of Bec. In short, Geoffrey (like James Joyce with *Ulysses*) found it easier to publish a book on 'a familiar place' in exile.[75] These remarkable conclusions, drawn from the work of Julia Crick and others on Galfridian manuscripts and the like, solve many problems and deserve wide attention. Seldom do we meet an approach to our texts at once so fresh and compelling.

After that, routine, with (for example) discussion of Welsh translations, which reveal 'no striking differences' of addition or omission on the Emperor Arthur, any pride of Welsh copyists being limited to a few 'embellishments' on their hero's family or attributes.[76] Below that, and deserving of scholarly reproof, is Professor McKenna of Harvard, who states (correctly) that 'Geoffrey's book was received enthusiastically in Wales' and (incorrectly) that the 'date of the *Four Branches of the Mabinogi*' must 'remain a matter of debate'.[77] It does nothing of the sort. Published research confirms views going back to Alfred Nutt (d. 1910) on those native tales as predating Geoffrey. Their author shows no knowledge of his work; Arthur is never mentioned. They will be of the late 1120s or so.

If the author of the *Four Branches* knew nothing of Geoffrey, others did, none more so as regards consequences than Edward I, citing this author in a famous letter of 1301 to Pope Boniface VIII. He and other English kings took their realm as 'the direct continuation of the ancient kingdom of Britain described by Geoffrey'. Hence their jurisdiction over Scotland, Wales, Ireland; a regalian right to which many (in Wales, Scotland, Ireland) were strangely unreceptive, and therefore began a political modification of (and selection from) their own past. Llywelyn II's advisers had already done this in a famous letter (of 11 November 1282) to Archbishop Pecham, where they dropped their prince's claims to descent from Locrinus son of Brutus (implying the British united sovereignty maintained by Edward), instead making out his ancestor as Camber, brother to Locrinus and ruler of allocated lands called 'Cambria' after him.

Llywelyn's rights were ancient. They came *a temporibus Kambri filii Bruti*, from the age of Camber, son to Brutus.[78] Llywelyn was not the only Welshman with his own ideas on Geoffrey's narrative. Another was the unknown author of *Vera historia de morte Arthuri*, from North Wales and perhaps of the 1180s. He took issue with Geoffrey's account of Arthur's last days, asserting that they were really at a Gwynedd church dedicated to the Virgin Mary. He had no truck with assurances from Glastonbury on Arthur's burial there.[79] Whether in politics or religion, whether in Wales or London or Somerset, the past was reworked for someone's advantage, as it ever shall be: a truth confirmed by attempts (in an account of Geoffrey) to dismiss Arthur's place on 'the historiographical radar'.[80] There can be no such doubts. Arthur really existed. In the same contentious vein is comment on Geoffrey as time-server for Norman ascendancy, his historical interpretations naturally at variance with those of the Welsh, who never forgot their 'autochthonous ethnicity and a political autonomy brutally shattered by the Saxons'.[81]

Now for a glitch. In a monograph on the Arthurian toponymy of Geoffrey and others, Tintagel is listed amongst locations 'tous fictifs'.[82] Yet Tintagel is a real place. It is a parish in north-east Cornwall, half-way along the coast between Padstow and Bude. The error is (for once) not Geoffrey's fault. Others were. How he long made April Fools of English antiquarians and historians is shown by a study of Galfridian geography, including Tintagel, where the French went further than he did, romantically seeing it as also 'the seat of King Mark in the Tristan stories'.[83] Not romantic at all is Geoffrey, racist. It is found in his treatment of giants, allegedly seen through a 'negative racial lens'.[84] Hence the need to exterminate them. They were 'indigenous' inhabitants to be wiped out by colonizing invaders.[85]

We end with a bang and a whimper. The first is a 565-page volume on Geoffrey and his school, its very title an acknowledgement to J. S. P. Tatlock's *The Legendary History of Britain* (Berkeley, 1950), and with its first 238 pages devoted to Geoffrey alone. It has limitations. Its author is an authority on Old French but not Celtic, leading to misconceptions. They include an unwavering belief in the ability of medieval scribes (also untutored in Celtic) faultlessly to reproduce obscure British names; which means failure to notice proofs for the historical Arthur (including genealogies of sixth-century princes called after him). Nevertheless, the volume outdates all its predecessors thanks (in part) to eighty-four pages on the first variant version. Diligent editing of Geoffrey's narrative reveals his changes of mind, as with Arthur himself, where in this version the 'trappings' ('wealth, generosity, splendour') of a social elite at his court are absent. It raises the question ('perhaps insoluble') on whether Geoffrey wrote this version *first*, with lavish ostentation as an afterthought.[86] But an answer was here supplied in 2000 by Rees Davies. It is more likely that Geoffrey cut out his dangerous initial prophecy on Welsh reconquest of Britain, than that he put it in later. The variant version represents second thoughts, not first ideas: a conclusion suggesting how Jean Blacker's book (fundamental for decades to come) helps deepen our understanding of Geoffrey. As for the second, it is a paper by Professor Melia of California and it is unfortunate. Publications duly and correctly cited by Jean Blacker seem to him quite unknown; and to that he adds his own gifts of inaccuracy, shown concerning the defiant missive from Llywelyn's council on 11 November 1282, written (need one say?) a month before that prince was ambushed and killed. It is the document on how Llywelyn's rights had come down *a temporibus Kambri filii Bruti*, more than two millennia previous. Professor Melia cites it (without page reference) from a 1935 calendar of correspondence (where it does not appear); states that Llywelyn wrote it to the King (when the addressee was Archbishop Pecham); imagines that that king was Henry III (who by 1282 had been dead for ten years); and concludes with allusions to Heidegger and William Faulkner (which tell us nothing about medieval Wales).

So our study of reception begins in January 1139, when Henry of Huntingdon was excitedly misled by a copy of Geoffrey's history at the monastery of Bec, Normandy; it ends in the present day with a professor in California (also misled). On the way has been much on Geoffrey's sources, purpose, impact; and how he created a myth of Arthur which has undergone unimaginable transformations in the nine centuries since, and will see ones still more amazing in the nine centuries to come.

Notes

1. John Rhŷs, *Celtic Britain*, 3rd edn (London, 1904), 144.

2. J. C. Morrice, *A Manual of Welsh Literature* (Bangor, 1908), 25-6.

3. J. E. Lloyd, *A History of Wales* (London, 1911), 523-8.

4. J. E. de Hirsch-Davies, *A Popular History of the Church in Wales* (London, 1912), 102.

5. Hugh Williams, *Christianity in Early Britain* (Oxford, 1912), 121-30.

6. *A Primer of Medieval Latin*, ed. C. H. Beeson (Chicago, 1925), 243-8.

7. E. K. Chambers, *Arthur of Britain* (London, 1927), 20-99.

8. Saunders Lewis, *Braslun o Hanes Llenyddiaeth Gymraeg* (Caerdydd, 1932), 40-1.

9. Robert Richards, *Cymru'r Oesau Canol* (Wrecsam, 1933), 390-1, 393.

10. A. H. Williams, *An Introduction to the History of Wales: 1063-1284* (Cardiff, 1941), 46-9.

11. *Brut Dingestow*, ed. Henry Lewis (Caerdydd, 1942), xiv-xvi.

12. J. de Ghellinck, *L'Essor de la littérature latine* (Bruxelles, 1948), 158-60.

13. T. D. Kendrick, *British Antiquity* (London, 1950), 4-15, 78-133.

14. Rachel Bromwich, 'The Character of the Early Welsh Tradition', in *Studies in Early British History*, ed. N. K. Chadwick (Cambridge, 1954), 83-136.

15. Thomas Parry, *A History of Welsh Literature* (Oxford, 1955), 84-6.

16. R. S. Loomis, *Wales and the Arthurian Legend* (Cardiff, 1956), 179.

17. Geoffrey Ashe, *King Arthur's Avalon* (London, 1957), 176-8.

18. C. N. L. Brooke, 'The Archbishops of St Davids, Llandaff, and Caerleon-on-Usk', in *Studies in the Early British Church*, ed. N. K. Chadwick (Cambridge, 1958), 201-42.

19. I. Ll. Foster, 'Geoffrey of Monmouth', in *The Dictionary of Welsh Biography* (London, 1959), 274-5.

20. A. O. H. Jarman, 'Geoffrey of Monmouth and the "Matter of Britain"', in *Wales Through the Ages: From the Earliest Times to 1485*, ed. A. J. Roderick (Swansea, 1959), 145-52.

21. J. J. Parry and R. A. Caldwell, 'Geoffrey of Monmouth' in *Arthurian*

Literature in the Middle Ages, ed. R. S. Loomis (Oxford, 1959), 72-93.

22. Geoffrey of Monmouth, *The History of the Kings of Britain*, tr. Lewis Thorpe (Harmondsworth, 1966), 17.

23. Geoffrey Ashe, 'The Visionary Kingdom' in *The Quest for Arthur's Britain*, ed. Geoffrey Ashe (London, 1968), 1-26.

24. Ceri W. Lewis, 'The Literary Tradition of Morgannwg', in *Glamorgan County History: The Middle Ages*, ed. T. B. Pugh (Cardiff, 1971), 449-554.

25. May McKisack, *Medieval History in the Tudor Age* (Oxford, 1971), 57.

26. *Brut y Brenhinedd*, ed. Brynley F. Roberts (Dublin, 1971), ix-xxxi.

27. Eugene Vinaver, *The Rise of Romance* (Oxford, 1971), 129.

28. R. Ian Jack, *Medieval Wales* (London, 1972), 26-30.

29. *Historia Gruffud vab Kenan*, ed. D. Simon Evans (Caerdydd, 1977), lvi-lvii.

30. Rachel Bromwich, *Trioedd Ynys Prydein*, 2nd edn (Cardiff, 1978), xcvi-xlviii.

31. Margaret Gibson, 'History at Bec in the Twelfth Century', in *The Writing of History in the Middle Ages*, ed. R. H. C. Davis and J. M. Wallace-Hadrill (Oxford, 1978), 167-86.

32. O. J. Padel, 'Geoffrey of Monmouth and Cornwall', *Cambridge Medieval Celtic Studies* 8 (1984), 1-27.

33. R. R. Davies, *Conquest, Co-existence, and Change: Wales 1063-1415* (Oxford, 1987), 106-7, 352.

34. Maureen Fries, 'Boethian Themes', in *The Arthurian Tradition*, ed. Mary F. Braswell and John Bugge (Tuscaloosa, 1988), 29-42.

35. Geoffrey Ashe, 'Geoffrey of Monmouth', in *The New Arthurian Encyclopedia*, ed. Norris J. Lacy (Chicago, 1991), 179-82.

36. B. F. Roberts, 'Geoffrey of Monmouth, *Historia Regum Britanniae*, and *Brut y Brenhinedd*', in *The Arthur of the Welsh*, ed. Rachel Bromwich, A. O. H. Jarman, B. F. Roberts (Cardiff, 1991), 97-116.

37. B. F. Roberts, *Studies on Middle Welsh Literature* (Lewiston, 1992), 37.

38. Ceri Davies, *Welsh Literature and the Classical Tradition* (Cardiff, 1995), 31.

39. A. Breeze, *Medieval Welsh Literature* (Dublin, 1997), 46.

40. Teresa Michałowska, *Średniowiecze* (Warszawa, 1997), 137.

41. Beate Schmolke-Hasselmann, *The Evolution of Arthurian Romance*

(Cambridge, 1998), 285-6.

42. R. R. Davies, *The First English Empire* (Oxford, 2000), 39-41.

43. Andrew King, *'The Faerie Queene' and Middle English Romance* (Oxford, 2000), 197.

44. D. H. Green, *The Beginnings of Medieval Romance* (Cambridge, 2002), 172.

45. N. J. Higham, *King Arthur: Myth-Making and History* (London, 2002), 223.

46. Derek Pearsall, *Arthurian Romance* (Oxford, 2003), 9.

47. Helen Cooper, *The English Romance in Time* (Oxford, 2004), 24.

48. Laurie A. Finke and Martin B. Schichtman, *King Arthur and the Myth of History* (Gainesville, 2004), 38.

49. O. J. Padel, 'Geoffrey of Monmouth and the Development of the Merlin Legend', *Cambrian Medieval Celtic Studies* 51 (2006), 37-65.

50. Robert M. Stein, *Reality Fictions: Romance, History, and Governmental Authority 1025-1180* (Notre Dame, 2006), 109.

51. Martin Aurell, *La Légende du roi Arthur* (Paris, 2007), 164.

52. Anon., 'Geoffrey of Monmouth', in *The Welsh Academy Encyclopaedia of Wales*, ed. John Davies, Nigel Jenkins, Menna Baines, P. I. Lynch (Cardiff, 2008), 309.

53. Simon Meecham-Jones, 'Where Was Wales?', in *Authority and Subjugation in Writing of Medieval Wales*, ed. Ruth Kennedy and Simon Meecham-Jones (Basingstoke, 2008), 27-55.

54. Helen Fulton, 'History and Myth', in *Companion to Arthurian Literature*, ed. Helen Fulton (Basingstoke, 2009), 44-57.

55. Jane Beal and E. D. Kennedy, 'Geoffrey of Monmouth', in *The Encyclopaedia of the Medieval Chronicle*, ed. Graeme Dunphy (Leiden, 2010), 681-4.

56. Thomas Bredehoft, 'The Gothic Turn', in *The Oxford Handbook of Medieval Literature in English*, ed. Elaine Treharne and Greg Walker (Oxford, 2010), 353-69.

57. Ceri Davies, 'Renaissance Latinists', in *Wales and the Wider World*, ed. T. M. Charles-Edwards and R. J. W. Evans (Donington, 2010), 99-117.

58. Siân Echard, 'Geoffrey of Monmouth', in *The Arthur of Medieval Latin Literature*, ed. Siân Echard (Cardiff, 2010), 45-66.

59. Karen Jankulak, *Writers of Wales: Geoffrey of Monmouth* (Cardiff, 2010),

75.

60. Patrick Sims-Williams, *Irish Influence on Medieval Welsh Literature* (Oxford, 2011), 24-6.

61. Fiona Tolhurst, *Geoffrey of Monmouth and the Feminist Origins of the Arthurian Legend* (New York, 2012), 53.

62. Oliver Padel, *Writers of Wales: Medieval Arthurian Literature*, rev. edn (Cardiff, 2013), 56-7.

63. Michael A. Faletra, *Wales and the Medieval Colonial Imagination* (New York, 2014), 25.

64. John Gillingham, 'Richard of Devizes and "A Rising Tide of Nonsense": How Cerdic Met King Arthur', in *The Long Twelfth-Century View of the Anglo-Saxon Past*, ed. Martin Brett and D. A. Woodman (Farnham, 2015), 141-56.

65. Laurence Mathey-Maille, 'De la Vulgate à la *Variant Versión* de l'*Historia regum Britanniae*', in *L'*Historia regum Britanniae *et les «Bruts» en Europe: traductions, adaptations, réappropriations*, ed. Hélène Tétrel and Géraldine Veysseyre (Paris, 2015), 129-39.

66. Natalia I. Petrovskaia, *Medieval Welsh Perceptions of the Orient* (Turnhout, 2015), 26-7.

67. A. Breeze, '*Historia Brittonum* and Britain's Twenty-Eight Cities', *Journal of Literary Onomastics* 6 (2016), 1-16.

68. Kurt Liebhard, *Suchen nach dem historischen Arthur* (Wiessenthurm, 2016).

69. Nikolai Tolstoy, *The Mysteries of Stonehenge* (Stroud, 2016), 42-3.

70. Harriet Archer, *Unperfect Histories* (Oxford, 2017), 56-7.

71. Joshua Byron Smith. *Walter Map and the Matter of Britain* (Philadelphia, 2017), 98.

72. Charlotte A. T. Wulf, 'Arthur's Channel Crossings', in *Arthur, la mer et la guerre*, ed. Alban Gautier, Marc Rolland, Michelle Szkilnik (Paris, 2017), 83-95.

73. A. Breeze, 'Salisbury's Welsh Names *Caergaradog* and *Caer Sallog*', *Wiltshire Archaeological and Natural History Magazine* 111 (2018), 301-3.

74. Nicholas Higham, *King Arthur: The Making of the Legend* (New Haven, 2018), 245.

75. Jaakko Tahkokallio, 'Publishing *The History of the Kings of Britain*', in

L'Historia regum Britanniae *et les «Bruts» en Europe: production, circulation et réception*, ed. Hélène Tétrel and Géraldine Veysseyre (Paris, 2018), 45-57.

76. Katherine Himsworth, '*Brut y Brenhinedd*', in *Arthur in the Celtic Languages*, ed. Ceridwen Lloyd-Morgan and Erich Poppe (Cardiff, 2019), 95-109.

77. Catherine McKenna, 'Court Poetry and Historiography Before 1282', in *The Cambridge History of Welsh Literature*, ed. Geraint Evans and Helen Fulton (Cambridge, 2019), 93-111.

78. Ben Guy, *Medieval Welsh Genealogy* (Woodbridge, 2020), 246-7.

79. Owen Wyn Jones, '*O Oes Gwrtheyrn*', in *The Chronicles of Medieval Wales and the March*, ed. Ben Guy, Georgia Henley, O. W. Jones, Rebecca Thomas (Turnhout, 2020), 169-229.

80. Rory Naismith, *Early Medieval Britain* (Cambridge, 2021), 89.

81. Helen Fulton, 'The Invention of Arthurian Britain', in *The Arthurian World*, ed. Victoria Coldham-Fussell, Miriam Edlich-Muth, Renée Ward (London, 2021), 35-48.

82. Flore Verdon, *Le Royaume arthurien* (Paris, 2022), 100.

83. Mary Bateman, *Local Place and the Arthurian Tradition* (Cambridge, 2023), 92.

84. Melissa Ridley Elmes, 'Arthurian Ethics Before the Pentecostal Oath', in *Ethics in the Arthurian Legend*, ed. Melissa Ridley Elmes and Evelyn Meyer (Cambridge, 2021), 8-34.

85. Natalia I. Petrovskaia, *This Is Not a Grail Romance: Understanding 'Historia Peredur vab Efrawc'* (Cardiff, 2023), 67.

86. Jean Blacker, *Arthur, Origins, Identities and the Legendary History of Britain* (Leiden, 2024), 20, 52-3, 190.

87. Daniel F. Melia, 'Territorial Narrative in the *Mabinogi*', in *Medieval Welsh Literature and Its European Contexts*, ed. Victoria Flood (Cambridge, 2024), 55-67.

CHAPTER SIX

LAꞫAMON'S *BRUT*

After a long march through Latin and Welsh (and then Latin again), we strike upon English and LaꞫamon's *Brut*. We there meet Arthur for the first time in the English language, beginning a line that includes *Sir Gawain and the Green Knight*, *Morte Arthure* (alliterative and rhyming versions), *The Awntyrs off Arthure*, Malory, Spenser's *Fairie Queene*, Tennyson's *Idylls of the King*, and versions high and low (in prose or verse) of our own time. If we know little of LaꞫamon, a Worcestershire priest active soon after 1200, he yet started something big.

His poem is big as well. It has 32241 lines (or 16095 in modern editions). If it perhaps has few readers, those taking it on often do so with zest. Men and women, usually with old-fashioned tastes in poetry (like C. S. Lewis), have responded with enthusiasm to its battles and campaigning. Altogether cooler, though, was W. P. Ker (d. 1923) of London, with whom we start. He made basic points. He did not praise LaꞫamon's metrics: his alliterative verse is 'uncomfortable', possibly from its translating 'a French rhyming version' (by Wace, a Jerseyman) of Geoffrey of Monmouth. Yet LaꞫamon has things 'neither in the Latin nor the French', which Ker regarded as perhaps added by the poet himself, who may have gone 'note-taking in Wales' (much as Tennyson in 1848 visited Polperro, Cornwall, on a quest for traditions of Arthur). All the same, despite the 'disagreeable and discordant' metrics, outcome

137

of a narrative in elegant 'French couplets' reassembled in 'corrupt' Germanic alliteration, Ker condescendingly found some 'memorable passages' amongst much that was 'heavy and prosaic'.[1]

Far more positive was a US bibliographer, also supplying fundamental information (dating, dialect, the two manuscripts, editorial history). For him, Laȝamon's *Brut* was amongst 'the most important works' in Middle English. It survives in two copies (London, British Library, MSS Cotton Caligula A.ix and Cotton Otho C.xiii), the first written between 1200 to 1225 or so, the second some five decades thereafter. (MS Caligula is today still placed in the thirteenth century, but several decades later.) Both are in South-Western dialect; the latter was 'badly damaged' in the fire of 1731 (also wreaking havoc on the *Beowulf* Manuscript), with some of the text now lost; nor does it derive from the former, presenting major differences between the two. As for the poet, we know from his opening lines that he was a priest *at æðelen are chirechen* ('at the noble church') of Areley Kings (across the River Severn from Stourport, in north-west Worcestershire), who rendered Wace's *Le Roman de Brut* (completed in 1155) into English verse, setting out the history of the Britons from the legendary Brutus (hence *Brut*), a Trojan exile and founder of a British kingdom, to their glory-days under Arthur and then final defeat by the Saxons. Arthur's deeds occupy over ten thousand lines, which is natural, because Laȝamon 'loves valor, vigor, energy, power, bold speech, a heroic fight'; he is 'no dull proser'; 'something is always happening in his accounts'. Examples include passages on the 'splendor' and festivities of Caerleon; Childric's flight, like a hunted fox's; and the fearsome ogre of Mont-Saint-Michel. Laȝamon 'expands greatly' the text of Wace known to us, thus adding lines on 'the elves at Arthur's birth' or developing 'a hint of the Table Round' or, above all (despite anachronism), making Arthur a patriotic Englishman, who if 'not much the king of chivalry', is at least not the 'crude hero of the Welsh' and 'is always generous and kind' (and chaste). Even the 'brutal giant of

St Michael' gets fair warning from him. (So Arthur undergoes yet another transformation at this poet's hands, including a change of nationality.) Laȝamon also had a 'mystic' taste for wonders not in Geoffrey or Wace (both down-to-earth on such matters), including the 'fairy elements of the birth and the passing of the hero', which seem unGermanic (and may be Celtic).[2] Those wonders have had a long history. They have left their mark on pre-Raphaelite painters and Tennyson and even those who now congregate at Glastonbury (in the belief that it was Avalon) or Tintagel. Without them, England would be a duller place.

After this admiring American portrait of Laȝamon and Arthur, a few sober comments on the text. It is much better preserved in MS Caligula, although MS Otho sometimes offers better readings; but the latter has undergone heavy cutting by a man 'mainly interested' in events, who left out many similes, epic repetitions, descriptive touches, so that 'much that is characteristic' of Laȝamon has vanished. In 1847 both versions became accessible in Sir Frederic Madden's classic edition. Textual corruption notwithstanding, features of the poet's dialect survive intact, including borrowings from Scandinavian (such as *dreng* 'man, warrior; retainer', *grið* 'the peace of society; cessation of fighting') and a few from French (such as *castel* 'castle', *latimer* 'interpreter'). This despite a French original, itself styled as 'prosaic' and thus offering 'strong contrast' to Laȝamon's 'delight in descriptions of feasting and music', as at a banquet where Rowenna, Hengist's dangerously attractive daughter, caught the eye of Vortigern:

> Bemen heo bleowen, gomen men gunnen cleopien,
>
> Bord heo hetten breden, cnihtes setten ther to,
>
> Heo æten, heo drunken, dræm wes i burhyen...

-- with trumpets sounded, games announced, tables set up; knights sat down to eat and drink, the town heard their clamour.[3]

It was a convivial prelude to treachery and Britain's fall to Saxon invaders. Laȝamon could create a dramatic scene. If this is clear, his debt to Welsh tradition has been less so, not least for Argante, wise woman and sorceress. Arthur is wounded at *Camlan* and his life is threatened. He bids his men take him to this otherworld being:

> And Ich wulle uaren to Aualun, to uairest alre maidene,
>
> To Argante there quene, aluen swithe sceone,
>
> And heo scal mine wunden makien alle isunde,
>
> Al hal me makien mid halweiye drenchen

--He will fare to Avalon, to the fairest of all maidens, to the Queen Argante, fairy-woman exceeding bright; she will cure all his wounds, making him well with healing drinks.

Sir Edmund Chambers made three points on the above. The first is fundamental. It seems that Laȝamon's source here was not Wace the Norman but an 'expanded *Brut*' by an Anglo-French poet. That explains why Laȝamon's text is so different from Wace's, incorporating 'signs of Celtic knowledge' which the Englishman hardly found out for himself. (No need to think of Laȝamon's touring Wales and interrogating the locals.) Second, that lost French text probably drew upon Geoffrey of Monmouth's *Vita Merlini*. Third, the name of Argante is 'best explained as a corruption of Geoffrey's "Morgen"' in that Latin poem. Besides that, the elves who bless the new-born Arthur 'are perhaps a borrowing from Teutonic rather than Celtic folklore' (nothing Celtic is known in this context).[4] The views of Chambers, however, did not reach Wales in time for one professor. Quoting the above lines from Laȝamon and noting that Argante features in his poem alone, W. J. Gruffydd (d. 1954) of Cardiff followed Sir John Rhŷs for links with Arianrhod, a Celtic goddess who dwelt on a rock off the Gwynedd coast, and a sinister presence in the twelfth-century *Four Branches of the Mabinogi*.[5] But the names are unlike. Argante is another Celtic immortal, Morgan le Fay, eventually made out as Arthur's sister or half-sister. We shall come to her again, in the meantime jettisoning almost everything said by Gruffydd on the subject.

With Oakden's survey of medieval verse we return to a sturdy English approach to Laȝamon. If Ker had little love for the poet, Oakden admired him greatly, quoting eulogies by the fellow-admirer H. C. Wyld (d. 1945), Oxford professor of English (and *bête noire* of the young C. S. Lewis). The poet loved England: her heroes, customs, scenery, mead-halls, joys of the chase, fields of battle. He loved as well 'the ancient poetic compounds' derived from older verse and abounding in his work. Especially to be praised was the long description of how Arthur pursued Childric, who fled like a fox in the chase, where:

> Hunten thar talieth, hundes ther galieth,
> Thene vox driueth, yeond dales and yeond dunes

-- hunters bellow, hounds bark, they drive the fox over dales and downs.

This passage on Childric, fugitive king, is an addition to the text and makes powerful reading. Also displaying Laȝamon's gusto are descriptions of scenery, including ones on the eeriness of Loch Lomond (in Scotland), on the sea, and on warfare (as with on the arming of Arthur). While Ker was discomfited by Laȝamon's metrical see-sawing and frequent 'heavy, prosaic' writing, Oakden quoted Wyld for him as a poet who 'never fails to interest the reader' and whose work is 'lofty, chivalrous, and noble'.[6] Which is an overstatement: for it puts him and his Arthur into Victorian dress, leaving his *Brut* as too much like *Idylls of the King*. All ages tend to make the past anew. An Oxford professor might thus well see an Arthur of King John's reign as if he were a foreign royal visiting Queen Victoria and Prince Albert at Balmoral.

There are four points in a brief biographical guide to Laȝamon. His *Brut* is styled 'one of the most entertaining' compositions of the period, which demonstrates rehabilitation from the strictures of Ker (all thanks to Wyld, whose essays on him are called 'Indispensable'); its date is 'controversial', but perhaps of between 1173 and 1207; material not found in Wace may reflect 'contemporary Welsh tradition' (where we yet recall that the English poet hardly knew it directly, as Chambers observed). A last point is singular. 'An edition by M. S. Serjeantson and the late E. V. Gordon is in preparation for the EETS.'[7] That society brought out volume one in 1963, volume two in 1978; but volume three (with general introduction, commentary, glossary) is unpublished yet. It enhances respect for the poem's first editor, Sir Frederic Madden (d. 1873). He evidently had Victorian qualities of diligence or staying-power.

In the same year appeared further appraisal, with remarks on the 'numerous vivifying touches' in Laȝamon's (apparent) additions. Despite vague comments by others on supposed use of 'oral tradition', we now hear how most of those 'touches' occur in French or Breton-French writing of the time: 'there is little evidence for a Welsh origin.' After analysis of his style *vis-à-vis* that of Old English verse, his indifference to dress and ceremonial, his relish for accounts of hunting and battles and storms at sea and weapons, come words on Arthur. He has a 'poetic glamour' not known to Wace, together with a new stress on 'marvellous elements': the elves at his birth, the properties of the Round Table, his mysterious departure for Avalon. Arthur is now also a 'Germanic hero', not a 'knight of chivalry'.[8] The clock has turned back. Much of this was repeated in summary form (with mention of Tatlock's 1950 study of the 'legendary history of Britain'), followed by seven extracts. First come the opening lines on the poet as a priest of Areley *on-fest Radestone* or beside Redstone, a sandy cliff above the River Severn; then a leap to the poem's last part. We hear of feasting and magnificence at Arthur's court, where even the servers *gold beren on honden*, 'carried gold in their hands'; of his battle with Colgrim, whom he attacked like a wolf racing out of woodland *bihonged mid snawe* or snow-laden (wolves in winter being hungry and more likely to attack flocks); and of the humbling of Childric, like the doomed fox which hunters dig out of his *hol* or den. After that, the arming of Arthur with his coat of mail, Wygar, and his sword, Caliburn; his coming to haunted Loch Lomond, with grim *nikeres* or monsters below its waters; and his final battle and departure for Avalon, where he lives still *mid fairest alre aluen* ('with the fairest of the elf-folk'), awaiting his return *Anglen to fulste* 'as aid to the English'.[9] Assuredly, the stuff of legend.

Several of these points were taken up in a discerning account of Laȝamon and the hand that fed him: the hand of Germanic alliterative poets, such as the eighth-century Mercian who composed *Beowulf* and his predecessors. Hence a common interest in battles, revelry, voyages, sea-storms, terrors in the night; whereon 'a few rough alliterative lines' (preserved in a thirteenth-century Latin sermon) on the Teutonic god Wade indicate missing links. (Those lines and sculptures of Wade figure below in a paper of 2023.) All the same, if Laȝamon lacked the professional 'variety and flexibility' of pre-Norman bards, he could still present 'mystery' (as in the passage on Arthur's departure to Avalon) and ferocity (as on Arthur attacking like a wolf). Laȝamon was less modern than Wace, at once his source and 'antithesis'. The latter, known at Henry II's court, makes the most of a chivalric knight's 'noblesse', or of the 'signs of love' which Uther sent Ygerne. Quite unlike Laȝamon, no court versifier but an English country priest and proud of it, telling us of his Worcestershire home in provincial (even rustic) style. His speech is 'almost free from French words', despite his 'good knowledge of the language'. Was this due to 'conscious preference for what was traditional among the English'? He certainly had no respect for Norman invaders. He thought that they 'destroyed this people'. If his English patriotism (for us) jars with his praise of British heroes, at least he had no doubt of his country's 'long and often glorious past'. His poem is 'astonishingly

English'. His Arthur is atavistic. That king (unlike Wace's) is known for his grand household, with 'thanes of noble birth', so that he resembles not a feudal monarch but a *hlaford* or lord in *Beowulf*. Like an Old English poet, Laȝamon was also 'not interested in romantic love', toning down even the little that Wace offered.[10]

What was perceived above by a scholar in Oxford compares with equivalents by another scholar in New York. Loomis, who followed Tatlock for the present poem as of Richard I's reign (1189-99), further noted how Laȝamon gloried in the name of Englishman, despite using a poem by Wace in which the English 'are held up to execration'. (Plenty of revisionism there, then.) Laȝamon also vastly improved on his French source in a 'feeling for the concrete and the dramatic', as in similes already discussed, or in an account (with their speeches) of how six Saxons wheedled their way into Uther's court at Winchester so as to poison him; or of Arthur's dream of himself astride a hall, with Modred hewing at its wooden pillars and Queen Guinevere pulling at its roof, so that Arthur fell and broke his right arm, but was avenged when he used his other arm to grasp a sword, decapitate Modred, and hack Guinevere to bits. Given such brutality, small wonder that Loomis regarded Laȝamon as 'a barbarian at heart', as when, following quarrels (at a Christmas banquet), men are beheaded and women have their noses sliced off. The Worcestershire poet had a 'ferocious streak'. As for supposed Celtic symptoms in the text (elves at Arthur's birth, Avalon, the Round Table), Loomis thought them derived from French sources, whatever their ultimate origins. Emphasis on Laȝamon's savagery notwithstanding, Loomis yet concurred with Oxford writers in seeing the poet as very English. Anyone familiar with Old English verse 'will feel at home' with him.[11]

For a third exercise on essentials, we have C. S. Lewis himself. He listed six of them. The poem's very language made it 'sterner, more epic, more serious' than French verse of the time, as in the 'hammer-like' phrase *mid orde and mid egge* 'with [a weapon's] point and edge'). Its world is more archaic than Wace's, one of 'heroes and thanes', not 'knights and courtiers'. Lewis yet thought it 'kinder' than its source. Its warriors have 'tender hearts': Brennus aids Roman refugees, Vortimer plans to liberate slaves. (Loomis, we recall, took a harsher view.) Finally, it shows interest in signs and marvels; displays a gift for dialogue; and contains a 'wealth of simile'.[12] Lewis's manly love of older English poetry is evident. In the same year appeared an edition of the poem's first half, with explanation of how the task was first allocated to E. V. Gordon (editor of *Pearl* and co-editor of *Sir Gawain and the Green Knight*), whose premature death in 1938 brought work to a halt.[13]

After that, a sensation, conveniently indicated by Jacobus Swart of Amsterdam. It is this: Herbert Pilch's proposition (made public in 1960) that Laȝamon took much of his material from a Middle Welsh translation of Geoffrey of Monmouth's *Historia*, which is best preserved in Aberystwyth, National Library of Wales, MS Llanstephan 1. The English poet's use of this *Brut y Brenhinedd* ('Chronicle of the Kings') hence does away with 'laying any stress at all' on a lost text by the Anglo-Norman versifier Gaimar. Less contentiously, Swart acknowledges the 'many gory details' of the English poem, even quoting Loomis on 'a Nazi streak of ruthlessness and cruelty'.[14] A grimmer and more disturbing or troubling text than one would gather from C. S. Lewis. Yet any debt of the English *Brut* to the Welsh *Brut* cannot be maintained. Apart from the improbability of any English author's learning Welsh (and never mentioning it), there is the fatal objection that versions of *Brut y Brenhinedd* postdate Laȝamon (as we shall see).

The noble description of Arthur's final voyage 'to Aualun' in a barge where *twa wimmen þerinne wunderliche idihte* (= fairy women 'wonderfully arrayed') will attend him, was well edited by Jack Bennett, who indicated Laȝamon's creative attitude to his French original, and how he was the first to tell stories of King Arthur (and Lear) in English and thereby spread their glamour. Bennett also cited Irish analogues, including the eighth-century tale of Froech (whose aunt or mother was Boann, goddess of the River Boyne), wherein women carry that wounded hero to a fairy hill, entrance to the Other World, which the Celts saw as underground home to the feasts of joyous and blessed immortals.[15] Laȝamon had little direct knowledge of Welsh and Irish tradition (despite what Pilch and Tatlock believed). Yet the eerie quality of Arthur's final journey is certainly a Celtic trait, *Avalon* being a British toponym (compare Welsh *afallen* 'apple-tree'). English poetry will thus have a debt (unsuspected by many) to Britain's pre-English inhabitants. Tribute is paid in Worcestershire itself to the poet of Areley Kings (a mile or so from Stourport and the River Severn) by inscribing of his name on the church's Norman font; while at nearby Radstone can still be seen a hermitage 'cut into the sandstone cliff by the Severn', a place to be dismissed by Hugh Latimer (d. 1555), fierce Protestant bishop, as a dwelling equally ready to house five hundred 'thieves and traitors' as 'true men'.[16] Such was the Laȝamon country's history.

Another wise voice from the post-war period, that of Birmingham's Geoffrey Shepherd, had telling observations. Born not much than a century after the Conquest, Laȝamon curiously and 'without irony' presented Britain's legendary past as if containing the history of his own race, and that one of 'fierce glory', wherein Arthur is no 'benign but passive presence' behind the feats of his knights, instead being a 'war-leader, the captain of his host', the whole treatment being 'pre-chivalric'. Unremarkable, then, if the poet used 'old heroic terms', even if he often had no 'clear idea of their meanings', as shown by differences between the Otho and Caligula texts; which all the same prove that 'the work was read as well as heard'. It was also reactionary. Writing in a century of 'profound and disturbing change', Laȝamon saw 'the present with anxiety, the past with regret'. He had no part in twelfth-century Europe's intellectual awakening or rebirth. In no way did he share 'the vivid excitement of the age'.[17] What he did had prodigious consequences for the future; surprisingly, for he himself was backward-looking.

An aspect of that future is inclusion of the Death of Arthur in a classic anthology, and how the Welsh yet say that he did not die and *That an Arthur shulde yete cum Anglen to fulste* (= an Arthur will come again to aid the English).[18] A bland appropriation. Welshmen then and now might hear with disbelief and irritation such assurance on Arthur's love of England. A specific remark on the arming of Arthur underlines Laʒamon's difficulties with past as well as with future. He tells us that the royal coat of mail, called Wygar, was forged by Witege the smith (a descendant of the mythical Weland). It may be that by Laʒamon's day the descent of Witege (or Wudga) from Weland was the one thing 'still remembered of him'. A lost text also relevant to Laʒamon is a vernacular life of St Wulfstan (Bishop of Worcester 1062-95), written soon after his death, but with its text surviving in a Latin translation only. All the same, that original is proof of how Old English literary culture flourished at Worcester under Wulfstan's eye.[19] Less remarkable, then, if a century later we find that tradition revived at nearby Areley Kings. Conclusions: on the one hand, Germanic legends familiar to Alfred three centuries previous were all but dead; on the other, sufficient of the past remained in Worcestershire for Laʒamon to compose his own tribal lay.

There is proof of a further kind in a useful volume (with an admirable account of Geoffrey of Monmouth's influence in Wales). It has this statement. The Middle Welsh translation of *Historia Regum Britanniae* in MS Llanstephan 1 is of 'the thirteenth century'.[20] So it postdates Laʒamon. That shoots through the heart Pilch's case for its influence on the poet. Perhaps awaiting another bullet is assertion, in a book which is (alas) a cornucopia of Leavisite opinion (but without Leavis's insights), on how 'we couldn't call Laʒamon' an English poet 'within the range' of the phrase's meaning.[21] That although others thought him very

English indeed. Hence comments on him as a writer from Worcestershire, where 'a strong tradition' of interest in the vernacular survived the Conquest (proved by the life of St Wulfstan and by the thirteenth-century 'tremulous hand' glossing Old English texts in Worcester's cathedral library). This cultural survival may be due partly to Wulfstan himself, partly to 'powerful conservative families of the Western Marches'.[22] We shall see below how Laʒamon the cleric-poet of battle and slaughter had an unacknowledged predecessor at Worcester in 937. It accords with comment on Laʒamon as living less than twelve miles north of 'the great centre of Old English learning at Worcester', and with perceptions of him as 'an archaist' in language and politics; a 'patriot'; and (in frequent battle-descriptions) 'aggressive, violent, heroic, ceremonial': the opposite of the 'calm, practical, rational' Wace.[23] Further understanding comes from discussion of his (somewhat bookish) vocabulary in the context of Old English heroic poems, including the tenth-century *Battle of Brunanburh*.[24] At this time appeared too the remaining part of the poem, edited to modern standards.[25]

His text now being secure, an excursus, relating it to *The Battle of Brunanburh* as cited by Turville-Petre. Its author boasted of how King Athelstan vanquished Norse-Irish foes at this combat (fought in 937 near the River Browney, south of Lanchester, County Durham). They fled back to Dublin 'on dingesmere', to be corrected as *on dingles mere* 'over the abyss of the ocean', where *dingle* 'a hollow or cleft (between hills and so on)' is a West Midlands word.[26] (Hence the puzzlement of West Saxon scribes, who miscopied it.) Now, also of the West Midlands was Cenwald, Bishop of Worcester and witness (in 934 and 946) to charters of Athelstan and Eadric. This book-loving cleric and court chaplain can now (after a conjecture by Sarah Foot of Christ Church, Oxford) be identified as author of *The Battle of Brunanburh*, with its 'mere of the dingle' (not 'Ding's mere') showing it as by a West Midlander, and its source (noted long ago by Brandl and Klaeber) as Joshua 10:1-27 (when Joshua reconquered Gibeon, made 'the sun stood still', and slew five enemy kings).[27] Bishop Cenwald, wishing to praise his royal master, saw Athelstan, reconqueror of the North, as a latter-day Joshua, reconqueror of Gideon. So we have a Worcestershire continuity. If it seems curious that Laȝamon the priest in about 1200 wrote a bookish alliterative poem on battle-slaughter, he had a precedent in Cenwald the bishop, who in 937 wrote a bookish alliterative poem on battle-slaughter. Worcester being less than twelve miles from Areley Kings, it implies that Laȝamon's *Brut* had links with *The Battle of Brunanburh* even closer than those indicated by Professor Turville-Petre.

Reminding us of another kind of poetry is an extract from Wace's *Roman de Brut*, with information on his birth in Jersey; his career in Normandy and beyond; his completion of the poem in 1155; his there mentioning for the first time the Round Table, 'symbol of altruistic knighthood'; and his conception of Arthur and his followers as 'defenders of Christian civilization', equivalent to the *Chanson de Roland*'s Charlemagne and his Twelve Peers.[28] There is a return to another literary tradition (its heart in Oxford) with observations by Derek Brewer and Jack Bennett, both from the school of Tolkien and C. S. Lewis. Brewer and Bennett were all for Laȝamon, praising him at length. The first spoke of the poet's 'novel personal enthusiasm' quite unlike the tone of Old English verse, which could yet have a 'majestic movement' not found in his *Brut*. Nor did it resemble Wace's 'crisp and lively narrative'. Laȝamon had a different objective, whereon (same word again) his 'enthusiasm never flags'. Expressions prompted by his chronicle of invasion and conflict are 'fierceness', 'a noble vigour of feeling; nothing is mean'; but also 'compassion' and (at times) a 'calm archaic sense of wonder', especially in the 'superbly elegiac account of Arthur's death' and departure for another world. In Avalon, Arthur's wounds will be healed, so that he will one day return to the Britons *mid muchelere wunne*, 'with great joy'. 'Profound, complex image of the death of the king!' was Brewer's verdict.[29] He spoke with a weight and pregnancy heard elsewhere on what he termed 'almost an English national epic'.

Brewer's admiring appreciation has a complement and contrast in an entire chapter by Jack Bennett (d. 1981), who was more down-to-earth. Bennett acknowledged the difficulties. Laʒamon is read solely by literary historians. For other readers, the language of his *magnum opus* is 'inaccessible', 'difficult or uncouth'; while the poem itself is (for English narrative verse) exceeded in length only by *The Faerie Queene*, which it 'foreshadows' in its Arthurian subject and 'archaistic' style. Studies of Homer by Milman Parry and others are thus 'a good starting point' for reading Laʒamon. Bennett noted surprises. Although the work of a priest, the chronicle 'is bare of Christian sentiment'. It is yet 'of epic scope'. If its author really did *gon lithen wide* ('travel widely') in a quest of material, he might have found manuscripts of Old English poetry not far away (at Worcester, Pershore, Evesham, Much Wenlock) on a *voyage littéraire* resembling that of John Leland three centuries later. Bennett even reckoned the battle-scenes of Laʒamon's *Brut* 'not far removed' in spirit from those of *The Battle of Brunanburh*. (That poem being attributed by Sarah Foot to Bishop Cenwald of Worcester, it would strange if Laʒamon did not know it.) Narrative skill appears in passages where a leader appeals to his warriors, so that Arthur cries out *To horse, to horse, halethes gode!* ('Worthy champions, mount your steeds!'); or when warriors fight, and *Urnen tha brockes of reden blodes* ('The brooks streamed with red blood'); or when bad news arrives, as with Modred's treachery. Silence at once fell in Arthur's hall, until *Tha umbe stunde stefne ther sturede* ('Then before long a murmur arose'). There was (in Bennett's words) shock; a subdued noise following; a final 'roar of anger'. Of interest too are what the poet left out. If he (like the author of *Sir Gawain and the Green Knight*) had a passion for hunting, he had no time for tournaments or the *courtoisie* by which 'bright eyes rain influence'. He leaves out the Scriptural allusions given by Wace. But he had plenty of time for

Arthur, presented without the 'glamour' or 'refinements' of later romance. This Arthur is 'savage', a 'monarch of the chase', albeit one 'more eloquent' than he is for other writers. As regards English literature, then, Laȝamon established 'the Matter (or Myth) of Britain, and of Arthur'; he provided national history (or pseudo-history) with 'a dress, language, and colour' to be appropriated by romancers.[30] If Laȝamon's readers are few, his place in English tradition is yet secure.

Brewer and Bennett providing ample reflections on Laȝamon and his conception of Arthur, comment by another will seem meagre. Yet it is rightly noted that the poet's supreme warrior-king is shown in 'the Anglo-Saxon' heroic manner, 'the new chivalric manners' being avoided; his Arthur is now 'a hero worthy of celebration' by Englishmen, annexing a British champion (as they long before annexed British territory). Laȝamon nevertheless stopped short of the 'blind patriotism' with which some Elizabethan poets fended off doubts on Arthur. He merely laid 'the groundwork' for them.[31] Difficulties for modern readers are admitted by another critic. Laȝamon's *Brut* is 'five times the length of *Beowulf*'. Its first (lengthy) part takes us from the Fall of Troy and settlement by refugee Trojans of 'a giant-inhabited Albion' up to the arrival of the Saxons under Hengist. The central part is an 'Arthuriad'; thereafter are a few thousand lines on 'the sad fate' of subsequent British kings and Athelstan's 'consolidation of English power' in the tenth century. The whole is not a history of Britons but of Britain, which has a personality surviving 'continual conquest'. Hence the identification of 'Britain' and 'England' (to the chagrin of real Celts). After stimulating remarks on the poet's perception of feudal landscape, in 'an unstable world where violence and treachery are commonplace', comes a conclusion. To maintain order, 'strong, even ruthless, kingship' is imperative. It brings us to the 'ferocious' Arthur. Although 'strong and virtuous', he is devoid of 'the chivalric qualities' that he had in Wace's *Brut*. His knights lack them too. They are the thugs who (for example) throw Roman diplomats to the ground and 'tear them by the hair'. They may be a reason for this absence of finesse. Laȝamon's English readers perhaps too often saw 'mounted soldiery' to mistake them for *beaux chevaliers*.[32] After this frank analysis, then, strange to hear that Laȝamon 'developed the chivalrous aspect' of the Arthur legend.[33] Here 'unchivalrous' seems nearer the mark. An explanation by Hallam Tennyson (the laureate's son) on how in *Idylls of the King* his father used Laȝamon, Malory, Charlotte Guest's *Mabinogion*, and 'his own imagination' reminds us of Arthurian malleability.[34] Laȝamon's Arthur has no chivalry: Tennyson's is its quintessence.

In the 1990s came another survey of Laȝamon in a handbook of Arthuriana. It contains acknowledgement of his portraying a society 'much rougher, more brutal' than that of Wace. Arthur besieges and captures Winchester, burning it down and massacring its inhabitants; Gawain, learning of Guinevere's intrigue with Modred, threatens to have her tied to horses and ripped in half. Not much chivalry there. Laȝamon still had a gift for the dramatic, though, as with Saxon assassins (disguised as paupers) begging for alms outside Uther's castle, or Arthur's nightmare of his banqueting hall destroyed by Guinevere and Modred. Further consensus, then, on the kind of writer that Laȝamon was.[35] Access to him is also advanced by a volume of over 500 pages (it has introduction, bibliography, translation, notes).[36]

In a new and different tone is discussion of love as perceived by women. There is little of it in Laȝamon's *Brut*. Nor is that text a 'romance' (so a chapter-heading is here misleading). Where it does happen, its results can be catastrophic, so that (after Françoise Le Saux) one learns how it drove Guinevere into the arms of Modred to 'combine in treachery' against her husband. Later, bereft of her lover, the Queen finds herself in misery at York, 'saddest of women', as Laȝamon dwells on 'the bitterness of her grief' but (unlike Wace) says nothing on any sense of 'shame' or 'repentance'.[37]

In an engaging collection of essays is (a) recognition of how Laȝamon's 'national epic' parades heroes 'noble and brutal' together with 'traitors and cowards' in 'a history unsoftened by the chivalry, courtesy, or love-interest of the Norman overculture'; (b) comment on how Arthur's slain foes in their armour are called *stelene fisces* 'steel fish' as they lie below the River Avon's waters (prompting comparison with the riddling mode of Old English verse); and (c) summing-up of the chronicle as offering 'fascinating and complex negotiation' of diverse identities (Celtic, English, Norman).[38] All this is due to what is called Laȝamon's 'clear transformation' of Wace's *Brut*.[39]

As a break from critical reception of Laȝamon's *Brut*, we glance at the career of its first editor, Sir Frederic Madden (1801-73), who spent sixteen years on the task. The text's eventual publication in 1847 came at a time of violent Chartist demonstrations, agitation in London by Marx and Engels, unrest prompting the revolutions of 1848. It was a *Zeitgeist* reinforcing Madden's 'hatred of democracy' (with consequences for him as an editor).[40] Returning to the poet, we find learn how, when Romans attacked Britons and took few (*lut*) prisoners, but left many dead, Laȝamon was indebted to Old English forms of litotes 'bleak in their exploitation of grim irony'.[41] What he owed to earlier poets was deeper and more pervasive than one might think.

After this, the cheering sight of conference proceedings with a wealth of insight. Significant for a study of Arthur is a paper on how Laȝamon represented that monarch, to whom he allocated 1021 lines additional to those in Wace (as demonstrated in 1989 by Françoise Le Saux). The result is 'a conqueror ruthlessly successful in the pursuit of his imperialistic objectives', who (for example) in Ireland encourages knights 'to slaughter and destroy'. (This except at places of sanctuary, which his army has 'strict orders to respect'; because Arthur is a 'Christian king' with veneration for 'holy relics'.) His merciless struggle for power notwithstanding, there remains a curious 'preoccupation with treason', subject of 'so many of the amplifications' in the Arthurian part of Laȝamon's verse-saga, where the warrior-king occupies (in Le Saux's phrase) the 'centre and culmination' of the poem.[42] This obsession with treason is puzzling. It seems never to have been explained. Nothing in Arthur's rule accounts for it. It lacks narrative motivation.

In the same year as the above, there appeared a book-length study (on context, language, interpretation) of Laȝamon's *Brut*.[48] It is less useful than one might expect. Its theme is prophecy, and this was something fundamental in Welsh tradition. But what its author says on the subject is enfeebled for two reasons: the writer does not know Welsh, and therefore cannot deal with original sources and commentary in this language; and further neglects material on Welsh traditions that has been published in English. That means inconclusiveness (and inaccuracy). Not a volume, one fears, from which we learn anything remarkable.

Better is an account by D. A. Pearsall, including a portrait of Laȝamon's Arthur. Wace stressed how the king 'surmounted all in courtesy'. Laȝamon 'excises all comment' on that, instead offering a ruler 'of extravagant heroism and kingliness, steeped in religious awe' (the last an emotion for which Pearsall had scant sympathy). Yet the battles come across with 'brilliant panache', as also the poet's considerable 'fury and indignation', which Pearsall related to the author's occupation. It kept him away (we hear) 'from any actual fighting'. If Wace, in his presentation of Arthur and elsewhere, is 'calm, practical, rational' (and realistic on 'war and strategy'), Laȝamon is 'aggressive, violent, heroic, ceremonial, and ritualistic'. The poet yet gave serious attention to Arthur in another guise, as a ruler establishing 'an ordered kingdom under the rule of law'. This is done in a 'unique way'. It might mean executing brawlers at a feast and cutting off the noses of their womenfolk (so that nobody will marry the latter and 'the tribe will die out'). Even so, Laȝamon can be scrupulous. If he makes much of the Round Table (briefly mentioned by Wace), so that we learn that it is hollow (= not a solid disc), capable of seating 1600, and nevertheless going with Arthur everywhere, he still relates it to 'fables' of the Britons. As concerns Arthur's return from Avalon, the poet distanced himself in another way. It was all a prophecy of Merlin, whose 'sayings were true'. A somewhat oblique utterance. All the same, here and throughout Laʒamon presents himself 'as a historian, and not a romancer'.[44]

In commenting on what is known of Areley Kings and local ruling families in Laʒamon's day (where English-speaking gentry were presumably his patrons, rather than grandees whose first language was Anglo-French?), reference is made to his poem as predating 1216 (according to Françoise Le Saux), even if others think it of about 1250.[45] In paragraphs on concrete aspects of the poet's literary status (his quills and parchment) and more subjective ones of his literary persona (the 'artificiality and illusoriness' of the text's 'single speaking subject'), the work is dated to 'about 1220' (no word on why).[46] Also concrete is landscape. If the verse-chronicle opens with lyrical praise of Areley and the Severn, both of them *sel* or 'pleasant' to the poet, and later has lines on how Brutus saw the *muntes feire and muchele* ('beautiful high mountains') and meadows and woods and cornfields of his new home, we can find as well the reverse of any *locus amoenus*. By Laʒamon's time Worcestershire abutted the Welsh border, which bristled with castles. Their remains are still there, proof of an ugly former insecurity. They underline the poem's theme of 'conquest, invasion, and conflict'.[47] Conflict and slaughter exist even in the text's fantasies. When attacking Gaul, Arthur deals with the Giant of Mont St Michel and the Giant with a Cloak of Beards, who together prompted a 1999 study by J. J. Cohen on how the two relate to 'the psychic space of imperial conquest'.[48] If giants are potent symbols, the Round Table is one too. Created by a Cornish joiner, after Arthur had had brawlers at a banquet beheaded (together with their parents) and *le nez de leur femmes* cut off, the *égalitaire Table Ronde* and knights drawn to it were to dim *un peu de l'aura et de la brilliance* bestowed on Arthur by Geoffrey of Monmouth.[49] The table was a literary Trojan Horse. That other wooden item had brought together warriors, with destructive results. If a horse constructed by Greeks was bad news for Troy, the table constructed by a Cornishman was bad news for Arthur, whose adventures were to be eclipsed and diminished by those of his knights.

Enigmatic contradictions in Laȝamon's attitudes to nation and government may (or may not) be smoothed away by Christopher Cannon's remark of 2004 on British 'continuity'. Quoted in a collection on border studies, it suggests that the poet–chronicler took 'ancient law' and 'modern law' as one and the same because neither conquest nor usurpation 'have ever altered a timeless custom'.[50] Laȝamon's name is Germanic and means 'lawman, one skilled in the law'. Perhaps, besides his name, he received a knowledge of law from an ancestor trained in it? Whatever his views on law, however, he assuredly cared little for the sea. A study of 1926 by R. A. Kissack is quoted on how for him it was 'cold water and very little else'; it (supposedly) lacked the creative possibilities exploited by older poets (like the authors of *Beowulf* or *The Seafarer*).[51] Even so, if Laȝamon was no seafarer, he was a translator, allowing updating on his achievement and a reference (after Rosamund Allen) to his writing during the Interdict of 1208-12, and in Worcestershire, where Old English texts were still read. There are other insights, some of them novel and stimulating. His audience has been seen as 'racially mixed'. His knowledge of (Anglo-)Norman was unusual for an Englishman of his day. He admired a 'strong ruler' and was 'intolerant of paganism' (if still intrigued by it). If he is violent, it is not done gratuitously. It is there 'to serve order'.[52] All in all, Laȝamon is a more complex writer than one might imagine. Nostalgic, yes; primitive, no.

That qualifies attitudes in a more straightforward discussion, which (after E. G. Stanley) contains acceptance of the poet's 'antiquarian sentiments' and offers details on the two surviving manuscripts. Their scribes were the poet's first known critics. MS Cotton Caligula is usually thought 'the better version'; MS Cotton Otho (damaged in the Ashburnham House fire of 1731) has a text with many cuts (no credit given now to the work of Wace) and its language modernized. The attitude of the latter scribe becomes more intelligible (and less reprehensible?) if we accept that Laȝamon did not have 'a widespread and multiple audience' in mind. It explains why only two copies of his work have come down to us (in contrast to those of Geoffrey and Wace).[53]

That is less remarkable when we recall that Laȝamon considered himself a careful historian (not a romancer or even a writer of epic). He thereby finds himself in a dictionary of historians, where we learn this. His poem will not postdate 1236, when Henry III wedded Eleanor of Provence, because an opening allusion to an Eleanor who 'wes Henries quene' (and who in 1155 received Wace's original text) must be to Eleanor of Aquitaine, Henry II's spouse. He died in 1189 (providing a *terminus post quem*). As for the poet, his sympathies were with the Britons and 'certainly not the Saxons'. Even so, if critics once thought that Laȝamon wrote his *Brut* to express 'anti-Norman English nationalism', they now see more 'ambivalence' in the Celtic-Saxon-Norman question.[54] The work has subtlety and complexity (and brutality).

The subtlety appears in comment on Arthur's voyage to Avalon. Wace had spoken of how the Britons think that Arthur 'will return'. Laȝamon is more circumspect. He cites Merlin on 'an Arthur' who will come to 'help the English'. The indefinite article makes a difference; so does 'English' and not 'Britons'. It is all part of 'English appropriation of the Arthurian legend', leading to the (illogical) belief found in Malory (and still heard today) that Arthur was an Englishman.[55] There are further emphases in an extended study, anatomizing Laȝamon's overriding concern with kingship. He had plenty of instances to work from, and his convictions on what it entailed (nobility in action, rather than in descent; justice; resolution in war) are fundamental and 'pragmatic'. Fundamental too is the poet's loathing of treachery, 'most heinous of crimes'. Rosamund Allen is quoted on how Laȝamon four times gives 'definitions of the ideal ruler' in writing of Arthur, whom he styles 'noblest of kings'. Arthur as paradigm is further revealed by words of Merlin, foretelling not how Arthur will return to the Britons, but how *an* Arthur will come to aid the English (a people who have inherited 'an innate nobility' from the Britons whom they dispossessed). A lesson, then, on how 'British history for the English' came about.[56]

Laȝamon's veneration of nobility and the like was not obvious to another. In a curt and negative tone, his *Brut* is styled 'hard to read, hard to date, hard to gauge, textually unstable'; many readers now will also find it repugnant, given its 'enormous length, horrific violence, and harsh vision of the world'.[57] Which contains some truth (even if Laȝamon was not responsible for his scribes or issues of dating). It would, naturally, be unfortunate if Laȝamon were smothered by bouquets of admirers; and the *via negative* often provides lessons. Similar testing is on offer in discussion of 'displacing feminist legend in Laȝamon', taking up the subject of male supremacy and women. Its conclusions are interesting. Geoffrey of Monmouth described women with 'access to political power' who used it 'competently'; he in addition expressed 'sympathy for the sufferings of female figures'. How unlike Wace and Laȝamon, intent on 'villainizing and disempowering Arthurian females'.[58] Time-travellers to the England of 1200 would soon discover the sickening and the abominable; and it is well to recall that, especially as concerns women.

Such reflections on society return us to kings and to Arthur as king. In a stimulating collection of essays, attention is given to politics. Medieval thinkers knew from the Book of Proverbs (chapter twenty) that a monarch's throne 'is upholden by mercy'; this Jewish and Christian ideal notwithstanding, little was heard before the seventeenth century on any 'well-defined notion of constitutionally limiting' the royal prerogative or regality. The playing-out of consequences is visible with Laȝamon's kings (there are 114 of them) in a study which unfortunately has nothing on Arthur. But it leaves material for development, with the two following remarks in mind. First, no doubt 'peace for and within his realm' was a wise king's prime objective; all the same, in a 'battle against heathen foes, a Christian king must show no moderation'. Second, Laȝamon's political views, although termed 'complex and noble', differed sharply from 'the politics of modern democracies'.[59]

In a volume on Geoffrey of Monmouth's *Nachleben*, Françoise Le Saux comments both on Laȝamon's respect for clerical learning (as with his mention of Pellitus, Spanish priest and adviser to King Edwin), and on how the scribe of MS Cotton Otho not only smoothed away the poem's archaic diction, but also showed impatience 'avec les passages technique ou érudits' (above all, medical ones).[60] Each of these observations implies a poet-priest who was also a scholar. A further aspect of his reception has not been much noticed. In a 1995 book, J. B. Friedman discovered mention of 'three copies of Layamon's *Brut*' in wills from the late medieval North (the ecclesiastical jurisdictions of York, Durham, Carlisle). The poem had more readers than one might think; circulated in the fourteenth and fifteenth centuries; and was favoured in Northern England, away from the West Midlands of its author.[61] Scrutiny of those who possessed his text (Yorkshire clerics with old-fashioned tastes in poetry?) would be revealing. From dry-as-dust probate deeds, then, come flashes of insight for critics and historians.

For those who think the poet unscholarly on history, there is ingenuity (or sophistry?) in K. J. Tiller's 2007 monograph on the chronicler, which is quoted on how 'objective' truth was peripheral to Laȝamon's remit, what mattered being discourse 'edifying and sufficiently verisimilar' to be convincing history.[62] Related to that (on what the poem was meant to be) is a verdict on military sea-faring and the like. Geoffrey had no great interest in it, his concerns being 'the greatness of the British people' and civil war's futility; Wace (born on the island of Jersey and thus familiar with ships) used sea-pictures mainly to 'entertain his audience'; Laȝamon was different again, because for him they are 'entertaining as well as educational' (geography and logistics and direct speech being added to the history).[63] That was Laȝamon, country schoolmaster on his mettle.

More recent accounts here tend to confirm established opinions on Arthur. He was a 'worthy', unyielding in battle. But there is an emotional focus on his court which is absent from Geoffrey and Wace. We have already encountered Laȝamon's loving account of its feasting and largesse, Arthur being *mete-custi* or 'generous' with every man alive. His cup-bearers and chamberlains and footmen bear gold and are dressed in fine cloth; his cooks are fighting men; even a squire is always a 'bold thane'. This (we recall) was interpreted as a harking-back to the world of *Beowulf*. But it is understood now as also denoting movement in the opposite direction. Arthur is 'a father to his young subjects'; a 'comfort to the old, a stern voice to the unruly, and a fair lord', thereby transcending the 'feudal governance system'. That has (we are told) an unforeseen result: it provided 'a gateway into the later medieval romances, where Arthur takes a secondary role' and his knights occupy the foreground.[64] An interesting consideration. What might seem backward-looking, a return to the mead and benches of Heorot, was yet (allegedly) an enabler of change. If cooks were warriors and squires were thanes, we may hear of their feats: a process that, from a literary point of view, would tend to crowd Arthur out. The innovative meets the archaic.

Some final notes. On kingship and Arthur's coronation (after Geoffrey) at Silchester, comparison of MSS Cotton Caligula and Otho bring out the way that scribal caprice impairs traditions (even fake ones). While the former has 'Silchester', the latter has 'Cirencester' (the same thing occurs in manuscripts of Geoffrey and of Wace).[65] One sees what happened. Silchester, site of the vanished Roman city of *Calleva* (its name related to Welsh *celli* 'grove, wood'), is a deserted spot by Hampshire's border with Berkshire. Even in the thirteenth century it was less famous than Cirencester, crowned by a great Augustinian abbey (now also vanished). For an obscure toponym, a scribe put a better-known one. It is a common process. We found it with Arthur's battles in chapter one. Texts of Geoffrey, Wace, Laȝamon all provide a lesson on scribal unreliability. As for the archaic, mention above of Laȝamon and a Middle English verse-fragment on Wade (Germanic demi-god of the sea) is now related to Viking sculptures of Wade in north-west Wales.[66] If a modern aspect of Laȝamon is not often noticed, ancient ones need no emphasis, as here.

Lastly, two thought-provoking commentaries on Laȝamon and Wace. The first deserves attention even if one disagrees with it (as in its description of the original Arthur as a 'king' who 'drove Germanic invaders out of Britain'). So, then, with its conclusion on Laȝamon. One accepts that he presented kings and lords in a way unlike that of Geoffrey or Wace, each of the three differing (in language, culture, audience) from the other two. Less evident is the claim that Laȝamon subverted 'the "great man" theory of history' by emphasizing lesser folk who 'formed a layered network of efficient causes for the progression of history'. In writing of Arthur, Laȝamon thus (we learn) displaced 'chivalry' (figuring primarily in that king) by 'a ethical system exclusive to the ruling class' in which anyone might attain 'chivalry'.[67] The argument appears forced. One feels that, if Laȝamon (with his portrait of Arthur, conqueror of nations) had been congratulated on how he depicted the rise of ordinary people, he would have been puzzled and surprised. As for our second item, it will not detain us for this reason. Despite extended analysis of Geoffrey and Wace, it has virtually nothing on Laȝamon, except in implications on (for example) Wace's 'blatant endorsement on territorial appropriation for its own sake' (= might is right) which might well apply to the English poet.[68]

Extending from 1912 to 2024, our tour of Laȝamon's *Rezeptionsgeschichte* reveals shifts. We began with remarks on defects of metre or dullness of treatment, accompanied by grudging admission of a gift (at times) for powerful writing. Praise of the poet's Englishness and love of what is old then came to the fore; thereafter, an admission of his nonchalance as regards cruelty; finally, stress on his complexity. At the centre of this is Arthur. Nowadays the leader created by Laȝamon would be condemned as a war criminal. An interesting transmogrification of our sixth-century commander. That this no more worried the poet than his theft of the Celtic past is perhaps the oddest and most striking aspect of his excursion into Britain's older history.

Notes

1. W. P. Ker, *English Literature: Medieval* (London, 1912), 118, 207.

2. J. E. Wells, *A Manual of the Writings in Middle English* (New Haven, 1916), 32-5, 191-5.

3. *Selections from Early Middle English*, ed. Joseph Hall (Oxford, 1920), 108, 450, 463, 477.

4. E. K. Chambers, *Arthur of Britain* (London, 1927), 105-6, 220.

5. W. J. Gruffydd, *Math vab Mathonwy* (Cardiff, 1928), 186-97.

6. J. P. Oakden, *Alliterative Poetry in Middle English: A Survey of the Traditions* (Manchester, 1935), 20-3.

7. W. L. Renwick and Harold Orton, *The Beginnings of English Literature to Skelton* (London, 1939), 308-10.

8. R. M. Wilson, *Early Middle English Literature* (London, 1939), 206-13.

9. *Early Middle English Texts*, ed. Bruce Dickins and R. M. Wilson (Cambridge, 1951), 17-28.

10. Dorothy Everett, *Essays on Middle English Literature* (Oxford, 1955), 28-45.

11. R. S. Loomis, 'Layamon's *Brut*', in *Arthurian Literature in the Middle Ages*, ed. R. S. Loomis (Oxford, 1959), 104-11.

12. C. S. Lewis, 'Introduction', in *Selections from Laʒamon's'Brut'*, ed. G. L. Brook (Oxford, 1963), vii-xv.

13. Laʒamon, *Brut*, ed. G. L. Brook and R. F. Leslie (London, 1963), v.

14. J. Swart, 'Laʒamon's "Brut"', in *Studies in Language and Literature in Honour of Margaret Schlauch*, ed. Mieczysław Brahmer, Sławomir Helstyński, Julian Krzyżanowski (Warszawa, 1966), 431-5.

15. *Early Middle English Verse and Prose*, ed. J. A. W. Bennett and G. V. Smithers, 2nd edn (Oxford, 1968), 145-57, 341-9.

16. Nikolaus Pevsner, *The Buildings of England: Worcestershire* (Harmondsworth, 1968), 71.

17. G. T. Shepherd, 'Early Middle English Literature', in *The Middle Ages*, ed. W. F. Bolton (London, 1970), 67–106.

18. *The Oxford Book of Medieval English Verse*, ed. Kenneth Sisam and Celia Sisam (Oxford, 1970), 1–4.

19. R. M. Wilson, *The Lost Literature of Medieval England*, 2nd edn (London, 1970), 7, 90–1.

20. *Brut y Brenhinedd*, ed. Brynley F. Roberts (Dublin, 1971), xxix.

21. Ian Robinson, *Chaucer and the English Tradition* (Cambridge, 1972), 286.

22. R. N. Bailey, 'The Development of English', in *The Mediaeval World*, ed David Daiches and Anthony Thorlby (London, 1973), 127–62.

23. Derek Pearsall, *Old English and Middle English Poetry* (London, 1977), 108–13.

24. Thorlac Turville-Petre, *The Alliterative Revival* (Cambridge, 1977), 7, 11–13.

25. Laȝamon: *Brut*, ed. G. L. Brook and R. F. Leslie (Oxford, 1978).

26. E. J. Dobson, *The Origins of 'Ancrene Wisse'* (Oxford, 1978), 117 n. 3.

27. *English Historical Documents c. 500–1042*, ed. Dorothy Whitelock, 2nd edn (London, 1979), 219–20, 550, 552.

28. *A Medieval French Reader*, ed. C. W. Aspland (Oxford, 1979), 73–82.

29. Derek Brewer, *English Gothic Literature* (New York, 1983), 9–14.

30. J. A. W. Bennett, *Middle English Literature* (Oxford, 1986), 68–89.

31. Christopher Dean, *Arthur of England* (Toronto, 1987), 67–8.

32. Michael Swanton, *English Literature Before Chaucer* (London, 1987), 175–87.

33. John Taylor, *English Historical Literature in the Fourteenth Century* (Oxford, 1987), 156.

34. David L. Boyd, 'Tennyson's Camelot Revisited', in *The Arthurian Tradition*, ed. Mary Flowers Braswell and John Bugge (Tuscaloosa, 1988), 163–74.

35. E. D. Kennedy, 'Layamon', in *The New Arthurian Encyclopedia*, ed. Norris J. Lacy (Chicago, 1991), 274–6.

36. Lawman, *Brut*, tr. Rosamund Allen (New York, 1992).

37. Flora Alexander, 'Women as Lovers in Early English Romance', in *Women and Literature in Britain 1150-1500*, ed. Carol M. Meale (Cambridge, 1993), 24-40.

38. Ian Johnson, 'Language and Literary Expression', in *An Illustrated History of Late Medieval England*, ed. Chris Given-Wilson (Manchester, 1996), 127-51.

39. Beate Schmolke-Hasselmann, *The Evolution of Arthurian Romance* (Cambridge, 1998), 293 n. 23.

40. David Matthews, *The Making of Middle English, 1765-1910* (Minneapolis, 1999), 134.

41. Jane Roberts, 'Two Notes on Laȝamon's *Brut*', in *New Perspectives on Middle English Texts*, ed. Susan Powell and Jeremy J. Smith (Cambridge, 2000), 75-85.

42. James Noble, 'Laȝamon's Arthur', in *Laȝamon: Contexts, Language, and Interpretation*, ed. Rosamund Allen, Lucy Perry, Jane Roberts (London, 2002), 285-97.

43. Kelley M. Wickham-Crowley, *Writing the Future* (Cardiff, 2002).

44. Derek Pearsall, *Arthurian Romance* (Oxford, 2003), 17-19.

45. Laurie A. Finke and Martin B. Schichtman, *King Arthur and the Myth of History* (Gainesville, 2004), 229 n. 9.

46. A. C. Spearing, *Textual Subjectivity* (Oxford, 2005), 13-15.

47. Catherine A. M. Clarke, *Literary Landscapes and the Idea of England, 700-1400* (Cambridge, 2006), 134-6.

48. Robert M. Stein, *Reality Fictions: Romance, History, and Governmental Authority, 1025-1180* (Notre Dame, 2006), 238 n. 13.

49. Martin Aurell, *La Légende du roi Arthur* (Paris, 2007), 189.

50. Simon Meecham-Jones, 'Where Was Wales?', in *Authority and Subjugation in Writing of Medieval Wales*, ed. Ruth Kennedy and Simon Meecham-Jones (New York, 2008), 27-55.

51. Sebastian I. Sobecki, *The Sea and Medieval English Literature* (Cambridge, 2008), 19.

52. Thea Summerfield, 'Chronicles and Historical Narratives', in *The Oxford History of Literary Translation in English: To 1550*, ed. Roger Ellis (Oxford, 2008), 332-63.

53. Thomas A. Bredehoft, 'The Gothic Turn and Twelfth-Century English Chronicles', in *The Oxford Handbook of Medieval Literature in English*, ed. Elaine Treharne and Greg Walter (Oxford, 2010), 353-69.

54. Elizabeth Bryan, 'Laȝamon', in *The Encyclopedia of the Medieval Chronicle*, ed. Graeme Dunphy (Leiden, 2010), 989-90.

55. E. D. Kennedy, 'Glastonbury', in *The Arthur of Medieval Latin Literature*, ed. Siân Echard (Cardiff, 2010), 109-31.

56. Lucy Perry, 'Legendary History and Chronicle', in *A Companion to Medieval Poetry*, ed. Corinne Saunders (Chichester, 2010), 219-36.

57. Julia Marvin, 'The English *Brut* Tradition', in *Companion to Arthurian Literature*, ed. Helen Fulton (Chichester, 2012), 221-51.

58. Fiona Tolhurst, *Geoffrey of Monmouth and the Feminist Origins of the Arthurian Legend* (New York, 2012), 112.

59. Eric Stanley, 'The Political Notion of Kingship in Laȝamon's *Brut*', in *Reading Laȝamon's 'Brut'*, ed. Rosamund Allen, Jane Roberts, Carole Weinberg (Amsterdam, 2013), 123-35.

60. Françoise Le Saux, 'La Grande-Bretagne, Patrie des Sciences?', in *L'Historia regum Britanniae et les 'Bruts' en Europe: Traductions, adaptations, réappropriations*, ed. Hélèle Tétrel and Géraldine Veysseyre (Paris, 2015), 157-75.

61. Caroline D. Eckhardt, 'The Manuscript of *Castleford's Chronicle*', in *The Prose 'Brut' and Other Late Medieval Chronicles*, ed. Jaclyn Rajsic, Erik Kooper, Dominique Hoche (Woodbridge, 2016), 199-217.

62. Harriet Archer, *Unperfect Histories* (Oxford, 2017), 56.

63. Charlotte A. T. Wulf, 'Arthur's Channel Crossings', in *Arthur, la mer et la guerre*, ed. Alban Gautier, Marc Rolland, Michelle Szkilnik (Paris, 2017), 83-95.

64. Audrey Martin and David Mason, 'Arthur Among the Nine Worthies', in *The Arthurian World*, ed. Victoria Coldham-Fussell, Miriam Edlich-Muth, Renée Ward (London, 2022), 49-68.

65. Mary Bateman, *Local Place and the Arthurian Tradition in England and Wales, 1400-1700* (Cambridge, 2023), 109.

66. A. Breeze, 'The Germanic Hero Wade and Wat's Dyke, Wales', *Language – Culture – Politics* 1 (2023), 117-28.

67. B. Christopher Jensen, 'Translation Praxis and the Ethical Value of Chivalry in the Caligula *Brut*', in *Ethics in the Arthurian Legend*, ed. Melissa Ridley Elmes and Evelyn Meyer (Cambridge, 2023), 109-30.

68. Jean Blacker, *Arthur, Origins, Identities and the Legendary History of Britain* (Leiden, 2024), 333.

CHAPTER SEVEN

SIR GAWAIN AND THE GREEN KNIGHT

If works of literature are like paintings in a gallery (where the visitors are on trial, rather than the exhibits), then *Sir Gawain and the Green Knight* offers a gamut of tests, some of them unusual. Amongst them is its ascent in the last two centuries from oblivion to world fame (in 2021 reaching a *ne plus ultra* with an epic-medieval-fantasy-adventure film, *The Green Knight*). Another is a demonstration published in 2023 (and developing observations of 1999 by the US scholar Ann W. Astell) on *Sir Gawain and the Green Knight* as written in 1387 by Sir John Stanley (d. 1414), Cheshire magnate. A third is the light which the discovery in turn casts upon previous discourse. Some of it emerges as careful and perceptive. Readers, now with grandstand seats for evaluation of critics from the early twentieth century onwards, will see how many scholars of the period (including W. P. Ker, Tolkien, Laura Loomis, John H. Fisher, Gervase Mathew) emerge with their credit enhanced.

As elsewhere, we start with Ker. His account teems with insights. This 'most original' romance begins with Arthur 'keeping high festival' at Christmas and awaiting a 'marvel'; which he has in the form of the Green Knight, riding his horse into the banqueting hall and challenging courtiers to a 'beheading game'. Gawain accepts the 'jeopardy' and decapitates the intruder, whose body then runs forward to retrieve the head; it bids Gawain meet him at 'the Green Chapel' in a year and a day for 'the return blow'. The rider thereafter exits briskly into the night, sparks flying from the hoofs of his steed. Although Ker dated the poem to the age of Edward III (d. 1377), his other observations are exact. A 'fabulous' story has been treated with the realism of a 'modern novelist'. Its author, probable author of other poems in the same manuscript (*Pearl, Cleanness, Patience*), was an 'educated man' (if no 'original philosopher'), also possessed of 'great force of will', an awareness of life's difficulties, 'high spirits', and professional knowledge of the chase. His later descriptions of hunts (for deer, boar, fox) come from life, not books. He excelled in winter scenes: hill-mists, icicles on stones, swollen becks. As for Gawain, he is the protagonist of 'a chivalrous *Pilgrim's Progress*'.[1] Ker's analysis still prompts reflection; even if his dating the text to before 1377 veiled (for him) implications of its youthful Arthur, resembling Richard II, who in 1387 (when the poem was written) was just twenty. (One might reflect too on how the great hall at which the Green Knight was an uninvited guest would resemble that of Chester Castle, demolished in 1788-1822 for the Greek Revival ensemble which is today a centre of local government.)

If Ker wrote well on the romance, so did Wells, despite locating it to about 1370 and linking it with Edward III and his Order of the Garter. Like Ker, Wells praised the author's 'keen eye' and unique 'power for description', whether of a hunt or an icy winter's day (or intimate conversations in a bedroom). Wells similarly had little on Arthur.[2] It is true that in the poem the King's role seems peripheral. But the sustained criticism cited below of his and Camelot's supposed failings shows him less on the margins than imagined. Knowledge of when the text was written and by whom thus has obvious implications for Richard II and politics in 1387. It further underlines the variations which Arthur's *persona* has undergone since the 530s. In a classic handbook, Sisam placed *Sir Gawain* within the period 1350-75; paid tribute to Sir Frederic Madden's edition of 1839; and dismissed attempts to identify the poet as 'unsuccessful'.[3] James Oakden similarly exalted the narrative, concurring with Wells on the realism of its winter scenes, with the 'icy rain' and 'hills lost in mist' of Welsh mountains or Pennine hills, and at the same time the author's skill in making us believe the unbelievable: a rare gift, shared by few artists.[4] Others were more subdued, giving the date as about 1370 and the author as 'unknown'.[5] The pre-war period came to a conclusion with the EETS edition and editorial comments on how *Sir Gawain* and three related poems, plus *St Erkenwald* (by the poet's brother?), have a special connection with the alliterative *Wars of Alexander* (of the decades about 1400).[6] The 1989 edition of the last (also from the EETS) will here present fresh opportunities for enquiry.

More philosophical and wide-ranging than the above are Mathew's observations on how by 1390 the chivalric ideals subscribed to by Gawain had 'at Eltham or at Sheen' come to seem naïve, 'old-fashioned', 'insular'. A telling remark, as penetrating as his notes on the lavish original manuscript of the four poems ('commissioned by a magnate of wealth not much before 1390'), with the surviving copy of them (from 'some such town as Chester') dismissed as clumsy and 'slovenly'.[7] One does not know which to admire more: recognition as far back as 1948 of links between the Green Knight poem and Cheshire's ruling classes in about 1390; or perception of its narrator's ideals as by then somewhat provincial. Had Mathew (who in 1968 suggested connections between the poems and John Stanley) developed these insights, the *Gawain* Poet might have been compellingly identified in 1950 (not 2023). Kane then had subtle observations on *Sir Gawain*, as (for example) on how its author 'scarcely developed Bercilak's enchantment by Morgan la Fay', magic presumably being 'not greatly to his taste', so that, when the supernatural came in, he treated it 'quietly'. He further attributed the 'brilliant achievement' of the narrative to the 'remarkable visualization of action and setting' rather than to the 'conceptions of conduct' motivating those involved.[8]

Gordon, in an exemplary edition, spoke of the author's having 'little trace of the priest' yet perhaps being 'a member of a noble household'.[9] (He was not a priest; and the 'household' was ruled by him.) Dorothy Everett, influenced by Tolkien and Gordon's edition of 1925, thereupon put the poem in the fourteenth century's last quarter (making it effectively of Richard II's time, not Edward III's) and by an author not identified. She yet noted his 'considerable reading': secular, religious, English, French, Italian (of Dante, a feature most unusual); his 'intimate knowledge of the Bible' and (despite that) his 'independence of mind'; his intimate knowledge of courtly or aristocratic society.[10] Beyond that she did not go. She (like later writers) did not perceive implications of his Cheshire dialect or knowledge of North Wales and the Wirral, indicating an audience of Cheshire men and women, and surely a connection with Chester Castle, king's court, seat of government. Nor (like Gordon) did she take on board his passion for hunting; or his sophisticated familiarity with love as the sport of lords and ladies.

What Dorothy Everett said on the writer still gets us further than comments on *Sir Gawain* as 'clearly a midwinter festival poem' wherein the 'Green Knight whose head is chopped off' but remains 'magically alive' relates to the 'Green Man' of English village festivals and to 'vegetation' gods.[11] Better are sober views of Laura Loomis (except where misled by her husband's notions on Celtic tradition). Of the first importance is her suggestion on the poet as perhaps 'a man of rank and wealth', at home with royal 'pleasures' and 'luxuries'.[12] He walked with kings; but retained the common touch. Because the poet knew King Richard, of interest is his representation of King Arthur. So much can be inferred from a study of major significance and now grievously neglected. John Fisher cited with approval a 1959 paper by Hans Schnyder, who proposed that 'the depiction of Arthur' in the Green Knight poem embodied comments on kingship. Arthur is styled 'sumquat childgered' or childish, just as (in his *Vox Clamantis*) 'Gower scolds Richard'. Fisher yet added that the northern poet in no way questioned 'the aristocratic system'. His values were very firmly those of 'the agrarian aristocracy'; not for him the 'issues that troubled Langland and Gower'.[13] Because we regard the *Gawain* Poet as a Cheshire magnate who was *de facto* if not *de jure* an agrarian aristocrat, no surprise; writing just before the constitutional crisis of 1387-8, if he thought Arthur/Richard lacking the calibre for high office, again, no surprise. Another US scholar perceived *Sir Gawain* as a text 'remote in time' and attitudes for modern people, so that it 'requires historical study' for proper understanding.[14] If we accept that it was composed on the eve of December 1387's attempted *coup* (so that it surely never had its intended public reading at Chester Castle that Christmas), we clear our way as regards the poet's attitudes to politics and kingship.

Also clearing our way is demolition of Speirs's notions on Gawain's host Sir Bertilak as *eniautos daimon*, a 'year-king' annually killed and resurrected, this entity being of much interest a century ago to students of Greek tragedy.[15] Since then, little has been heard of such approaches. Better, too, is analysis of the poet's singular interest in Cheshire topography.[16] Blurring that focus are words of a Polish-American Marxist, who thought that the text (although 'a jewel of medieval narrative') was 'provincial' and (as regards modern fiction) 'antiquarian'.[17] But (at least in his art) the poet was not backward-looking, so that Ker's comparison in 1912 of him to a modern novelist is today reinforced a hundred times by modern explorations of fantasy; while the poem also repays analysis even in Marxist terms of class and money and power (see recent authors cited below).

Attention to Arthur's defects, initiated by Schnyder and accepted by Fisher, was taken further by Burrow. There is (naturally) no 'outright denunciation of the king'. But the poet was not a 'professional publicist'. He does not admire Arthur 'unre-

173

servedly'. With *childgered* (line 86) and its negative implications of boyish merriment is *rechles* (line 40) 'reckless, heedless', a term normally carrying 'sinister implications' of rashness.[18] Burrow's careful analysis tallies with the case for *Sir Gawain* as of 1387, with Richard II's actions already prompting concern, as when in the previous year he made Robert de Vere a duke; while, after the summer of 1387, when Robert and his Central European partner had gone through plenty of *rechles* merry-making at Chester Castle (with John Stanley as their host), the courtiers there had seen plenty of upper-class excess.

An anthology of twelve (mainly US) critical essays prompts mixed reactions, some of them having worn better than others.[19] Preferable is a study of values amongst the high-born, which are listed as religious faith, integrity, respect for others, politeness, beauty, humour, self-control, courage. They all come under the heading of 'courtesy'.[20] Works of the *Gawain* Poet thus reveal (uniquely) the mentality of an English provincial magnate, here seen more positively than by Fisher in 1961. One notes too how Richard II possessed few of the qualities set out by Brewer. Even details will confirm this. The sense of *fare* lacked by Gawain at night and alone in wintry Welsh mountains has been disputed. It will yet be 'food'. An army marches on its stomach. Knights have stomachs too. The allusion is proof of the poet's 'humour – even ironic humour' and practical sense.[21] *Le style est l'homme même*; and this man appreciated the quartermaster's role (as Arthur/Richard II perhaps did not). Curious that this military man should thereafter have read Dante.[22] If Italian poetry was unknown to him in 1387 (no reference to it in *Sir Gawain*), it was seemingly known to him by 1390, when *Pearl* was composed.

After food and *terza rima*, allegory; and scepticism (with useful references) on those seeing *Sir Gawain* as an allegory.[23] Thereafter sound judgement (in an exemplary edition) on the poet's knowledge of hunting, fortification, armour, naval architecture, court etiquette, the Vulgate, patristics, French poetry; on his language,

'strongly provincial' but 'highly sophisticated'; and on his indifference (unlike Chaucer) to astrology or 'Boethian' problems of
free will.[24] Artist, courtier, politician, landowner, forester: he was
a man with wide experience of life and not an academic intellectual. He was not, however, the author of *St Erkenwald*
(despite what is claimed).[25] It is identical in dialect but different in
style (and so was perhaps by the poet's brother). Amongst our
poet's other concerns were jewels and numerology; and (after
Kean, and against the doubts of Tolkien and Gordon) Boethian
questions of destiny and fate.[26] Perhaps between 1387 and 1390
his interest in such matters had been stirred by a reading of Dante?

In 1968 appeared a (heavily cut) reprint of Mathew's paper on
knighthood, with some by others.[27] In that year Mathew himself
shed brilliant light on issues. Not only was he the first person to
relate *Pearl* and its fellow-poems to Sir John Stanley (as their poet's
supposed patron), but he also unkindly pointed out that Stanley's
desertion in 1399 to Henry IV (when it 'became apparent that
Richard would be defeated') was 'treason'. The King had well and
truly 'alienated his natural supporters'.[28] Events in 1399 bring us
back to 1387 and qualms upon King Arthur/King Richard. They
also prompt questions on Gawain's fidelity and loyalty to his
plighted word. What Stanley did in 1399 implies that, for him in
life and Gawain in art, perfection is not to be expected.

There is an eloquent study of the *Gawain* Poet and Latin
prayers for the dead.[29] It was a subject of which (like butchering
the corpses of deer or boar) he knew much, creating problems for
modern readers (few of us being familiar with either the liturgy or
cutting-up of game). As if that was not enough, there is the
probability (after Pamela Kean) that he derived his Pearl-Maiden,
who is at once 'allegorical' and 'individual', from a reading of
Dante.[30] That Italian connection helps date the poems. There
being no trace of it anywhere but *Pearl*, it puts the poem after *Sir
Gawain and the Green Knight* and not, as Anderson supposed,
before.[31] The poet, amazing polymath, had interests (besides

these) which are museum curios today, but were for him matters of immediate concern, such as heraldry, whereon he spent 'nearly fifty lines on one device'.[32] Another man valuing that kind of knowledge was G. T. Shepherd, stressing how the dismemberment of a slain deer's carcass was set out by the *Gawain* Poet in the 'technical language of an elaborate ritual'.[33] He regarded most of it as beyond even the original audience's ken. Yet auditors in the great hall of Chester Castle at Christmas 1387 would have included many professionals from the Forest of Wirral. They might have heard those gory details with a relish bewildering to us. Returning to Arthur, we find acknowledgement of how the youthful prime of his court's 'fayre folk in her first age' (line 54) implies 'potential' but also 'dangers' in the King's 'restlessness' and boyish temperament; which leads to comparison with the 'impatient but glorious' youthful hero of *The Wars of Alexander*.[34] Again, implications not only for Richard II in 1387, but for work on intertextualities pointed out in 1940 by Mabel Day.

In 1970 appeared an influential monograph on the author. Amongst much of interest is citation of Norman Davis's paper of 1966 on the phrase 'Krystez dere blessyng and myn' in *Pearl* (line 1208). In medieval texts it is always used in greetings 'from parent to child'.[35] So the poet was a father and a layman. Influential too was a comparative study (centring on style, structure, irony), but never bringing us close to the poet in the way that tauter comments by Gervase Mathew do, as with a characteristic vague aside on the *Sir Gawain*'s audience as 'in the household of some magnate'.[36] For that, after Mathew's insights, we can now read 'in the great hall of Chester Castle at Christmas 1387 in the presence of Sir John Stanley and before Cheshire courtiers, retainers, foresters, huntsmen' (although we think that the political crisis of December that year meant that the poem was never actually 'performed'). There are varied comments elsewhere: on Gawain as 'knight errant' fighting bulls, bears, satyrs (like the Alexander of medieval romance); on the garden in *Pearl*; on Gawain as an individual; on descriptions of women and of beheading.[37] More significant, however (because it enables us to harden opinion into knowledge), is thorough and conclusive proof that Gawain and its three fellows are of 'common authorship'. The same poet wrote all four works.[38]

Which gets us somewhere. Others perhaps do not. So we pass by observations on *Gawain* as 'a criticism of life' or 'sport', and not by the author of *Patience*.[39] So too as regards its 'mimetic effects' (in lines 421-6, for example, beginning 'Gawain gripped to his ax').[40] Given what is said below on the poet's astonishing sophistication, we may still note the Middle Irish and Old French sources of his narrative, and their transformation by the author.[41] On texts known to him, amongst much that is wrong-headed in discussion (after Gollancz) of Ralph Strode the Oxford philosopher = the *Gawain* Poet, there is yet an insight on how *Troilus and Criseyde* (of the mid-1380s) influenced him.[42] *Pearl* deriving its Pearl-Maiden from Chaucer's *Prologue* to his *Legend of Good Women*, and Chaucer's tales of Squire and Wife of Bath respectively taking their horseman-in-a-hall and Arthurian knight (with a year and a day to avoid decapitation) from *Sir Gawain and the Green Knight*, the link deserves investigation.

Genuinely insightful, however, is discussion of the Green Knight's 'astounding entry' into Arthur's hall and his challenge. There is silence. Courtiers sit 'ston-stil'. The Knight mocks them, wondering aloud if this is Arthur's house. The King is outraged; 'blod shot for scham into hys schyre face' (line 317); he seizes the axe, ready to do the deed himself; but Gawain, in a speech of superlative tact, described as having 'qualification and modification' in a manner worthy of Henry James, takes over, never for an instant implying that Arthur needs his help, or would lose face by withdrawing, or that his offer is meritorious, or that any 'blame' attaches to the court.[43] Stevens's entire account has a significance beyond what he could have imagined, and (with others) repays careful reading, because it displays both the poet's amazing skill in discourse and his veneration for kingship. Arthur (here taken as Richard II) is young. He is not calm; his anger comes swiftly. But he is ready to risk his life. He is no coward. As for Gawain, his words breathe an utter respect for royal authority. It is absolute, unquestioned. In short, it contains a theory of sovereignty as something sacred. Which has obvious implications for attitudes to Richard II in 1387, as also 1399, when even loyalists deserted him. Stevens's reading of 1973 should of necessity be read with Fisher's socio-political conclusions of 1961. Much has been written about Richard II's exalted views of his prerogative and the divine nature of his office. In the light of the above, more might be said on it; for Arthur's portrayal in *Sir Gawain and the Green Knight* brings us close to Richard II, as also to Ricardian theories of regalian right.

A paper on 13 October as Richard II's special day, being the feast of the Translation of Edward the Confessor (amongst his patron saints), has tangential significance for *Gawain*, for it was the day on which Richard granted favours (in 1398, to Chaucer himself).[44] So in 1386, when he further ennobled Robert de Vere as Duke of Ireland (see below), the first non-royal duke in England's history, Richard's infatuated decision outraged the nobility, all now inferior to Robert. Hence implications on how Gawain was brave enough to be made 'a duk' (line 678); also dating the poem to *after* October 1386 and *before* Robert's fall in December 1387. In the tangle of criticism that has sprung up about *Gawain*, it is useful to have a plain introduction, making the fundamental point (easily neglected) that the poet may have been translating 'a French romance which has not yet been identified'.[45] From the same source is the proposition that Chaucer borrowed the horseman of the Squire's Tale (of 1400?) from *Gawain* (which will be correct), and that the pearl-lady of his *Prologue* to the *Legend of Good Women* derives from *Pearl* (which will be wrong, *Pearl* postdating the *Prologue*).[46] Also prompting revision is comment on how Gawain in his fine new clothes seemed the 'ver by his uisage verayly' (line 866).[47] His appearing verily the *ver* or spring will be a hit at Robert de Vere (a notorious fop). The sally may be taken with a verdict on *Cleanness* and its three fellows as about 'respect for God' (or its reverse); for purity (and the sacrament of penance by which sinners regain it) relates to being true to one's word in *Gawain*, innocence in *Pearl*, acceptance of God's will in *Patience*.[48] The poet was a moralist; if one with a sly sense of humour, something unusual for moralists.

On the last, there is a task for readers on whether *Pearl* (after Carleton Brown in 1904) really has a debt to neo–Augustinian ideas on grace and free will in Bradwardine's *De causa Dei*.[49] Here one should not be over-refined, historically or otherwise. Metaphysics (of Boethius, Dante, William of Occam, Thomas Bradwardine) perhaps seeming remote from Arthur, martial hero, one may echo Pearsall's cautions on 'over-sophisticated' commentators who perceive 'irony in the portrayal' of Camelot.[50] John Stevens's interpretation of Gawain's words to Arthur points to the poet's unquestioned loyalty, not subversiveness. Writing of 'details of courtly life' in the Green Knight poem, another envisages its audience as one of gentry and the like.[51] We can go further. Every account of medieval Cheshire, county palatine, underlines its unique relation to the monarch. Chester and its Castle were royalist to the core (whatever was thought about some in the royal entourage). They were the reverse of rebels. Risky, then, to seek flaws in the Arthur of *Gawain*.

One may on that basis follow Davenport against Benson and Moorman on a refusal to see mere 'pride and hedonism' at Camelot, and agree with him that Arthur is, rather, 'a worthy master of a worthy house'.[52] According with this is comment on how Arthur's welcome to the Green Knight (even a request for him to dismount) is 'courteous and hospitable in the extreme'.[53] It was the correct response to the Green Knight's taunts and insolence; it demonstrated powers of self-control essential for a wise ruler. We may thus agree with Brewer, rejecting those who see the entire episode as an attack on a court's 'childishness and responsibility'.[54] Others will not have it. Gawain's failure in integrity (we hear) reflects failure in Camelot, with its 'superficial response to his deposition'.[55] Or there is shrugging of shoulders in print, with wry dismissal of how the 'testing' in the Green Knight narrative, regarded as 'written for a local magnate with a family and manor' (when we maintain that it was written *by* a magnate of fabulous wealth and political power), 'has puzzled' so many critics.[56] Yet a surer guide against the irrelevant and facile is to think that poet took seriously the words of St Peter (in his first epistle, chapter two), 'Fear God. Honour the king.' With them he would take the matter of being true to oneself.

Dante, a poet greater than the author of *Gawain* (yet also with views on kingship), might have provided the latter with ideas by way of Antonio de Romanis, the Neapolitan physician who in 1387 was John Stanley's personal doctor and accompanied him to Ireland (where Stanley acted as deputy to Robert de Vere, Duke of Ireland, who never stepped foot in the place).[57] It would be surprising if, in the evenings at Dublin Castle, a graduate like Antonio never spoke of Italy's national bard. Derek Brewer thereafter restated opposition to 'modern' perceptions of 'irony' in *Gawain*'s depiction of Arthur's court.[58] In far stronger language (and using research by anthropologists) John Burrow condemned unhistorical attitudes to honour and shame at Camelot and Hautdesert.[59] This may go to the heart of the matter better than a conclusion (in an otherwise admirable edition) on conclusions of 'love and laughter among one's fellows' in the world of Arthur.[60]

With Jack Bennett we encounter criticism of substance (and things not-so, as on dates or splitting of authorship). Like commentators of a century ago, he commented on the text's wintry scenes, far from the comforts of courts royal or lordly. But he could spring surprises. The tale begins 'not with the usual appeal for a hearing, but with a deliberate deployment of rhetoric and learning' that takes the matter back to Troy.[61] Even from this one might infer a writer of exalted rank. When he stood up, people went quiet. No need to call for silence. Hence the special interest of his views on kingship. Also with unsuspected implications for these opening lines is a comparison of them to those the Wife of Bath in her story. The first are 'serious and single-minded'; the Wife's are 'comic and distracted'. In this, Chaucer's one poem with 'an Arthurian setting', the Wife turns expectations 'up-side down'.[62] Literary analysis also upsets expectation; for the Wife's tale (a late one) shows that Chaucer knew *Sir Gawain and the Green Knight* and subverted its story of an axe-threatened hero (whom the Squire mentions by name, as he does a horseman-at-a-banquet). As for Arthur, there are stimulating comments on how his encounter with the Green Knight shows him 'not as weak as his court'. 'Once aroused, he is abrupt and stern.'[63] It adds to the debate on whether Camelot is weighed and found wanting. After much on the poem's beginning, a note on its ending and that of *Pearl*, in neither case with 'any pretence that all problems are solved', but still with a sense of artistic closure that 'leaves us exhilarated and satisfied'.[64] Which is well said. Perhaps it brings us nearer the poet-artist than supposed reminders in *Gawain's* first part on Camelot's 'moral turpitude' and 'eventual passing'.[65] It may (?) be due to the narrative's having 'the structure of a very ancient myth'.[66]

As a reminder of scholarship to avoid is assurance on the Green Knight poem as composed 'to unmask the hollowness of Arthur and his court' from the rider's entry to its very end, when Gawain's 'reintegration into the Table Round is impossible', because 'the court lives by 'insufficient moral standards'.[67] The same is true of further assurance on how the common authorship of the four MS Cotton Nero A.x poems 'is far from proved'.[68] This even though Vantuomo proved their common authorship in 1971. Better, in indicating a road that repays exploration, is further comparison between Arthur and Richard, between 'monarch and nobleman, metropolis and hinterland', between a court in the provinces (surely that of Chester Castle) and a court at Westminster. We are asked to consider whether the poet saw Arthur in terms of Richard.[69] The answer is Yes, albeit in complex terms: for Chester's court was royal *and* provincial; its attitude to Richard II was loyal and provincial. Not the black-and-whitism envisaged by simplistic readers.

Once grasped, this point has a wondrous effect on what we are told thereafter by others. So with comment on how the Green Knight poem brings courtly culture 'to the bar of a moral and religious inquisition', its author's viewpoint being 'clerkly', like that of Langland.[70] But its poet was not a clerk, as indicated by his unclerkly familiarity with hunting, court ritual, love-talking. So equally as regards the 'failure of the Round Table' in *Gawain*'s opening scene and (supposed) implications of 'rejection of worldly chivalry' and the like.[71] Or, with a new and neo-Marxist note, stress on the Green Knight poem's (assumed) 'overlay of knightly and mercantile values' indicating an audience of 'sophisticated and wealthy merchants and knights' whose 'obvious location' is 'London'.[72] Why London auditors should be engrossed by a narrative from a Cheshire poet in Cheshire dialect with allusions to Cheshire forests is not explained. So again, quoting Jill Mann's words above, the London card played with reference to the *Gawain* Poet's knowledge of Dante and Boccaccio, because only in London 'with its community of Italian bankers and merchants' would Italian literature be 'readily accessible' to English writers.[73] Fatal to those assertions are (a) absence of Italian influence in *Sir Gawain*, dated to 1387; (b) presence at Chester Castle that very year (as noted in 1983 by Wendy Childs) of Antonio de Romanis, Italian physician, a man presumably aware of the *dolce stil novo*; (c) a consequent influence of Italian writers on *Pearl*, dated on other grounds to 1390. After that is a smaller heap of declarations on how the Gawain poem 'reminds one of Bakhtinian linguistic carnival' (they imply that it postdates *Pearl*, which it does not).[74] After that, refreshing to meet Derek Pearsall's sweeping-away of facile modernism, whether on Gawain's (alleged) maturing by 'healthy confrontation' with Nature (mountains, ice, snow, green giants), or failure to grasp that 'the joy of the chase, and the joy of the kill' felt by early hunters are 'something that we shall just have to learn to appreciate and share'.[75] What is sauce for medieval attitudes to deer and wild boar is, one might also think, sauce for kings, including Arthur. It would be strange if sensibilities of the 1380s were identical to ours.

That applies increasingly as we approach our own time and encounter new questions and issues and fashions, certainly provoking thought (now that the date and authorship of *Gawain* are confidently established) on whether they aid progress or get in its way. Examples include a condemnation of Arthur's court for being 'fearfully young and inept', its ways 'mannered and effete', and so possessing a 'vulnerability' seen as 'feminine'.[76] Still more curious is an entire book on the present narrative with much on both kings and even Sir John Stanley (as the poet's patron); but, in its 442 pages, no suspicion at all that he actually *was* the poet.[77] Consideration of *Sir Gawain*'s opening lines on the Siege of Troy in the context (after W. R. J. Barron) of 'truth and treason' and (after Malcolm Andrew) history's alternate 'blysse and blunder' yet usefully offers a refocus on Ricardian (and perennial) issues, both political and personal.[78] Difficulties in sizing up the romance are revealed by observations on it as a 'morally earnest' text (as if its author were St Dominic listing errors of Albigensians) that at the same time has a delicate 'erotic' description of the 'revealing dress' worn by the chatelaine of Hautdesert (a passage implying a writer who inhabited a court, not a cloister).[79] Welcome scepticism then followed (as regards those who find fault with Camelot) in praise of how Arthur displays 'courtly self-discipline' in the face of a churlish Green Knight.[80]

In 1999 came a literary bombshell which was noticed by nobody at the time, not even by the lady who dropped it, but which had a time-fuse destined to explode twenty-four years later.

It came in analysis of *duk* 'duke' in line 678 and *ver* 'spring' in line 866 of the narrative. They will be quiet jokes at the expense of John de *Vere*, Earl of Oxford and (from 1386) *Duke* of Ireland.[81] In 2023 these would be interpreted to show that *Sir Gawain and the Green Knight* (a) was composed later than October 1386, when Richard II's elevation of de Vere, his favourite, to a dukedom antagonized other peers; (b) predates December 1387, when Robert's career collapsed and he fled into exile; and (c) was composed in late 1387 to be Christmas entertainment at Chester Castle to courtiers who had had their fill of de Vere's extravagances when he was John Stanley's guest there that summer (the poem yet surely never being presented to an audience, because of crisis in 1387's last weeks). It provides a lesson.

While Professor Astell's bomb was ticking away, *Gawain* scholarship continued its stately progress. Ray Barron contrasted its 'utopian' (but 'unprepared') Camelot with 'superficially similar' Hautdesert (yet with aspects 'concealed' and 'ambiguous').[82] Remarks on how Cheshire gentry would be its 'primary audience', and how Macclesfield Forest is described in it, offer a picture of those expected to be at Chester Castle during the Christmas of 1387.[83] They would understand its Cheshire dialect; relish its jokes about de Vere (678, 866), of late their unloved guest, and also about men of Wirral (701-2); and be absorbed by its accounts of hunting. After reading that, one is jerked to a halt on reading Madden's description of the work and its three fellows as 'Scottish'.[84] Which underlines progress since he edited it in 1839. Despite that, one fears that a study (with others) of the poem's background does not aid that advance.[85] Nor does comment on its message: that the harmony of Arthurian society is 'hollow'.[86] The same may be said on supposed deployment of 'the model of royal theatrics partly to critique the very power of that form to self-create the image of the court'.[87]

The millennium passed, we find a welcome placing of the poet against power and class and money in Richard II's age, including references to John Stanley as the poet's assumed patron.[88] Not a word on him as poet, though. All the same, material set out here (on Cheshire and the court for example) will be enhanced once that is understood, and deserve re-reading (not least for perception of Arthur). Serious too (despite baseless doubts on whether the *Gawain* Poet also wrote on *Pearl* and the like) is recognition of Camelot's innocence. It was 'full of youth and joy', being (as the poet puts it) in its first age. Not yet had adultery by Lancelot and Guinevere cast a long 'shadow'.[89] A corrective to critics who smell rats behind tapestries.

After that, an extended paper, setting out for the first time linguistic and other arguments for John Stanley as the *Gawain* Poet.[90] In the same year came ubiquitous generalization, with comment on how the Garter motto (added to the unique Cotton Nero A.x manuscript) perhaps shows that 'a Garter knight' was the poet's patron.[91] Exploration of that could have meant break-through. But the critic looked, saw nothing, passed by. Preferable therefore (for an intriguing view of the romance's narrative) are conclusions, made with a nod to post-structuralism, on the poem is a *fabula* (which is 'untrue') 'pretending to be *historia*'.[92] In another study, which (in principle) starts from the texts, we encounter an ambiguous view of Camelot. 'Chivalry is evidently in his blood' is what we read of the poet. Correct. Yet ('especially if he is a cleric') his dwelling on 'conspicuous consumption' and 'luxury' at Camelot and Hautdesert 'may imply disapproval'.[93] There is middle-class guilt in that perception. It would be hard to prove it from the narrative. The lesson given by John H. Fisher in 1961 on the poet's politics as solidly conservative (as opposed to those of Langland or even Chaucer) is forgotten. Need one comment too on there being nothing in *Pearl* and the like to indicate a clerical author or a layman other than man of power and wealth?

Elsewhere one finds oneself in full agreement when *Sir Gawain* is envisaged as written to be read aloud 'at a Christmas feast'; and

185

the very opposite on how evidence for Dante's influence on *Pearl* 'is lacking', even if with the admission that Italian visitors to England (merchants, bankers, friars) may have come with *La Commedia Divina* in their luggage.[94] On this we say again that the 'Christmas feast' would have been at Chester Castle in 1387; and that (after Wendy Childs in 1983) it was a doctor, the Neapolitan physician Antonio de Romanis present at Chester Castle earlier in 1387, who was the only begetter for Dantean echoes in *Pearl*. Chester (for a while) resembled Urbino, which Yeats styled 'That grammar school of courtesies / Where wit and beauty learned their trade'; there being no lack of courtesy and wit and beauty in *Sir Gawain and the Green Knight*. Readers wondering how those desirable qualities were paid for will find clues in a volume (citing Marx's *Economic and Philosophic Manuscripts of 1844* and recent Marxian critics) on court life, with Hautdesert defined as where 'By explicit and immediate but inexact reciprocity, the exchange of winnings game at the castle gives regulated, potentially lethal consequence to personal relations in the context of a single visitor's encounter with a single household.'[95] The *Gawain* Poet's identity today being certain, more can be said on these lines (for class, power, money, politics) not only for the court of Chester in 1387, but for the courts of Camelot and Hautdesert. King Arthur and the Prophet of the British Museum's Reading Room find themselves in unexpected (but potentially enlightening) juxtaposition.

One major court activity (the original sport of kings) was the joyful labours of the chase; which brings us to the ravine of Ludchurch.[96] It is in Macclesfield Forest (of which John Stanley was Forester), and was known to the poet, who had a professional's knowledge of hunting. Economic historians could tell the rest of us much about the implications of pursuing game for class and political control in the Green Knight romance. Rather different from expertise in killing animals and butchering their corpses is the poet's skill (we hear) in manipulating 'generic expectations'.[97]

Concerning his politics, reference at *Sir Gawain*'s beginning and end to Britain's legendary origins at Troy brings up concepts of 'a unified British nation' which allegedly suffers 'damage' from the Green Knight's rude incursion and what follows.[98] The subject deserves investigation in the context of Arthur. As for Camelot, its presumed location at Caerleon in south-east Wales has been followed up to give impressions of its traditional splendour.[99] So there are fruitful ideas in the above, all awaiting further analysis.

Now for more opinions. The theme of the 'Beheading Game' was (we are told) here used to 'lay bare the contradictions at the heart of chivalric ideals', chivalry itself being an 'ideology' expressed in 'practices devoted to cultural and economic and social exploitation', its connections with Christianity being an 'appropriation of value, rather than an absorption of significance', with the poet therefore 'subtly but ruthlessly' undermining romance 'to expose the emptiness of its own highest values'.[100] Really? Did he engage in acts of betrayal or deconstruction to demonstrate chivalry's absurdities? Certainly, opportunities here for revaluation of works by a poet whom (we recall) John Fisher in 1961 regarded as a king's man, a reactionary; which goes well with John Stanley, Knight of the Garter and colonialist oppressor of the Irish; not so well with the subversive bard envisaged by Professor Ashe. More cautious and persuasive, then, was W. A. Davenport, on whether (for example) we are 'meant to disapprove of Camelot?'[101] Answer (it seems, after Brewer and Fisher and Davenport himself), probably not; for the poet as a Cheshire magnate had the most vested of interests in maintaining Arthur/Richard II (even if Ann Astell spells out his disobliging opinions of Robert de Vere, whom Richard idolized). The point is underlined by remarks on Richard's 'special relationship' with Cheshire and the unique prerogatives that were there his right.[102] As a jolt from politics and power is a reminder of 'erotic and menacing sides' of women in the tale, whether Bertilak's lady or Morgan le Fay: eerie folkloric aspects with an enigmatic relation to Camelot.[103] In the real world,

Cheshire–Staffordshire forests of *Gawain* again came under Turville-Petre's quizzical gaze, as well as places in related poems (such as the whale's belly of *Patience*, with Jonah in it).[104]

And now, post-colonialism. The Green Knight poem conveys 'anxiety about the alienness and intractability of the Welsh'; other concerns are the doubleness of gender and the 'recognizably Welsh' hostility of Bertilak's wife to Gawain, her 'feigned desire' for him (supposedly) masking 'an insistent colonial fantasy about the subjugated order'.[105] One may say two things. Nothing shows Gawain's would-be seducer as Welsh, because he had left Wales for the Wirral before reaching Hautdesert. It will have been in England. On the other hand, Stanley knew a lot about colonialism. In 1387 he was running the English colony in Ireland (where he died in 1414); in the next century he reported to Henry IV on the rising of Owen Glendower, passing on information received from spies (as discussed in this writer's 2004 paper in *Arthuriana*); when he became king of the Isle of Man, he actually had his own personal colony to run (it remained a family possession until George III's day). So, more material on colonialism (and its opposite) here than one might expect. Material of a different kind (on the poem's Morgan as 'Oresteian Mother' and the like) appears elsewhere in a sub-Freudian phantasmagoria, with many interesting and original approaches to the text, where Arthur's allowing Gawain to accept the Green Knight's challenge is termed 'an abdication of personal power that foreshadows the end of Camelot'.[106] In earlier texts, Arthur had been overmighty; now he is undermighty. Which will be right?

Doubts of another kind surface for what is now the essential edition. Its statements on provenance and scribal dialect, are important; not important are those on the poet as perhaps a 'cleric' in 'minor orders'.[107] There is no evidence for such statements. As justiciar in Ireland, Stanley controlled a national budget and English military forces. He was not (in James Joyce's phrase) a 'shy monkish guest' at any feast, but a man with imperial responsibilities. Himself running a court, he would have a view on Camelot and Hautdesert that was at an angle to those in the academy, who know nothing of such things.

So we come back once more to questions on money, class, power, colonialism, capital, exchange, violence, community: all with the virtue of stress upon actuality. Here one may respond to propositions after Jill Mann (and others) that *Gawain* 'was directed to a mercantile audience' who naturally depended on *trewthe* in its various meaning to underwrite their business dealings.[108] In one sense this barks up the wrong Marxian tree. Since the poem was demonstrably intended, not for London merchants and their circle, but for Chester courtiers, her case as it stands must collapse. Yet Chester was a major commercial centre. Sea-going trade was once its lifeblood. Shifted from the Thames to the Dee, much of what is said on courts (Arthurian or the like) and the cash that kept them afloat may repay examination. We shall see more clearly what relation the Green Knight's irruption into Arthur's banqueting hall bears to an assumed 'decaying seigneurial culture' and alleged 'divergent gender and economic hierarchies at Camelot and Hautdesert'.[109] Despite appearance in a volume which hardly mentions the Green Knight romance, a conclusion on how the politics of Arthurian literature are 'best understood by paying attention to regions, not to modern nations' is well said in the present context.[110]

Proofs for Sir John Stanley as the *Gawain* Poet (with a chapter on how *St Erkenwald* is not by him, but perhaps by Sir William Stanley of Hooton, his elder brother) appeared thereafter.[111] In the same year arrived a survey of the 'new spaces and possibilities' that post-colonial theory offers for *Sir Gawain and the Green Knight*. True, Hautdesert was not in Wales (with authors cited against others who imagine it was). It may yet be that the poet modelled it upon the *caput* of a Marcher lord: that is, a castle of adventurers who from the late eleventh century invaded Wales piecemeal and turned its petty kingdoms into domains (including the lordships of Glamorgan, Gower, Pembroke, Brecon, Oswestry, Denbigh) highly profitable to themselves, because they appropriated the royal revenues and rights from the Welsh kinglings whom they dispossessed.[112] The idea is attractive. More could be made of it. With the Marcher lordships of Hawarden or (to the south, including Wrexham) Bromfield and Yale on their doorstep, Chester administrators knew much of Marcher institutions (eventually abolished by Henry VIII's acts of union). For a different approach to the poem is a singular item (privately published and so found in few libraries), given by its author to the present writer.[113] Its very title shows it as revealing on literary *Realpolitik*.

That in mind, we come to 2024 and a final kaleidoscope of opinion, some of it informed, some less so. We start with Professor Helen Cooper, denying the case set out above, after Ann Astell, for *Sir Gawain and the Green Knight* as composed in late 1387 and for John Stanley as the *Gawain* Poet.[114] Readers thus have an admirable opportunity to see if Professor Cooper refutes what is said, or quite fails to do so. Thereafter an account of *Gawain* and fourteenth-century Marcher politics, concluding with reference to understanding of its 'cultural geography', yet without mention of the poem's Cheshire links, indicated by several writers.[115] More acceptable, then, is discussion of the romance's associations with Chester in 1387, which does take account of its apparent digs (in lines 678 and 866) at Robert de Vere, Duke of Ireland.[116] Older views appear in a statements on the likely audience as 'dans une ville comme Londres', where 'une communauté de clercs' from Lancashire and Cheshire occupied 'des postes d'importance'.[117] But, whatever the nature of Northerners in London, there were always more Northerners in Chester. Last of all, an expert account of dialect and provenance for *St Erkenwald*, a poem set in London and on a London saint, but in a dialect identical to that of the four verse texts of MS Cotton Nero A.x.[118] It offers another way ahead. Comparison may be made with the writer's book of 2023 and the observation (by John Burrow) there cited regarding the less involved style of *St Erkenwald*, different from the *Gawain* Poet's. It may yet be the work of his brother. Hence an identical dialect and non-identical style; a hypothesis supported by the manuscripts of each, both (it seems) from Cheshire, and the latter compiled for a family linked to the Stanleys by marriage.

We began with the metaphor of an art gallery; and above are collected the comments of viewers over twelve decades. They offer a multitude of lessons: on good ideas neglected or forgotten; on erosion in recent years of good scholarly technique or practice; and on the enduring power of Arthur. If there is to be progress for his portrayal in *Sir Gawain and the Green Knight*, it will be through scrutiny of the texts involved, and based upon what is demonstrable for London and Cheshire in the age of Richard II.

Notes

1. W. P. Ker, *English Literature: Medieval* (London, 1912), 137-40.
2. J. E. Wells, *A Manual of the Writings in Middle English* (New Haven, 1916), 54-7.
3. *Fourteenth-Century Verse and Prose*, ed. Kenneth Sisam (Oxford, 1921), 44.
4. J. P. Oakden, *Alliterative Poetry in Middle English: A Survey of the Traditions* (Manchester, 1935), 46-7.
5. W. L. Renwick and Harold Orton, *The Beginnings of English Literature to Skelton* (London, 1939), 350.
6. Mabel Day, 'Introduction', in *Sir Gawain and the Green Knight*, ed. Israel Gollancz (London, 1940), ix-xxxix.
7. Gervase Mathew, 'Ideals of Knighthood', in *Studies in Medieval History*, ed. R. W. Hunt, W. A. Pantin, R. W. Southern (Oxford, 1948), 354-62.
8. George Kane, *Middle English Literature* (London, 1951), 73-6.
9. *Pearl*, ed. E. V. Gordon (Oxford, 1953), xliv.
10. Dorothy Everett, *Essays on Middle English Literature* (Oxford, 1955), 68-9.
11. John Spiers, *Medieval English Poetry* (London, 1957), 219.
12. L. H. Loomis, 'Gawain and the Green Knight', in *Arthurian Literature in the Middle Ages*, ed. R. S. Loomis (Oxford, 1959), 528-40.
13. John H. Fisher, 'Wyclif, Langland, Gower, and the *Pearl* Poet on the Subject of Aristocracy', in *Studies in Medieval Literature*, ed. MacEdward Leach (Philadelphia, 1961), 139-57.
14. Marie Borroff, *'Sir Gawain and the Green Knight': A Stylistic and Metrical Study* (New Haven, 1962), 27.
15. C. S. Lewis, 'The Anthropological Approach', in *English and Medieval Studies*, ed. Norman Davis and C. L. Wrenn (London, 1962), 219-30.
16. J. McN. Dodgson, 'Sir Gawain's Arrival in Wirral', in *Early English and Norse Studies*, ed. Arthur Brown and Peter Foote (London, 1963), 19-25.

17. Margaret Schlauch, *Antecedents of the English Novel* (Warszawa, 1963), 28.

18. J. A. Burrow, *A Reading of 'Sir Gawain and the Green Knight'* (London, 1965), 6-8.

19. *'Sir Gawain' and 'Pearl'*, ed. Robert J. Blanch (Bloomington, 1966).

20. D. S. Brewer, 'Courtesy and the *Gawain*-Poet', in *Patterns of Love and Courtesy*, ed. John Lawlor (London, 1966), 54-85.

21. Henry L. Savage, *'Fare*, Line 694 of *Sir Gawain and the Green Knight'*, in *Studies in Language and Literature*, ed. M. Brahmer, S. Helsztyński, J. Krzyżanowski (Warszawa, 1966), 373-4.

22. P. M. Kean, *The Pearl* (London, 1967), 208.

23. Dieter Mehl, *The Middle English Romances of the Thirteenth and Fourteenth Centuries* (London, 1967), 203-4.

24. *Sir Gawain and the Green Knight*, ed. J. R. R. Tolkien and E. V. Gordon, 2nd edn (Oxford, 1967), xxiv-xxv.

25. Edward Vasta, 'Introduction', in *The Pearl*, ed. Mary Vincent Hillmann (Notre Dame, 1967), vii-xiii.

26. Ian Bishop, *'Pearl' in Its Setting* (Oxford, 1968), 28, 140 n. 4, 142 n. 51.

27. *Twentieth-Century Interpretations of Sir Gawain and the Green Knight*, ed. Denton Fox (Englewood Cliffs, 1968).

28. Gervase Mathew, *The Court of Richard II* (London, 1968), 164, 166.

29. James P. Oakden, 'The Liturgical Influence in "Pearl"', in *Chaucer und seine Zeit*, ed. Arno Esch (Tübingen, 1968), 337-53.

30. Elizabeth Salter, 'Medieval Poetry and the Figural View of Reality', *Proceedings of the British Academy*, liv (1968), 73-92.

31. *Patience*, ed. J. J. Anderson (Manchester, 1969), 5.

32. Basil Cottle, *The Triumph of English 1350-1400* (London, 1969), 279-80.

33. Geoffrey Shepherd, 'The Nature of Alliterative Poetry in Late Medieval England', *Proceedings of the British Academy*, lvi (1970), 57-76.

34. D. J. Williams, 'Alliterative Poetry', in *The Middle Ages*, ed. W. F. Bolton (London, 1970), 107-58.

35. A. C. Spearing, *The Gawain-Poet* (Cambridge, 1970), 133 n.2.

36. J. A. Burrow, *Ricardian Poetry* (London, 1971), 33.

37. Pamela Gradon, *Form and Style in Early English Literature* (London,

1971), 134–5, 195–211, 245–6, 289–91.

38. William Vantuono, '*Patience, Cleanness, Pearl,* and *Gawain*', *Annuale Medievale*, xii (1971), 37–69.

39. Ian Robinson, *Chaucer and the English Tradition* (Cambridge, 1972), 231.

40. A. C. Spearing, *Criticism and Medieval Poetry*, 2nd edn (London, 1972), 29.

41. Elisabeth Brewer, *From Cuchulainn to Gawain* (Cambridge, 1973).

42. Stephen Medcalf, '"Piers Plowman" and the Ricardian Age in Literature', in *The Mediaeval World*, ed. David Daiches and Anthony Thorlby (London, 1973), 643–96.

43. John Stevens, *Medieval Romance* (London, 1973), 90–5.

44. Sumner Ferris, 'Chaucer, Richard II, Henry IV, and 13 October', in *Chaucer and Middle English Studies*, ed. Beryl Rowland (Kent, 1974), 210–17.

45. *Poetry of the Age of Chaucer*, ed. A. C. and J. E. Spearing (London, 1974), 82.

46. A. C. Spearing, *Medieval Dream Poetry* (Cambridge, 1976), 111.

47. Philippa Tristram, *Figures of Life and Death in Medieval English Literature* (London, 1976), 29.

48. *Cleanness*, ed. J. J. Anderson (Manchester, 1977), 3, 5.

49. Barbara Nolan, *The Gothic Visionary Perspective* (Princeton, 1977), 156.

50. Derek Pearsall, *Old English and Middle English Poetry* (London, 1977), 174.

51. Thorlac Turville-Petre, *The Alliterative Revival* (Cambridge, 1977), 46.

52. W. A. Davenport, *The Art of the Gawain-Poet* (London, 1978), 145.

53. *The Poems of the Pearl Manuscript*, ed. Malcolm Andrew and Ronald Waldron (London, 1978), 217 n. 254.

54. Derek Brewer, *Symbolic Stories* (Cambridge, 1980), 73–4.

55. W. R. J. Barron, 'Knighthood on Trial: The Acid Test of Irony', in *Knighthood in Medieval Literature*, ed. W. H. Jackson (Cambridge, 1981), 89–103.

56. Janet Coleman, *English Literature in History 1350–1400* (London, 1981), 44, 167.

57. Wendy Childs, 'Anglo-Italian Contacts', in *Chaucer and the Italian*

Trecento, ed. Piero Boitani (Cambridge, 1983), 65-87.

58. Derek Brewer, *English Gothic Literature* (New York, 1983), 158.

59. J. A. Burrow, *Essays on Medieval Literature* (Oxford, 1984), 130.

60. *Sir Gawain and the Green Knight*, ed. Theodore Silverstein (Chicago, 1984), 14.

61. J. A. W. Bennett, *Middle English Literature* (Oxford, 1986), 202-3.

62. J. A. Burrow, 'The *Canterbury Tales* I: Romance', in *The Cambridge Chaucer Companion*, ed. Piero Boitani and Jill Mann (Cambridge, 1986), 109-24.

63. Christopher Dean, *Arthur of England* (Toronto, 1987), 78.

64. A. C. Spearing, *Readings in Medieval Poetry* (Cambridge, 1987), 215.

65. Stephen Coote, *English Literature of the Middle Ages* (Harmondsworth, 1988), 238.

66. Christopher Wrigley, '*Sir Gawain and the Green Knight*: The Underlying Myth', in *Studies in Medieval English Romances*, ed. Derek Brewer (Cambridge, 1988), 113-28.

67. Joerg O. Fichte, 'Grappling With Arthur', in *Poetics: Theory and Practice in Medieval English Literature*, ed. Piero Boitani and Anna Torti (Cambridge, 1991), 149-63.

68. V. J. Scattergood, '*Sir Gawain and the Green Knight*', in *The New Arthurian Encyclopedia*, ed. Norris J. Lacy (Chicago, 1991), 419-21.

69. Lee Patterson, 'Court Politics and the Invention of Literature', in *Culture and History 1350-1600*, ed. David Aers (Hemel Hempstead, 1992), 7-41, at 19-20.

70. Derek Pearsall, *The Life of Geoffrey Chaucer* (London, 1992), 62.

71. Geraldine Barnes, *Counsel and Strategy in Middle English Romance* (Cambridge, 1993), 125, 137.

72. Jill Mann, 'Price and Value in *Sir Gawain and the Green Knight*', in *Medieval English Poetry*, ed. Stephanie Trigg (London, 1993), 119-37.

73. Ad Putter, '*Sir Gawain and the Green Knight*' and French Arthurian Romance* (Oxford, 1995), 192.

74. R. J. Blanch and J. N. Wasserman, *From Pearl to Gawain* (Gainesville, 1995), 18.

75. Derek Pearsall, 'Madness in *Sir Orfeo*', in *Romance Reading on the Book*, ed. Jennifer Fellows, Rosalind Field, Gillian Rogers, Judith Weiss

(Cardiff, 1996), 51-63, at 56, 58.

76. Lynn Stacey, 'Julian of Norwich and the Late Fourteenth-Century Crisis of Authority', in David Aers and Lynn Stacey, *The Powers of the Holy* (University Park, 1996), 107-78, at 150, 154.

77. *A Companion to the 'Gawain' Poet*, ed. Derek Brewer and Jonathan Gibson (Cambridge, 1997).

78. Malcolm Hebron, *The Medieval Siege* (Oxford, 1997), 103-5.

79. David Burnley, *Courtliness and Literature in Medieval England* (London, 1998), 44.

80. W. A. Davenport, *Chaucer and His English Contemporaries* (London, 1998), 161.

81. Ann W. Astell, *Political Allegory in Late Medieval England* (Ithaca, 1999), 124, 126.

82. W. R. J. Barron, '*Sir Gawain and the Green Knight*', in *The Arthur of the English*, ed. W. R. J. Barron (Cardiff, 1999), 164-83, at 182.

83. Michael Bennett, *Richard II and the Revolution of 1399* (Stroud, 1999), 113, 131.

84. David Matthews, *The Making of Middle English* (Minneapolis, 1999), 131.

85. Malcolm Andrew, 'Setting and Context in the Works of the *Gawain*-Poet', in *New Perspectives on Middle English Texts*, ed. Susan Powel and Jeremy J. Smith (Cambridge, 2000), 3-15.

86. Jeff Rider, 'The Other Worlds of Romance', in *The Cambridge Companion to Medieval Romance*, ed. Roberta L. Krueger (Cambridge, 2000), 115-31, at 119.

87. James Simpson, 'Contemporary English Writers', in *A Companion to Chaucer*, ed. Peter Brown (Oxford, 2000), 114-32, at 127.

88. John M. Bowers, *The Politics of 'Pearl'* (Cambridge, 2001), 17.

89. Derek Pearsall, *Arthurian Romance* (Oxford, 2003), 75.

90. A. Breeze, 'Sir John Stanley (*c.* 1350-1414) and the *Gawain* Poet', *Arthuriana*, xiv (2004), 15-30.

91. Helen Cooper, *The English Romance in Time* (Oxford, 2004), 52.

92. Tony Davenport, *Medieval Narrative* (Oxford, 2004), 23.

93. J. J. Anderson, *Language and Imagination in the 'Gawain'-Poems* (Manchester, 2005), 239.

94. A. C. Spearing, *Textual Subjectivity* (Oxford, 2005), 137, 172.

95. Elliot Kendall, *Lordship and Literature* (Oxford, 2008), 263.

96. Thorlac Turville-Petre, 'The Green Chapel' in *A Commodity of Good Names*, ed. O. J. Padel and D. N. Parsons (Stamford, 2008), 320-9.

97. K. S. Whetter, *Understanding Genre and Medieval Romance* (Aldershot, 2008), 90.

98. Robert W. Barrett, *Against All England* (Notre Dame, 2009), 154.

99. Ordelle G. Hill, *Looking Westward* (Newark, 2009), 55.

100. Laura Ashe, 'Introduction', in *The Exploitations of Medieval Romance*, ed. Laura Ashe, Ivana Djordević, Judith Weiss (Cambridge, 2010), 1-14, at 14.

101. Tony Davenport, '*Sir Gawain and the Green Knight*', in *A Companion to Medieval Poetry*, ed. Corinne Saunders (Chichester, 2010), 385-400, at 399.

102. Lee Patterson, *Acts of Recognition* (Notre Dame, 2010), 71-2.

103. Corinne Saunders, *Magic and the Supernatural in Medieval English Romance* (Cambridge, 2010), 195.

104. Thorlac Turville-Petre, 'Places of the Imagination', in *The Oxford Handbook of Medieval Literature in English*, ed. Elaine Treharne and Greg Walter (Oxford, 2010), 594-608.

105. Carolyn Larrington, 'English Chivalry and *Sir Gawain and the Green Knight*', in *Companion to Arthurian Literature*, ed. Helen Fulton (Chichester, 2012), 252-64, at 260-1.

106. Kristina Pérez, *The Myth of Morgan la Fey* (Basingstoke, 2014), 104, 114.

107. *The Works of the 'Gawain' Poet*, ed. Ad Putter and Myra Stokes (London, 2014), xv.

108. Walter Wadiak, *Savage Economy* (Notre Dame, 2017), 90-1.

109. David K. Coley, *Death and the Pearl Maiden* (Columbus, 2019), 127.

110. Kenneth Hodges, 'Spenser, Malory, and Regionalism', in *The Arthurian World*, ed. Victoria Coldham-Fussell, Miriam Edlich-Muth, Renée Ward (London, 2022), 83-94, at 92.

111. A. Breeze, *The Historical Arthur and the 'Gawain' Poet* (Lanham, 2023).

112. Steven Bruso, 'Contesting Royal Power', in *Ethics of the Arthurian Legend*, ed. Melissa Ridley Elmes and Evelyn Meyer (Cambridge,

2023), 173-97.

113. M. G. Gibson, *TRUTH, DARE, KISS ... CHEAT!: Being an Account of Some 'TRANSFOMATIVE DISCOVERIES' Regarding the Storytelling in the Poem 'SIR GAWAIN AND THE GREEN KNIGHT' Made in the Course of Publishing a Close Translation of It, Together with REVELATIONS of PLAGIARISM of That Translation by the POET LAUREATE* (Knutsford, 2023).

114. Helen Cooper, 'Five Blows of the Axe', *Studies in the Age of Chaucer*, lxvi (2024), 97-120.

115. Victoria Flood, 'A Romance of England and Wales', in *Medieval Welsh Literature and Its European Contexts*, ed. Victoria Flood (Cambridge, 2024), 114-30, at 130.

116. James Ross, *Robert de Vere* (Woodbridge, 2024), 235-6.

117. *Sire Gauvain et le Chevalier Vert*, tr. Olivier Simonin (Paris, 2024), 20.

118. *St Erkenwald*, ed. Thorlac Turville-Petre (Liverpool, 2024), 14-15.

CHAPTER EIGHT

THE ALLITERATIVE *MORTE ARTHURE*

The Alliterative *Morte Arthure* is a robust alliterative poem in East Midlands dialect, formerly placed in the 1360s, now dated to about the year 1400. It should not be confused with the Stanzaic *Le Morte Arthure*, a smoother and less virile text (occasionally mentioned below) of the fifteenth century, or with Sir Thomas Malory's *Le Morte Darthur*, anatomized in our final chapter. This triple-naming yet brings out the sway that Arthur had over men and women in late medieval England, and even England now; for the alliterative poem has admirers there (and beyond) to this day.

It survives in a unique copy, in the ponderous 'Thornton Manuscript', an *omnium gatherum* of vernacular prose and poetry copied in the 1430s by the Yorkshire squire Robert Thornton; and was first published in 1847 by J. O. Halliwell (d. 1889), literary historian and son-in-law of Sir Thomas Phillipps (d. 1872), bibliomane. (That Halliwell never acquired his father-in-law's stupendous library was a stupendous disappointment to him.) The *editio princeps* of 1847 was followed by the standard one of Brock (after George Perry) for the Early English Text Society, where the editor praised the unknown author, 'one of the greatest writers of his time', at once capable of 'freshness' or 'pathos' or 'a rapid flow and thundering force', and so a far better poet than Hoccleve or Lydgate or Skelton.[1] Others had similar feelings, including W. P. Ker. Grudging (as shown previously) on Laȝamon's *Brut*, he was warm and expansive on *Morte Arthure*. It is 'magnificent', to be mentioned in the same breath as *Sir Gawain and the Green Knight* (Ker thereafter styling both as of the fourteenth century); intended for an élite audience; 'remarkable'; and yet different, for *Morte Arthure* is not a romance but an 'epic', which Ker took as reflecting 'the glory of King Edward III', bellicose monarch).[2]

Brock and Ker led a procession of eulogists. Wells provided similar language, together with information (some of it now discredited). The poem has 4346 lines and (he thought) was from Scotland or northern England (so that some attributed it to the Scottish versifier Huchown; a baseless notion). Although its chronicle of Arthur's feats goes back to Geoffrey of Monmouth, 'the poet was very independent in his handling of his materials'. The result is dramatic. We encounter the 'terror' of Roman envoys before Arthur's fury; Guinevere's 'grief' on separation from her husband; a disturbing picture of a dragon dreamt of by Arthur; another disturbing image, of Fortune and her Wheel. Despite that, the author's concern was for the here and now, so he was silent on 'the mythical account' of the king's passing. But he had plenty to say elsewhere. Hence a lyrical description of a grove near Mont-Saint-Michel, or of an early-morning meadow near Metz; or humour, as with pithy comments by Sir Bedivere on encountering a giant; or pathos, in laments for the deaths of young and handsome knights; or tragedy, in Modred's betrayal of Arthur and its disastrous outcome. Pathos and tragedy notwithstanding, the poet tended to the actual and factual. He stressed 'accuracy and truth' (the narrative being presented not as legend or romance, but history), together with accounts of sieges, embarkations, musterings of troops, battles on land or at sea, all reading like those of an 'eye-witness' who knew much of war. He had a gift for 'constructive' detail and the creation of 'vivid' and 'veracious' scenes, whether of Arthur's rage against the 'terrified' ambassadors from Rome, or the 'last sad moments' of the dying king at Glastonbury. Important as a masterpiece (if one that, thanks to its anonymity, has never had due fame), *Morte Arthure* was, in addition, Malory's main source for 'the fifth book of his compilation' (thereby providing him with 'most that is of worth' there).[3]

Oakden assented to much of the above. *Morte Arthure* is 'more seriously historical' and 'more epic in quality' than other Arthurian poems. Its portrait of the king (the present book's central theme) also demonstrates subtlety. He is no Superman or world-conqueror set to 'defy the universe'; he does not 'dwarf all other warriors'. A change has taken place. By now, Arthur no longer monopolizes the text. The knights with him have their own exploits. All the same, he has enough 'vitality' to dominate the scene and give 'artistic unity' to the work. As for the plot, it is simple. We start with Arthur as having already conquered 'the bulk of Western Europe', so that we can concentrate on his showdown with the Roman Emperor, which leads to both triumph and disaster, because the king's doom is taken as a 'logical' outcome of his 'lust for power and territory'. On the way is no shortage of martial verse, 'throbbing' with 'the glamour and energy of fighting' and interspersed with other 'vivid' and 'picturesque' episodes, all 'described in the minutest detail'. An example is Arthur's grief on discovering the corpse of Gawain. He *glopyns* or 'is dismayed' at heart; he groans; tears well up in his eyes; and then:

> Knelis [he kneels] downe to the cors, and kaught it in armes,
>
> Kastys vpe his vmbrere [helmet's visor], and kyssis hyme sone,
>
> Lokes one his eye-liddis, that lowkkide [joined together] ware faire,

His lippis like to the lede [lead], and his lire falowede [face gone pale]!

British officers of those days did not always hide emotion; one notes too how the poet had often seen dead bodies and the way that their lips turn a leaden blue-grey. Small wonder that Oakden commented on the poet's 'masterly hand', so that Lady Fortune's wheel has the 'dazzling colours and splendour' of an 'oriental' treasure; giants are 'dreadful realities' (not something out of picture-books); so, too, are the deaths in a battle by land or sea. *Morte Arthure* is, then, an outstanding work, that does not 'suffer in comparison' even with *Sir Gawain and the Green Knight*.[4] More restrained, however, were Renwick and Orton, who summed it up as a 'fine poem' containing 'some good touches of nature and religion'.[5]

With George Kane we return to hyperbole (or something near it), plus faint praise for the stanzaic *Morte Arthure*. Like *Sir Gawain and the Green Knight*, the alliterative poem has 'a splendidly rich elaboration of imagery' and 'strength of both writing and conception'; the stanzaic poem, in contrast, never in its 3970 lines attains to 'brilliance'. It displays merely 'sober competence'. That is all. So the two provide an exercise in criticism. They could hardly 'differ more in intention, execution, and effect'. The alliterative poem is passionate, 'partisan', 'heroic', serious, dignified, 'stately', 'epic'; the stanzaic poem is one of 'half-tones' and 'no great stirring of emotion'. It is 'romantic and melancholy'; 'subdued, haunting'; an elegant and (within its limits) successful instance of medieval *'fin-de-siècle'*. Amongst further comments on its alliterative sibling are these. Its treatment of incidents is skilled, the author's intention being to glorify Arthur 'either directly or by reflection'. If it lacks the 'delicate effect of *cloisonné*' found in *Sir Gawain and the Green Knight*, it is 'more red-blooded', 'stronger', 'coarser'. Hence (for example) its 'exuberance' in describing the giant of Mont-Saint-Michel:

> Huke nebbyde as a hawke, and a hore berde
>
> And herede to the hole eyghne with hyngande browes;
>
> Harske as a hunde fische, hardly who so lukez,
>
> So was the hyde of that hulke hally al ouer

-- because this 'hulk' was 'hook-nosed', hoary-bearded, 'hairy' up to his 'hollow eyes', and ('for any careful observer') with a hide all over as harsh as a dogfish's. Certainly an ugly customer.

Quotation of these and other passages makes Kane's summary an admirable introduction to the poet's varied aspects. He is warm, vigorous, with an eye for the 'roo and the raynedere', the roe-deer and reindeer running through thickets by a river; but with an (unsentimental) eye too for death in battle, where (the doomed) Sir Idrus declares of his (equally doomed) father, 'He salle ferkke [go] before, and I salle come aftyre'. The old man is cut down now, with his son before long to follow him.[6]

Paralleling Kane's analysis is one by Dorothy Everett, who also regarded the work as 'thoroughly masculine', with its marvels of prophetic dreams and miraculous balms treated in a 'matter-of-fact' way. She had special words on Arthur's representation. He resembles less the hero of the romances than those of Old English poetry. He is the 'mighty conqueror, haughty to his enemies, generous to his knights, and undaunted in defeat'; his sole concern is fighting; his watchwords are 'courage' and 'loyalty'. For him and his officers, whether out on the battlefield or back in the mess, 'grim jests' are likelier than acts of 'courtesy' (that core medieval virtue). Arthur 'fights for personal glory' except when beginning his last campaign, where his ships sail under an ensign showing 'a chalke-whitte mayden /

And a childe in hir arme, that chefe es of hevyne' which is said to be the king's 'cheefe armes', even when hunting. This 'female figure with a child' (in the phrase of Belloc's ballade on 'illegal ornaments') marks Arthur as a Christian warrior, whose cause is just. Yet the poem has defects: too many giants, too many speeches, and 'far too much fighting'. They are perhaps due to the poem's sources, for its last part is 'far more engrossing' than the rest (thanks to fresh material?) and even stirring. In short, a Middle English poem with 'a sure sense of the dramatic' that is vastly different from conventional 'romances of chivalry'.[7]

The 1950s ended with a third fine assessment of *Morte Arthure*, in a volume which (even now) is an essential tool for researchers. The spirit of 'English expansionism' of the poem's 4346 lines is related to Edward III's reign, especially after the Treaty of Brétigny (1360), when the English controlled France from the region south of Nantes down to the Pyrenees. (The boisterous and confident and unrefined Arthur of the poem is certainly like Edward III, before the decline of his last years; and quite unlike Richard II, the over-refined and unwarlike grandson who succeeded Edward in 1377. It raises a critical question; for we now date *Morte Arthure* to about 1400 and thus later than 1387 and *Sir Gawain and the Green Knight*, with its quizzical representation of a youthful and capricious Arthur who curiously resembles Richard. Revisionism on dating ever shows the dangers of reading at face value.) After comments (now outdated) on the poem's authorship and dialect (which we pass over) is an observation on its text as 'reconstructed from memory'. Whole passages have been transposed or omitted; metre and phraseology have suffered. This is clear from comparison with Malory's prose version of the poem. As regards sources, the author's principal one was a version of Wace, but he made bold changes in its narrative, foregrounding Arthur by giving him 'exploits traditionally ascribed to his knights', where it is certain that deeds of Edward III and the Black Prince 'stirred the poet's imagination and patriotic ardour'. It included not only their routine sacking of French towns, or the prince's massacre of every man, woman, and child in Limoges (1356), or his father's near-success in having the Burghers of Calais put to death (1347), but also the king's defeat of a Spanish fleet (in French pay) off Winchelsea, Sussex (1350), which various lines of *Morte Arthure* reflect in 'specific detail'. Despicable aspects of the above notwithstanding, O'Loughlin called the poem an 'epic' with a 'noble, valiant' hero in Arthur, and thereby possessing an 'aristocratic appeal' not found in popular romances (like *Havelok* or *King Horn*); an interesting conclusion. He thought that, for all the difficulties of textual corruption and Northern dialectisms left by Robert Thornton, the poem should be recognized as 'a masterpiece of narrative art on a large scale'. O'Loughlin finished his account with a startling remark (possessing implications which he did not see). Although *Morte Arthure* survives in a unique copy, it once had 'a considerable circulation'. Its prophecies unmistakably influenced a long passage in *The Awntyrs off Arthure* (from the mid-1420s) on how Modred will commit treachery and at Carlisle will have himself 'crowned as king'; more startlingly, its description of a giant apparently influenced that of Nebuchadnezzar in *Cleanness* (so that, for example, *And herede to the hole eyghne with hyngande browes*, quoted above from Kane, lies behind *Holȝe were his yȝen and vnder campe hores*. The first is 'And hairy to the hollow eyes with hanging brows'; the second, 'Hollow were his eyes and under shaggy hairs').[8]

What this reveals on *Morte Arthure* deserves emphasis. An allusion to *Patience* in a revised version of Langland's *Piers Plowman* puts the former poem to before 1379; its sister-text *Cleanness*, identical in its Cheshire dialect and Biblical theme, may likewise be put in the 1370s; that might seem to locate *Morte Arthure* even earlier, after the diplomatic triumph of Brétigny in 1360 and before Edward III's decline began in 1369 (following the death of his queen). Yet (since the 1980s) the poem has been dated to about 1400, its author alluding to Richard II's fall. A surprising change. If so, either *Morte Arthure* echoes *Patience*; or it is a text of the 1360s that was revised in about 1400; or both echo a third lost text. The first seems most likely, but there is in any case a comparative task for investigators.

Thanks to the above writers (Kane, Everett, O'Loughlin), our knowledge of *Morte Arthure* rests on sure foundations. Later critics build higher. Marie Borroff underlined parallels between the poem and *Sir Gawain and the Green Knight*. Each, for example, starts its main narrative with a 'Rounde Table' banquet. In the former, Arthur 'at Carlele a Cristynmese he haldes' (that is, a Christmas celebration); in the latter, he 'lay at Camylot vpon Krystmasse'; and at both feasts were lords and ladies with good things to eat and drink.[9] Two works, then, from the same alliterative school. The provenance of the text known to Robert Thornton (a provenance not very different from that of the author's original?) then came under the scrutiny of McIntosh (in the Festschrift for J. R. R. Tolkien). He put it south of the Humber, 'somewhere not far north of Lincoln'; he also thought the West Midlands location often posited for the author was not 'satisfactorily proven', and instead tended to put him at or near Louth, in east Lincolnshire.[10] (Turville-Petre now prefers south Lincolnshire to east Lincolnshire.) Derek Brewer had an interesting observation (after Vinaver) on Malory's treatment of *Morte Arthure*. In the poem, Arthur's death was the sequel to his Roman triumph; but Malory 'postponed the tragic end' until the very close of his work, so that its second part is one of 'triumph' and perhaps a tribute to Henry V, who brought English troops into Paris and whose son Henry was later crowned King of France.[11] That would present an interesting juxtaposition of Arthur with three English kings. The Arthur of *Morte Arthure* is a belligerent Edward III; that of *Sir Gawain and the Green Knight*, a petulant (if courteous and spirited) twenty-year-old Richard II;

that of Malory (in part) a Henry V, England's supreme warrior-king. Writers can, after all, no more escape the affairs and politics of their age than they can jump out of their skin. We see Arthur-material ever modified by time. Such remakings appear not just with Malory and his predecessors but with Derek Brewer himself. He styled *Morte Arthure* a 'stern, pious' work, possessing 'a vein of repellent brutality as well as a hearty enthusiasm for battle'. He yet thought the author 'a cleric', despite the poem's obsessions with unclerical activities like hunting and fighting and feasting, and lack of reference to Scripture or ecclesiastical learning. (His opinion is not credible.) Brewer was on surer ground in noting how Arthur was there 'severely criticized', even if poet and audience were still 'on his side', especially given the seeming 'parallels with Edward III'; also undoubtedly correct is comment on the poem's 'extraordinarily vivid sense' of infantry fighting in the fourteenth century (and modern times). It is a work for 'middle-aged soldiers and politicians', and thus unlikely to 'attract women and undergraduates'.[12] Derek Brewer (the present writer's supervisor in the 1970s) was during the Hitler War a British Army officer. His experience of soldiering for the above perceptions is obvious.

There is an important and absorbing analysis of how the poet regarded Arthur in an edition of *Morte Arthure*, with fine words on its 'tragic, heroic close', together with cautious suggestions on where its author was from ('the general area of Louth', east Lincolnshire?) and still more cautious ones on when he lived (at some date between the middle of the fourteenth century and the early fifteenth).[13] We can jettison some of this. If *Cleanness* of the 1370s influenced *Morte Arthure* of about 1400, it aids us (after Turville-Petre) in the quest for its poet. Those with access to records of the Grantham-Sleaford-Boston region of Lincolnshire may now seek a local member of the gentry who, in war and peace, had (by 1400) long experience of the King's service. He will be a man of this period with appropriate military experience and speaking the local dialect. Ideally, he should belong to a family interested in reading (perhaps demonstrated by wills, medieval books being expensive items, often mentioned in bequests). The number of candidates being limited, a future researcher may be richly rewarded by identifying *Morte Arthure*'s poet. At risk of damping the zeal of investigators, one must yet recall that Middle English texts are contaminated by the dialects of their scribes, concealing those of the actual authors. If it is objected that the poet was perhaps his own scribe, thereby indicating a perfect match between his dialect and that of the original manuscript text, we may answer that a retired military man of means would employ a professional copyist for literary work (as did Chaucer and Gower, slightly lower in the social scale).

In discussion of the other and stanzaic *Morte Arthure*, a professor at Bonn declared that the author of its alliterative precursor was in comparison 'far more outspoken' on moral issues; he made 'no secret' of his convictions on and views of the events described.[14] If one poet was an obsequious courtier, the other was a bluff army veteran. Turning from *Morte Arthure* to *Le Morte Darthur*, we find in Vinaver's second edition a detailed analysis of how Malory treated this source for the tale of 'the Emperor Lucius'. The result seemingly alludes to 'the military and political triumphs of Henry V' (noted above after Brewer and Vinaver's first edition), as demonstrated by maps comparing Arthur's progress across France with Henry's.[15] John Finlayson then restated opinions (set out in his edited selections of 1967) on Arthur. The king 'hardly bears any resemblance' to the character in Wace's *Roman de Brut* (the English poem's main source). For one thing, he now has traits of 'grim irony' (readily coming to his lips in time of battle) and, better, a 'regard for his men' (like any good commander); despite that, the poet recognized Arthur's defects as a general (even a fearless one), as in his 'reckless engagement' with a superior force, leading to a 'last heroic stand' against Modred and 'the destruction of so much glory'.[16] Certainly the stuff of tragedy. Basil Cottle had other observations. He proposed that Chaucer's possible knowledge of *Morte Arthure*, 'a noble poem', is implied by his Knight's use of alliterative lines. Cottle gave further praise to the unknown author's 'great and aristocratic' work, and the opposite of praise for its account of Arthur's 'wasteful campaigns only too like' those of Edward III. Cottle made the further point that an account of 'coggez and crayers' transporting soldiers and their equipment from Sandwich, Kent, 'shows a mastery of the technical terms of fourteenth-century seamanship'.[17] Cottle's words collide with dating. Chaucer died in 1400. He might have known parts of the work, if (like James Joyce with *Ulysses*) the author published sections of it as work progressed. But he could hardly have *read* the entire work, especially in the 1380s, when he wrote his tale of the Knight. Again, a problem requiring reinvestigation.

Geoffrey Shepherd of Birmingham provided warm appreciation. He thought the poem a masterpiece written with 'assurance and panache'. Its Arthur is not the *roi fainéant* of so many romances, but a 'conqueror and ruler'. Shepherd stressed the contradictions implicit here, because the poet at the same time gave a zestful portrayal of war, despite its 'terrible ferocity', even if he could express 'pity at the loss that results'. The 'prevailing tone' is hence 'stern and sublimely heroic'; women 'play a small part'; there is 'considerable humour' of a rough, soldierly kind, as with Arthur's words on chopping off a giant's legs ('Thowe arte to hye by the halfe'); and understanding of war's sordid aspects, as with disembowelment, so that a rider's *filthe* and *guttes* thereafter leave a trail after his *fole fotte* ('horse's hoofs').[18] For anyone seeking descriptions of the trail of destruction left by English soldiery, there is a picture by Jean de Venette (d. 1370), French Carmelite. In a Latin chronicle (with words foreshadowing those of Burgundy in *Henry V*'s last act) he laments the devastation of his own birthplace, the village of Vedette (near Compiègne): vines 'not pruned or kept from rotting'; fields unploughed; roads deserted; houses and churches now 'smoking ruins'; nettles and thistles 'springing up on every side'.[19] Knights trailing bowels behind them, a village obliterated: they are the contrary face of *Morte Arthure*'s military glory.

After these insights, some misplaced confidence (alas) from Tony Spearing. He compares a line from *Morte Arthure* (3842) with two lines (2267-8) from *Sir Gawain and the Green Knight*. Both involve attack and how its object tried to dodge it. First is:

Bot the schalke for the scharpe he schowntes a littille

-- followed by:

And schranke a lytel with the schulderes for the scharp yrne.

That other schalk wyth a schunt the schene wythhaldes

-- where the sense in the former is that the man (Sir Modred) flinched a little on seeing the sharp weapon (a lance); in the latter, that (Gawain's) shoulders flinched a little, so that the other fellow jerked back the bright blade (of an axe).

A curious likeness, followed by Spearing's blandly informing us how there 'is no question here of the two poems being by the same author, or of one imitating the other'.[20] Indeed. It would be an innocent scholar who supposed the first, the *Gawain* Poet's dialect being of the north-west Midlands (and specifically Cheshire); but *Morte Arthure*'s of the north-east Midlands (probably Lincolnshire), as demonstrated by McIntosh in 1962. As for the assertion on how one poem cannot imitate the other, it makes strange reading in the light of lines (noted in 1959 by O'Loughlan) on Nebuchadnezzar in *Cleanness* and the parallels for a giant in *Morte Arthure*. The resemblances are no accident.

They are not due to poetic formulas. So the *Gawain* Poet's work was known to the author of *Morte Arthure* in about 1400, just as it was to Chaucer in his last years (see his tales of Squire and Wife of Bath). *Morte Arthure* was again known to Malory in the late 1460s. Such is the endless process of literary creation and recreation.

Two Oxford historians offer further insights on war. An outline of Edward's campaign of 1359-60 brings out its brutality, and yet ends with the words that, if the king had died in 1360, he would be considered 'one of England's most successful medieval rulers', despite the sickness and French attacks which had 'thinned the ranks' of what had been an immense host, so that he wisely came to terms.[21] It casts light on the mingled triumphalism and realism of *Morte Arthure*. As for the man who wrote it, an unromantic sketch of Edward III's commanders in the field and how they did well for themselves is illuminating. Many families (Cobham, Dagworth, Breadstone, Norwich, Bourchier, Scrope) gained status and profit from war. Those who rose (perhaps to the Garter, or even a title of nobility) might have begun as younger sons of the 'lesser gentry', as 'landless or near-landless adventurers'.[22] *Morte Arthure*'s author may (or may not) have been a Lincolnshire man of their number.

On his poem, a Cambridge professor laid stress on how in 'no other Arthurian romance' is that king 'so important and so impressive', in part because 'he usually has a huge army in support'; and the text is quoted with Finlayson's comments on it to bring out Arthur as there a 'royal hero', a Christian warrior-king who 'embodies the virtues of chivalry and knighthood'.[23] We may here yet recall Keen's words on the English retreat to Calais in spring, 1360, with thousands dying from disease or French harassment; or McFarlane's on plunder and English fortunes made. Stevens here never mentions Edward III. But it is hard to escape the idea of the narrative's Arthur as another Edward: potent, masterful, glamorous, flawed. Lodged in one's mind, it returns after reading how 'there are no better accounts of late medieval warfare' than that found in *Morte Arthure*, including its horrors, as on the slings and catapults used to bombard Metz. The poet's skill in description is one of many qualities that explain his 'high reputation' amongst the few who read him.[24] They contrast (one may add) with those of the stanzaic *Morte Arthure*, re-edited (under a variant title) at this time.[25] It was followed by an edition of the alliterative *Morte* which is welcome for its completeness, less so for its retrograde introduction. The editor is not helpful on dates, and similarly fails to take up remarks of McIntosh and Finlayson on the poet's Lincolnshire dialect, even proposing *Morte Arthure* and *The Awntyrs off Arthure* (of the 1420s and from the Carlisle region) as having 'common authorship'.[26]

Better, in bringing us back to British troops slogging their way across northern France, is an aside on how Arthur's deeds are in *Morte Arthure* treated as 'virtually contemporary'. Quite unlike the elegiac tone of 'long-past history' in its stanzaic namesake, or in Malory.[27] Derek Pearsall offered further praise on the poet's language. Its richness is 'flamboyant' and 'astonishing', yet 'never bookish'; it is often violent, as in 'thunderous' accounts of battle; sometimes 'wildly playful' (leading to comparison with diction in 'Shakespeare's time'); more often 'plain and serious'. It is a '*tour de force*' of 'profusion, richness, and vigour', and yet does not impede a 'pondered telling of the story'. As for Arthur, he is not stainless. In his second dream he is rebuked by Fortune. In imperialist wars he has 'schedde myche blode'; his pride brought death to innocent men, women, children. The consequence is a 'profound poignancy' rare in any poetry.[28] Another critic, providing expertise (on manuscript, metre, provenance, readership), was more restrained than Pearsall on the poet, whose tough-minded militarism is seldom assuaged by moral qualms: an artistic confusion which is 'nowhere resolved'.[29] For another problem, a collection of essays has many references to *Morte Arthure*, including Vinaver's suggestion that Malory's version of it (his 'Book II') was his 'first composition' (a proposal now thought unlikely).[30]

Twenty years after speaking up for *Morte Arthure*, Derek Brewer returned to the fray. He again stressed the poem's 'vivid sense of a real military campaign', although noting an oscillating 'ambivalence' on war's brutality vs. patriotism. Also indicative is its 'down to earth' conclusion: 'no mysterious boat, no queens' come to fetch the dying Arthur. Brewer dealt too with genre. K. H. Göller, the poem's 'chief modern student', styled it an 'anti-romance'; others call it tragedy, epic, history, even political tract, with a message to Edward III to 'take warning from Arthur's fate'.[31] Such is the almost infinite malleability of the Arthur theme (like John Donne's 'gold to airy thinness beat').

Now for a bombshell. Marty Hamel's 1984 edition develops arguments on the poem (after Larry Benson) as not being of the 1360s but of 1399-1402, and including allusions to Arthur's military advance from Luxembourg to Tuscany via the St Gotthard Pass, so that the poet would have known northern Italian cities at first hand.[32] The significance of this literary and scholarly *coup de théâtre* needs no emphasis. It casts telling light on a comment of John Burrow, who in his *Ricardian Poetry* (1971) spoke of 'Ricardian lack of interest in fighting', where Pearsall retorted that *Morte Arthure* has 'long battle-scenes'.[33] Our responses must be the servant of dating; not vice-versa.

In appraisal at once trenchant and judicious, Jack Bennett contrasted the alliterative *Morte Arthure* with the stanzaic one, the latter regarded as from the north-west Midlands or 'Gawain country' and written as the same time as *Sir Gawain and the Green Knight*. That poem being written in 1387 for (it seems) a Christmas entertainment at Chester Castle (a royal court, not a provincial one), it indicates new angles for the stanzaic *Morte*'s date and social context. As for the alliterative *Morte*, Bennett was clear-cut. It was composed 'in Lincolnshire or thereabouts'. Its poet had an inconsistent attitude to warfare. On the one hand he presented slaughter as if it were the finest sport under the sun. On the other, he had forebodings, an awareness of how Arthur's defects would bring doom to all. For all that, Bennett thought it wrong to read the text as 'a criticism of Arthur'. Like Froissart, the poet accepted the 'ebullient and rather bloody chivalry' of his age. Bennett had specific comments on Arthur himself. He is unlike the king of any earlier Arthurian text. He is fuller, more dynamic, no 'courtly king' but a 'world conqueror', an 'Alexander', who yet possesses 'the puzzling medieval mixture of ruthlessness and restraint'.[34] The debate may be followed in the work of others. One critic expressed no sympathy with the views of Göller and others on the text as an anti-war tract.[35] Another gave emphasis rather to the poet's (sometime excessive) skill in alliteration, if also invoking him in a critique of Burrow's phrase 'unheroic temper' as characterizing English poetry in the later fourteenth century.[36] The attitude is perhaps a more searching one than that of familiar comments elsewhere on a 'barbaric magnificence' of Arthur combined with his 'calculated' rather than 'natural' courtesy.[37]

In the 1990s updated attitudes to the narrative were conveniently supplied. It will be of about 1400; less easy to determine are its genre (romance? epic? tragedy?) and at what point the author came to regard Arthur's wars as 'unjust'.[38] Similarly, in a complete chapter on *Morte Arthure*, is acknowledgement of its allusions to 'the deposition of Richard II' (in 1399) with other evidence for its having been 'composed over a considerable period of time'.[39] Its afterlife offers problems as well, on how (for example) a reference unique in Malory's text to 'swearing by someone's soul' may come from a portion of *Morte Arthure* which reached Malory, but did not reach Robert Thornton.[40] During Edward III's campaigns there was no doubt plenty of swearing amongst English soldiery in France (compare Uncle Toby in *Tristram Shandy* on Marlborough's troops in

Flanders). Swearing by one's own soul or another's being a good manly mouth-filling oath, it takes us further on the poet's knowledge of life in the camp or on the battlefield. A particular aspect of that knowledge, the realistic passage (already mentioned) on the siege of Metz, is examined closely for inferences on the protagonist, if with a final admission of difficulties: do we see 'brutal but necessary efficiency' or an increasing 'moral degeneration of Arthur'?[41] More complex, certainly, than dismissal of the theme here as simply Arthur's 'arrogance and uninhibited lust for power'.[42]

Considerations on the poet's motives follow steadily. He wrote less 'to provide "gouty bailiffs" with a taste of martial adventure' than to 'prompt a knightly audience to give thought to the folly as well as the glory of war'.[43] Perhaps that is why the author was 'unusual in establishing Arthur clearly and firmly as the central character'?[44] Perhaps too, despite 'spread and sprawl in places', a narrative 'controlled by a clear overall sequences of events' from the 'opening challenge' faced by Arthur up to the 'sober' account of his end, 'completing the tale with laconic bleakness'.[45] There is comment as well on the distinctive 'emotional pitch' found throughout, whether on admiration for Arthur's 'martial achievements' or, in contrast, his representation in the story's 'final frames' as a 'grieving widow', who laments 'the loss of her loved ones'. They alike convey the power and weakness of 'noble homosocial bonds'. Larry Benson and Mary Hamel are also cited on the nature of the unknown poet to whom these perceptions are attributed: his dialect was of 'eastern Lincolnshire'; he wrote 'between 1399 and 1402'; he had 'diplomatic and bureaucratic experience'; was 'widely travelled' and knew Latin, French, and some Italian; and had access to a library 'through employment in the household of some lord'.[46] (That the author might actually have been the 'lord', using books that belonged to him, occurred to no one.) Yet the hypothesis removes several difficulties. The poem being composed in Lincolnshire dialect, this poet of rank may one day be identified. In about 1400 rather few people in that part of the world would know Italian and have had extensive political experience. Once again we indicate opportunities for literary detectives on Lincolnshire's nobility and gentry at the end of Richard II's reign.

The author's vision is further shown by his skill in giving shape to his narrative, as brought out by analysis.[47] There is a different take in observation on how Arthur's death was, for the alliterative poet, the 'necessary price to pay for historical credibility'; whereas the author of the stanzaic *Morte Arthure* divorced himself from 'the ineluctable process of time', so that his narrative 'ceases to be history' (whereas Malory has it both ways, providing an 'uncritical sense' that Arthur might return).[48] A more up-to-date perspective on the question appears in assertion on how the patriarchy epitomized by the King is 'not vulnerable to male aggression or female treachery'; only to 'the death of promise'.[49] More traditional is consideration of whether the text is to be regarded not as romance or even epic but 'tragedy'; one of many questions which make discussion of it 'a perennially fascinating activity'.[50] That very point is taken up in a complete chapter with comparison of *Morte Arthure* and the slightly earlier *Troilus and Criseyde*.[51] Elsewhere is consideration by another of its big subjects: war and medieval attitudes to war.[52]

More suggestive is a remark on the alliterative *Morte* as 'notable for the many British places' mentioned in it: Caerleon, Carlisle, Catterick, Cornwall, Dorset, Glastonbury, Sandwich, Wallingford, Watling Street, Winchester. Naturally, proper nouns are always useful for versifiers. They offer freedom and variety. Still, the critic's reference to relief of Roman diplomats on hearing 'the sound of the se and Sandwich belles' (line 490) when they flee abroad may tell us more.[53] The poem's numerous toponyms are consistent with authorship by an experienced traveller, not least on Sandwich, once a major trading and naval port (if now one of 'stranded pride', in Kipling's phrase). Also intriguing is a statement on *The Awntyrs off Arthure* (of the 1420s) as a romance which 'quotes from and alludes to both *Sir Gawain* [of 1387] and the *Morte Arthure*' (of about 1400), with obvious inferences for the intertextuality of these three 'northern Arthurian narratives'.[54] Again, a starting-point for researchers. So, too, for a thoughtful study of militarism, ending with a verdict on the unknown writer's 'ambivalently fatalistic vision' of the 'too often senseless bloodshed' in his narrative.[55] So, again (if for sharp disagreement with it), is a final claim that our not knowing the name of *Morte Arthure*'s author is because 'alliterative romance' was perceived 'as hostile to aristocratic claims to sovereignty'.[56] A strange remark. It goes flat in the face of a 1961 paper by Alfred Baugh (cited in the previous chapter) on the politics of *Sir Gawain and the Green Knight* and *Pearl*, which Baugh considered 'reactionary' (no surprise for the work of a Cheshire magnate). Baugh's reasoned conclusions will be a template for political analysis of a Lincolnshire gentlemen-poet in about 1400, with a military-literary-diplomatic background, who might then have composed *Morte Arthure*.

Although one Arthurian collection of essays has almost nothing on the text, we note acknowledgement of it there as a sole late work in the *Brut* tradition to gain 'anything like canonical status in English literature'.[57] After that, a complete edition with translation. It should be a cheering sight. Alas, its editors (working in a French-speaking milieu) tend to outdated vagueness on date and provenance. On the first we hear merely of the fourteenth century's *dernier tiers*; on the second, *l'ancienne zone anglo-danoise du Danelaw* and a society *des Midlands et du Nord*. Arguments for the years immediately around 1400, and for Lincolnshire, have not been heard. Still, the process of re-editing is useful in bringing problems to attention. Examples include the puzzling corrupted Mediterranean toponyms in lines 570-601 (many of which yield to those with a historical atlas).[58] Published in the same year and by the same academic press is a study which, in contrast, deserves the closest attention, not least on offering doubts on McIntosh's advocacy in 1962 for the Louth region, and modifying that to one for the poet's dialect as that of 'south Lincolnshire'.[59] That means an authorial quest for a retired military commander and experienced man of affairs in Boston or its hinterland; with Boston (still a working North Sea port) perhaps accounting for the many Scottish words in his vocabulary, thanks to mariners from Leith or Crail or Aberdeen who were seen and heard by England's east coast harbours?

Compared with the above, a paper of major significance, more recent offerings tend to the lightweight. Two critics remark on how the poem's Arthur is 'unique for his self-awareness of his own place in the typology'.[60] Still lighter are words, in a volume which (in general) cannot be recommended, on how *Morte Arthure* and *Sir Gawain and the Green Knight* can be 'termed "chronicle" romances'.[61] A poor substitute for what can really be said. Still, the alliterative *Morte Arthure*'s admirers can no longer complain of its neglect. The time is ripe for an in-depth account of the poem. If there is done for this work what Vinaver did for Malory, it will at last take its rightful place amongst the classics of English poetry.

Notes

1. *Morte Arthure*, ed. Edmund Brock (London, 1871), vii.

2. W. P. Ker, *English Literature: Medieval* (London, 1912), 24.

3. J. E. Wells, *A Manual of the Writings in Middle English* (New Haven, 1916), 36-8.

4. J. P. Oakden, *Alliterative Poetry in Middle English: A Survey of the Traditions* (Manchester, 1935), 35-8.

5. W. L. Renwick and Harold Orton, *The Beginnings of English Literature to Skelton* (London, 1939), 347, 391-2.

6. George Kane, *Middle English Literature* (London, 1951), 66-73.

7. Dorothy Everett, *Essays on Middle English Literature* (Oxford, 1955), 61-7.

8. J. L. N. O'Loughlin, 'The English Alliterative Romances', in *Arthurian Literature in the Middle Ages*, ed, R. S. Loomis (Oxford, 1959), 520-7.

9. Marie Borroff, *'Sir Gawain and the Green Knight': A Stylistic and Metrical Study* (New Haven, 1962), 100-1, 103-4.

10. Angus McIntosh, 'The Textual Transmission of the Alliterative *Morte Arthure*', in *English and Medieval Studies*, ed. Norman Davis and C. L. Wrenn (London, 1962), 231-9.

11. D. S. Brewer, 'the hoole book', in *Essays on Malory*, ed. J. A. W. Bennett (Oxford, 1963), 41-63.

12. D. S. Brewer, 'Courtesy and the *Gawain*-Poet', in *Patterns of Love and Courtesy*, ed John Lawlor (London, 1966), 54-85.

13. *Morte Arthure*, ed. John Finlayson (London, 1967), 15-20, 33-4.

14. Dieter Mehl, *The Middle English Romances of the Thirteenth and Fourteenth Centuries* (London, 1967), 192.

15. *The Works of Sir Thomas Malory*, ed. Eugène Vinaver, 2nd edn (Oxford, 1967), 1366-1405.

16. John Finlayson, 'The Concept of the Hero in "Morte Arthure"', in *Chaucer und seine Zeit*, ed. Arno Esch (Tübingen, 1968), 249-74.

17. Basil Cottle, *The Triumph of English 1350-1400* (London, 1969), 45,

75-80.

18. *English Historical Documents 1327-1485*, ed. A. R. Myers (London, 1969), 103.

19. G. T. Shepherd, 'Early Middle English Literature', in *The Middle Ages*, ed. W. F. Bolton (London, 1970), 67-106, at 129-32.

20. A. C. Spearing, *Criticism and Medieval Poetry*, 2nd edn (London, 1972), 24.

21. M. H. Keen, *England in the Later Middle Ages* (London, 1973), 139-42.

22. K. B. McFarlane, *The Nobility of Later Medieval England* (Oxford, 1973), 162-4.

23. John Stevens, *Medieval Romance* (London, 1973), 90-5.

24. *King Arthur's Death*, ed. Larry D. Benson (Indianapolis, 1974), xv.

25. *Le Morte Arthur*, ed. P. F. Hissiger (The Hague, 1975).

26. *The Alliterative Morte Arthure*, ed. Valerie Krishna (New York, 1976), 7-10.

27. Philippa Tristram, *Figures of Life and Death in Medieval English Literature* (London, 1976), 123.

28. Derek Pearsall, *Old English and Middle English Poetry* (London, 1977), 162-6.

29. Thorlac Turville-Petre, *The Alliterative Revival* (Cambridge, 1977), 103.

30. Terence McCarthy, 'The Sequence of Malory's Tales', in *Aspects of Malory*, ed. Toshiyuki Takamiya and Derek Brewer (Cambridge, 1981), 107-24.

31. Derek Brewer, *English Gothic Literature* (New York, 1983), 150-4.

32. *Morte Arthure*, ed. Mary Hamel (New York, 1984).

33. Derek Pearsall, *The Canterbury Tales* (London, 1985), 334.

34. J. A. W. Bennett, *Middle English Literature* (Oxford, 1986), 184-7.

35. Christopher Dean, *Arthur of England* (Toronto, 1987), 193 n. 14.

36. A. C. Spearing, *Readings in Medieval Poetry* (Cambridge, 1987), 140-1, 147.

37. Stephen Coote, *English Literature of the Middle Ages* (Harmondsworth, 1988), 234.

38. Dhira B. Mahoney, 'Alliterative *Morte Arthure*', in *The New Arthurian Encyclopedia*, ed. Norris J. Lacy (Chicago, 1991), 5-6.

39. Lee Patterson, 'The Romance of History', in *Medieval English Poetry*, ed. Stephanie Trigg (London, 1993), 217-49.

40. P. J. C. Field, 'Malory's Mordred and the *Morte Arthure*', in *Romance Reading on the Book*, ed. Jennifer Fellows, Rosalind Field, Gillian Rogers, Judith Weiss (Cardiff, 1996), 77-93.

41. Malcolm Hebron, *The Medieval Siege* (Oxford, 1997), 63.

42. Beate Schmolke-Hasselmann, *The Evolution of Arthurian Romance* (Cambridge, 1998), 287.

43. Michael J. Bennett, 'The Historical Background', in *A Companion to the 'Gawain' Poet*, ed. Derek Brewer and Jonathan Gibson (Cambridge, 1997), 71-90, at 80.

44. Norris J. Lacy and Geoffrey Ashe, *The Arthurian Handbook*, 2nd edn (New York, 1997), 123.

45. W. A. Davenport, *Chaucer and His English Contemporaries* (London, 1998), 183.

46. Lesley Johnson, 'Dynasty Romance: The Alliterative *Morte Arthure*', in *The Arthur of the English*, ed. W. R. J. Barron (Cardiff, 1999), 90-100.

47. Rosamund Allen, 'Performance and Structure in *The Alliterative Morte Arthure*', in *New Perspectives on Middle English Texts*, ed. Susan Powell and Jeremy J. Smith (Cambridge, 2000), 17-29.

48. Andrew King, *'The Faerie Queene' and Middle English Romance* (Oxford, 2000), 123.

49. Felicity Riddy, 'Middle English Romance: Family, Marriage, Intimacy', in *The Cambridge Companion to Medieval Romance*, ed. Roberta L. Krueger (Cambridge, 2000), 235-52, at 246.

50. Derek Pearsall, *Arthurian Romance* (Oxford, 2003), 79.

51. Tony Davenport, *Medieval Narrative* (Oxford, 2004), 210-37.

52. Andrew Lynch, '"Peace is Good After War"', in *Writing War*, ed. Corinne Saunders, Françoise Le Saux, Neil Thomas (Cambridge, 2004), 127-46.

53. Siân Echard, 'Insular Romance', in *The Oxford Handbook of Medieval Literature in English*, ed. Elaine Treharne and Greg Walter (Oxford, 2010), 160-80, at 169.

54. Rosalind Field, 'Arthurian and Courtly Romance', in *A Companion to Medieval Poetry*, ed. Corinne Saunders (Chichester, 2010), 308-28, at

317.

55. Alex Mueller, 'The Historiography of the Dragon', in *Studies in the Age of Chaucer*, xxxii (2010), 295-324.

56. Yuri Fuwa, 'A "Just War"? A Further Reassessment of the Alliterative *Morte Arthure*', in *War and Peace: Critical Issues in European Societies and Literature 800-1800*, ed. Albrecht Classen and Madia Margolis (Berlin, 2011), 349-75.

57. Julia Marvin, 'The English *Brut* Tradition', in *Companion to Arthurian Literature*, ed. Helen Fulton (Chichester, 2012), 221-51, at 232.

58. *Les 'Mort d'Arthur' moyen-anglaises en vers*, ed. Colette Stévanovitch and Anne Mathieu (Turnhout, 2017), 265-6, 312.

59. Thorlac Turville-Petre, 'The Vocabulary of the Alliterative *Morte Arthure*', in *Pursuing Middle English Manuscripts and Their Texts*, ed. Simon Horobin and Aditi Nafde (Turnhout, 2017), 43-61, at 51.

60. Audrey Martin and David Mason, 'Arthur Among the Nine Worthies', in *The Arthurian World*, ed. Victoria Coldham-Fussell, Miriam Edlich-Muth, Renée Ward (London, 2022), 49-68, at 62.

61. Victoria Flood, 'A Romance of England and Wales', in *Medieval Welsh Literature and Its European Contexts*, ed. Victoria Flood (Cambridge, 2024), 114-30, at 122.

CHAPTER NINE

THE AWNTYRS OFF ARTHURE

The last Arthurian poem dealt with in this book comes from the 1420s and was composed in the English dialect of Cumbria. *The Awntyrs off Arthure* (= 'The Adventures of Arthur') is a text so Northern in dialect and setting that early critics regarded its unknown author (very likely a cleric) as Scottish. He will yet have been a Lake District poet with a story of eerie encounters between the living and the dead upon Cumbrian moorland. Nine centuries after the historical Arthur fell in battle at Castlesteads or *Camlan*, not far from Carlisle (his fame leaving permanent traces in the region's ballads and place-names), a local writer took inspiration from his legend to produce a narrative which is at once a ghost story, a call to repentance, a celebration of married love, and a political morality intended for the Nevilles and other families that dominated Border politics. Conscious of the vanity or *néant* of human wishes, he presented an Arthur challenged or confronted. Great poetry, then, came out of the Lake District and Borders long before Wordsworth and Scott discovered their possibilities. *The Awntyrs off Arthure* has another aspect worth noting: its twentieth-century rise in reputation. It is underlined in a backhand or negative way by Ker, never mentioning the poem in his study of the period, despite an enthusiasm for Northern literature (Border ballads, Icelandic saga) natural for a Scot.[1] A contrast to our own day, when it is regarded as one of the strangest and most powerful of medieval English poems (comparable in that to *St Erkenwald*, another minor masterpiece on death and after-death, in this case by a Cheshire author of the 1390s).

If Ker ignored this Cumberland poem of the supernatural, Wells gave a full account of it, owing to a fortunate (if mistaken) belief in its belonging to the middle or late fourteenth century and not the early fifteenth (later than his chosen period). He gave details on its four surviving manuscripts and (of 1792) its *editio princeps*. Title notwithstanding, it is 'largely to the glory of Gawain' (not Arthur) and in one version consists of 702 alliterative lines. Its plot is this. Arthur sets off from Carlisle to go hunting. Guinevere 'rides out', attended by Gawain. A 'terrific storm' breaks out, a 'horrible female' appears, 'covered with toads and snakes'. It is Guinevere's mother, come back from the dead, urging the Queen to abandon her sinful life, and requesting masses for own soul, in order to help free it from Purgatory and to reach Heaven. The ghost also makes prophecies (in the manner of ghosts). Arthur is 'too courteous'; a 'knight by treason' will usurp his throne; King and Round Table will meet their doom on the Cornish coast. The storm clears, the poem's second part commences. Arthur and his court go to supper. While they dine, a fine lady and 'gorgeously armed' knight make their entrance. He is Galeron of Galloway (in Scotland's far south-west), seeking return of his domains, which Arthur has unjustly granted to Gawain. Galeron and Gawain engage in combat; the latter has the best of it; eventually, the Queen induces Arthur to stop the fighting. Galeron yields up his rights, but Arthur achieves a solution by regranting his lands to him, compensating Gawain with estates in Wales and Ireland and France. Everyone moves to Carlisle, Galeron marries the beautiful lady, becomes one of Arthur's knights, all ends happily. Wells commented further on two headaches for scholars today: the major differences between the four manuscript copies (in part due to oral transmission), and scribal miscopying of place-names. (It leads to some curious explanations by editors.) Wells also mentioned the text's lack of a known source; its poet-preacher's 'eye for color and glitter and show' (useful for one acquainted with the nobility's dames and horses and banners, but who still regarded the pride of life as play-acting); and his powers of description, whether for the storm, the ghost, hunting, banqueting, or the 'splendid' Galeron and his lady.[2]

The poem has faults. If Oakden praised it, he (like Wells and others) thought its Arthurian title misleading, because it is really 'concerned much more with Gawayn'; he added that condemnation of two major sins (lust, cupidity) was not a natural theme for Arthurian verse, especially its alliterative branch, so that 'form and construction' suffer. Still, Oakden followed S. O. Andrew (in 1929) for there being more cohesion than supposed. In the first part the spirit condemns Arthur's lust for war (as well as Guinevere's more conventional lust); in the second, that same royal belligerence has dispossessed Galeron, who with courage appeals for justice and gets it. Oakden also noted how, if the bard was poor on construction, he could 'describe vividly and imaginatively' varied things: hunting, Gawain and Guinevere at dalliance below a laurel tree, sudden darkness and thunder and lightning, an apparition, a banquet, an uninvited knight and his lady, a trial by combat; all appear with 'colour' and 'minute detail' and 'psychological' realism. So with a dead and blackened woman wreathed in snakes, gliding along, her eyes glowing *as a glede* or live coal. Her screams make dogs bolt for the wood; sensing evil, bold hunting-hounds flinch; 'birdes' on the branches 'skryke' or cry aloud.[3] Like *Sir Gawain and the Green Knight* (with its film version of 2021), *The Awntyrs off Arthure* has possibilities for a Hollywood or other director. It has more to offer than the faint praise of 'a very fair vigorous romance' suggests.[4]

The 1950s were a period of critical discord or dissonance, apparent from three accounts: cold, then gushy, cold again. Coldness appears in a condemnation of its 'minor' author, possessing 'too much talent and too little art' and telling a 'weak and meagre' tale.

Among terms that follow are 'static', 'objectionable', 'retarding', 'derivative', 'boredom'.[5] This languid dismissal was thereafter followed by bouncy neo-paganism, with the romance promoted as 'masterly', having 'splendidly easy' art and 'exuberant' imagery, the result being 'magnificent poetry', often 'dazzling' or 'glowing'. More precisely and helpfully, the analysis also alerted us to folklore and myth. Gawain guides the Queen until *vnder a lorre ho lighte* (she dismounted to rest below a laurel), and we hear how in such narratives trees were known for 'influence of the supernatural'. They were risky places to take repose. So it happens. The light fails, as if it were 'mydniʒt myrke'. From the nearby Tarn Wadling (now merely an area of damp grassland) arises an apparition in 'the lyknes of Lucyfere', moving swiftly and with a terrible clamour towards the pair (and reminding us how lochs in Celtic tradition are exits from the Other World).[6] The poet had a feel for the uncanny, so that (using work by Kenneth Jackson and others) one can here discover elements paralleled in early Welsh and Irish texts; for the Border region was rich in Arthurian and other Celtic tradition, Carlisle being a Cumbric-speaking city until the twelfth century, and Galloway (to the north-west) a Gaelic-speaking area until the seventeenth.[7] Even if Arthur, sixth-century North British hero, tends to be absent from the present romance's centre, he belonged originally to Strathclyde and Cumbria (not Wales, Cornwall, Brittany). The 1950s ended with another somewhat cool dismissal, of a mere three paragraphs, if with interesting comments on how *The Awntyrs* borrows from the alliterative *Morte Arthure* and (for its hunt scene) *Sir Gawain and the Green Knight*, a result of the latter perhaps being that Gawain, not Arthur, becomes its 'chief character'. If the author is described as 'naïve' in joining (supposedly) ill-matched tales of Guinevere's mother and of Galeron, he admittedly had 'a not inconsiderable art', his difficult stanza-form being 'well handled', his descriptions having 'vigour and realism'.[8]

After veering perceptions of the 1950s, some ideas (and mis-conceptions) of the 1970s. First is description of *The Awntyrs* as of the 'late fourteenth' or 'early fifteenth' centuries (only the latter is correct), and influence acknowledged on it (as regards 'Arthur's career and change of fortune') of the alliterative *Morte Arthure*, if with doubts on any debt to *Sir Gawain and the Green Knight* (the hunting scene of Arthur in Cumberland perhaps being quite 'in-dependent' of it); plus stress on its 'courtly' and 'moral' aspects. The author had 'no mean skill'; he enhanced his story by setting it in places which his audience knew. Despite the chorus of critics on the text as about Gawain rather than Arthur, the poet's lavish words on the King (when enthroned in splendour) indicate artistic subtlety. When Galeron asks for royal redress of grievance, there is a pause before he replies. The majesty of Arthur, 'soueraynest sir sitting in sete', is described in detail, if with an implication (we are told) that 'the value of all this is doubt, since Arthur has been called covetous'.[9] Later writers will bring the poem closer to a 'courtly' audience (and its moral failings), gathered for a magnifi-cent wedding at Carlisle in the 1420s. They also call off a literary wild-goose chase unwittingly prompted by Andrew Wyntoun, canon of Aberdeen, who mentioned an *Awntyr of Gawane* by 'Hucheon of the Aulde Realle'.[10] Wyntoun dying in about 1420 and our Cumbrian text postdating that, it cannot be by 'Hucheon' or any other Scot. It will be by an unidentified Englishman, per-haps a dignitary of Carlisle Cathedral in the 1420s. It similarly rules out statements on how *The Awntyrs* belongs to the 'period 1370-1400'.[11] Not so. It is of Henry VI's reign, not Richard II's.

Matters improved for the romance in 1974 with a new edition. It remains useful, even if one reads some of it with doubts: that the poem lacks 'topical allusion'; that the date of *Sir Gawain and the Green Knight* has no 'degree of precision' (undermining any quest for its influence); that *Morte Arthure* has links with 'Edward I' (an error for 'Edward III'). Preferable is a verdict on how *The Awntyrs* is probably of the 1410s.[12] It is not far from the 1420s proposed by

Ros Allen. Thereafter, Derek Pearsall (ruling out a Scottish author, while recognizing that poet had in mind contemporary 'relations between Scotland and England'). He once more observed
that the title is misleading, 'for the two adventures concern
Gawain', not Arthur. The King's frailties are yet made clear by the
'fearful wraith' who comes (her form blackened by purgatorial
fires) to denounce his 'overweening ambition and aggression',
qualities which are also a 'hollow and ruthless' presence in the tale
of Galeron. A connection with the alliterative Green Knight romance and *Morte Arthure* is taken as 'obvious' (but how exactly?);
each of them 'questions Arthur's militaristic values'.[13] The last
judgement is too simple. The clerical *Awntyrs* Poet no doubt held
military qualities in low regard; but the *Gawain* Poet hardly so,
being apparently a royal appointee who commanded English
troops fighting the native Irish. He was no left-of-centre anti-mil-
itarist egalitarian liberal. We shall be on firmer ground for that
with the poet of *The Awntyrs*, unimpressed by worldly show, and
with a sharp eye for the violence and chicanery that enabled it. His
Arthur is condemned in a way that the Arthur of *Sir Gawain* is
not.

On that matter, Turville-Petre offered gloom. For him, the
poet cast pearls before uncomprehending swine. Arthur and the
people of Camelot learn nothing. Even though a woman has (in T.
S. Eliot's phrase) 'come from the dead, / Come back to tell you
all', the results are meagre, pessimistic. Guinevere's life leads to
disaster, the Round Table is doomed. The 'proud knights and the
exquisite ladies continue with their struggles and extravagance as
if death and dissolution' were 'never to be'. If a 'gate has been
opened, Arthur's courtiers will not look outside.'[14] True or false,
this is more to the point than a belief that *The Awntyrs* belongs to
'Scottish poetry'.[15] A good Scot would not give so positive a picture of an 'English' Arthur, generously rewarding Gawain with
land outside England (in Glamorgan, Dyfed, Leinster, Brittany).

Jack Bennett left an admirable exposition of our Cumberland text, stressing the 'pertinent theological questions' asked in its first part (on 'the sin most grievous to God', for example), and noting the wrath to come for Arthur and his court. In the clear sky of romance, a cloud 'no bigger than a man's hand' has risen. It 'will grow to blot out the sun' and the whole world.[16] For all that, the forebodings of Turville-Petre and Bennett were not shared by another, who (in a volume with many acute observations) stressed the religious sources for the narrative's first part, where Arthur has 'virtually no role', but how in the second part he is 'a wise, generous, and prudent ruler who is firmly in charge of events'.[17] This is partly true. But if Camelot's *doughty bydene* (line 305) or 'valiant company' were so excellent, one wonders why 'one went unto them from the dead' (Luke 16:30) and bad them 'Fede folke for my sake' (line 319), like Lazarus, eating scraps from a rich man's table? Rosamund Allen was here forthright. The poem is 'a satire on the chivalric ethos cast in the form of courtly romance'.[18] Her radicalism deserves notice. One sharing it (in an essay on Arthurian romance-types) took *The Awntyrs off Arthure* and *Sir Gawain and the Green Knight* to be works equally 'critical of the Arthurian system of values'.[19] Yet care is needed. Differences matter more than similarities. The Cheshire poem is by a court insider, the Cumberland one by an outsider. That puts nuance on words of a contributor who (even if misdating the narrative to the 'late fourteenth century') notices 'unusual' features of the latter text, remarkable for the 'social criticism' of its dialogue of Gawain and a spirit condemned *in wo for to welle* (line 316) or 'boil in [purgatorial] anguish'.[20]

Further substantial advances on its audience and hence its date and background again came from Ros Allen, who envisaged those hearers as 'uneasily aware of the instability of power and wealth' and related them (and the text) to celebrations for a noble wedding or betrothal in 1424 or 1425.[21] It is a real step forward. It contrasts with asides on the romance which (one fears) tell us little.[22] Ros

Allen then noted the rise in our Cumberland text's prestige after Hanna's Manchester edition of 1974. Disobliging remarks on construction dwindled; significance was now perceived in 'the crowned king Arthur in the mid-point of the extant text', implying a sovereignty central to structure and theme alike; and there is further setting-out of associations in 1425 or so with the Nevilles of the Scottish March and with James I (d. 1437), King of Scots.[23] Small wonder that the poet emphasized redress for a Scottish knight. It does more justice to him than Sir Walter Scott's statements on how *Galoran of Galloway* (his name for the present poem) was by a fellow-Scot, so that a northern English text found itself 'dragged across the border to join' real Scottish ones like *Gawan and Gologras*.[24] Also misplaced are observations on the 'decomposing corpse of Guinevere's mother'.[25] They hardly deepen our understanding of the text, not least as regards souls in Purgatory, whose hope of salvation is certain (and can be speeded by prayers and other good works of the living).

After souls and cadavers, manuscripts. In a collection of essays on late medieval England, the four surviving ones of *The Awntyrs* (all of the fifteenth century) are given professional attention, with stress on how they demonstrate the romance's popularity, even in London, where it appears with writings by fashionable south-eastern authors (Gower, Hoccleve, Lydgate), which is a tribute to its readability, despite the textual havoc which an Essex scribe wreaked on its Cumberland dialect and toponyms.[26] The manuscript quartet (variously kept at libraries in Lincoln, Lambeth, Princeton, Oxford) is absorbing proof for the Arthurian legend in parts of England far from the British west and north. Despite warnings in its first half on 'the approaching downfall of the Round Table' as a result of greed, that popularity was due to 'a midpoint where Arthur is enthroned' and a second episode containing not the expected fall but 'a moment of triumph', the result of Arthur's 'noble generosity'.[27] Yes. Guests at a wedding-feast would not thank the *Awntyrs* Poet for a chronicle of catastrophe and death.

Attentive auditors or readers would still have qualified Arthur's 'noble generosity'. He is not so foolish as to grant domains in England to Gawain. They were in South Wales, being the lordship of Oysterlow (near Carmarthen) and Caerphilly Castle (in Glamorgan), together with the domains of Wexford and Waterford in south-east Ireland, as well as two 'baronrées in Bretayne' (= Brittany), where some of these toponyms (lines 664-71) have been problematic. Conclusion: Arthur was generous with territories of other peoples, the places named in Glamorgan and beyond having implications for families close (it seems) to the author in 1424-5.

The text was then defined as 'well-informed and non-deferential', an 'original and subversive remaking of Arthurian tradition'.[28] True. It shows yet again the shifting rewritings of Arthur, king and commander, which are our basic theme. Still, its 'subversive' radicalism is tempered, and of a literary-moral kind, rather than political. It offers no more than a brave preacher would think appropriate at a wedding-reception for those of rank. Hence his 'thoughtful interest in mutability and noble lordship'.[29]

Knowledge of what literary historians call 'background' will avert critical stumbling. It comes out as concerns a survey of the poem and what its author meant by it, much of which prompts assent, if often with the reaction 'Yes, but'. This is so with its opening epithet on the text as 'very uncourtly'; comments on 'the essential role' of women for it; and its 'happy ending'.[30] They provoke thought. On 'very uncourtly' we say that *The Awntyrs off Arthure* is not a manifesto for a Cumbrian rerun of the Peasants' Revolt. It is a story about courtiers for courtiers (male and female) and surely by a man who (if not himself a court chaplain) knew court chaplains. From that point of view *The Awntyrs* is very courtly indeed. Its message is yet a singular one for such a text. It preaches justice and temperance. Hence the role of women and (for the while) a happy ending. The original audience would contain fashionable men and women who expected entertainment. That is why the author, whatever his views on court morals, needed accommodation and restraint to make his narrative a success (that success being amply proved by its circulation throughout England).

So we have a balancing-act in verse. On the one hand are stern warnings, including one to Gawain: 'In a slake [valley, hollow] þou shal be slayne' (line 298). On the other is consideration for those listening, not least in 'debate over the culpability' of Arthur, when his ultimate fall as 'punishment for sin' should not have 'privileged' treatment.[31] Tact on the question is still imperative. Getting back to the grimness, we note that Guinevere's mother is most unlike Other World faeries encountered in romance (amongst them a *Mabinogi* tale from the 1120s of Prince Pwyll, or Breton lays like *Sir Orfeo*).[32] The poet has put his own twist on these beings, who in Welsh and Irish tradition inhabit an underground realm of feasting and every happiness. On artistic tactfulness, the writer's 'sense of an ending' is further emphasized, so that surgeons quickly *saned* (693) or healed the wounded, and a wedding took place with gifts and *garsons* (697) or treasures. Effective preachers and writers are skilled when it comes to impact. Hence this 'sermon dressed up as a romance'.[33] It was not, however, a composition of before 1400, as one scholar imagines.[34]

More up-to-date on that score is a further study, firmly relating the poem to Cumberland places mentioned in it.[35] Then comes regress with an edition reproducing errors in that of Hanna forty years previously, so that 'Criffones Castelles' (line 667) is again related to Crieff, Scotland.[36] This although lines immediately previously to it allude to Glamorgan and Wales; in a poem of Anglo-Scottish reconciliation, an English ruler would not grant an Englishman territory in Scotland; Crieff is not known for its castle; and Ros Allen and others had recognized that 'Criffones' is a corrupt rendering of *Caerphilly*, name of a castle squarely in Glamorgan. It offers lessons on textual criticism. There is a further lesson in a study of the alliterative *Morte Arthure* and how the *Awntyrs* Poet 'relied on it considerably' when writing his own poem.[37] It was a great help for the composition of intricate alliterative verse. Naturally, the two texts differ greatly on Arthur the warlord and his territorial aggressions: a revealing contrast.

It leads us to a stimulating Marxian analysis, developing work by Jill Mann and Ad Putter for class and power and value in *Sir Gawain and the Green Knight*. If their attempt to make out the Cheshire romance's audience as London knights and merchants is quite mistaken, a comparable approach to the Cumbrian text is still worthwhile. It confronts us with financial and political facts, even if we reject the proposition that Camelot is doomed because it suffers 'economic mismanagement' and cannot 'extend its gifts far enough'.[38] Naturally, the closer we focus on the poet and his mentality, the better we shall understand what he said. To the ideologies that figure above we can add that of colonialism, now recognized in comments on 'colonial tensions' in the text, with Guinevere's mother denouncing 'Arthur's wars of conquest' and with Galeron of Galloway (*not*, as stated, Galway) at its ending restored to his Scottish domains, Gawain being compensated with lands in Wales (also, Ireland and Brittany).[39] In a chapter on *The Awntyrs*, attention is paid to it (after Rosamund Allen) as a tract for the times, namely those of 1424-5, with a *rapprochement* (between London and Edinburgh) sealed by dynastic marriage with the royal house of Scotland.[40]

All texts belong to their age, if sometimes not just to their age. So with *The Awntyrs off Arthure*. In 1996, Ros Allen related it to the marriage of James I to Joan Beaufort the younger in February 1424. She was niece to Henry IV and hence a kinswoman of the powerful Ralph Neville, Earl of Westmorland, who had married Henry IV's half-sister. These and other events would place the poem in the period 1424-5 and suggest that Ralph perhaps commissioned it then from a cleric of St Mary's Priory, Carlisle, for marriage or betrothal festivities. They were possibly those for the youngest of his twenty-three children, Cecily, who was to marry Richard of York (1411-60). On dating, the book of 2023 cited above mentions a further event, the execution (for treason) on 25 May 1425 at Stirling of the Duke of Albany, two of his sons, and his father-in-law, the Earl of Lennox. A macabre occurrence, which may explain why the Lennox region figures (at line 420) in the poem, also locating its composition to between May 1425 and the following October, when Ralph Neville died. (We may add that that another Joan, Ralph's Countess, collected books by authors including Chaucer and Rolle, so that *The Awntyrs* perhaps gained circulation through her influence.) Once fixed securely in all its aspects (date, provenance, authorship), the romance will in any case all the more appear a radical or deviant reading of the Arthur legend, re-using his story to produce a critique of royal violence and outrage and lawlessness, so that it is a literary novelty: a narrative embodying unArthurian approaches to the customary Arthurian *Realpolitik*.

Notes

1. W. P. Ker, *English Literature: Medieval* (London, 1912).
2. J. E. Wells, *A Manual of the Writings in Middle English* (New Haven, 1916), 54-7.
3. J. P. Oakden, *Alliterative Poetry in Middle English: A Survey of the Traditions* (Manchester, 1935), 47-8.
4. W. L. Renwick and Harold Orton, *The Beginnings of English Literature to Skelton* (London, 1939), 392.
5. George Kane. *Middle English Literature* (London, 1951), 52-3.
6. John Speirs, *Medieval English Poetry* (London, 1957), 219.
7. K. H. Jackson, 'The Sources for the Life of St Kentigern', in *Studies in the Early British Church*, ed. N. K. Chadwick (Cambridge, 1958), 273-357.
8. J. L. N. O'Loughlin, 'The English Alliterative Romances', in *Arthurian Literature in the Middle Ages*, ed, R. S. Loomis (Oxford, 1959), 520-7.
9. D. J. Williams, 'Alliterative Poetry', in *The Middle Ages*, ed. W. F. Bolton (London, 1970), 107-58, at 132-3.
10. R. M. Wilson, *The Lost Literature of Medieval England*, 2nd edn (London, 1970), 108.
11. J. A. Burrow, *Ricardian Poetry* (London, 1971), 65.
12. *The Awntyrs off Arthure at the Terne Wathelyn*, ed. Ralph Hanna III (Manchester, 1974), 50-2.
13. Derek Pearsall, *Old English and Middle English Poetry* (London, 1977), 186, 321 nn. 71-2.
14. Thorlac Turville-Petre, *The Alliterative Revival* (Cambridge, 1977), 65.
15. *Anglo-Scottish Literary Relations 1430-1550*, ed. Gregory Katzmann (Cambridge, 1980), 8.
16. J. A. W. Bennett, *Middle English Literature* (Oxford, 1986), 178-81.
17. Christopher Dean, *Arthur of England* (Toronto, 1987), 79-80.
18. Rosamund Allen, 'Some Sceptical Observations on the Editing of *The Awntyrs off Arthure*', in *Manuscripts and Texts*, ed. Derek Pearsall

(Cambridge, 1987), 5-25, at 5.

19. Joerg O. Fichte, 'Grappling With Arthur', in *Poetics: Theory and Practice in Medieval English Literature*, ed. Piero Boitani and Anna Torti (Cambridge, 1991), 149-63, at 157.

20. Erick S. Kooper, '*Awntyrs off Arthure at the Terne Wathelyn, The*', in *The New Arthurian Encyclopedia*, ed. Norris J. Lacy (Chicago, 1991), 26-7.

21. Rosamund Allen, '*The Awntyrs off Arthure*: Jests and Jousts', in *Romance Reading on the Book*, ed. Jennifer Fellows, Rosalind Field, Gillian Rogers, Judith Weiss (Cardiff, 1996), 129-42.

22. Anne Rooney, 'The Hunts in *Sir Gawain and the Green Knight*', in *A Companion to the 'Gawain' Poet*, ed. Derek Brewer and Jonathan Gibson (Cambridge, 1997), 157-63.

23. Rosamund Allen, '*The Awntyrs off Arthure*', in *The Arthur of the English*, ed. W. R. J. Barron (Cardiff, 1999), 150-5.

24. David Matthews, *The Making of Middle English* (Minneapolis, 1999), 65.

25. Margaret Robson, 'From Beyond the Grave', in *The Spirit of Medieval English Popular Romance*, ed. Ad Putter and Jane Gilbert (Harlow, 2000), 219-36.

26. Andrew Taylor, 'Authors, Scribes, Patrons, and Books', in *The Idea of the Vernacular*, ed. Jocelyn Wogan-Brown, Nicholas Watson, Andrew Taylor, Ruth Evans (Exeter, 1999), 353-65.

27. A. C. Spearing, *Textual Subjectivity* (Oxford, 2005), 202.

28. Rosalind Field, 'Romance', in *The Oxford History of Literary Translation in English: Volume I, To 1550*, ed. Roger Ellis (Oxford, 2008), 296-331.

29. Douglas Gray, *Later Medieval English Literature* (Oxford, 2008), 386.

30. K. S. Whetter, *Understanding Genre and Medieval Romance* (Aldershot, 2008), 85-8.

31. Rosalind Field, 'Arthurian and Courtly Romance', in *A Companion to Medieval Poetry*, ed. Corinne Saunders (Chichester, 2010), 308-28, at 318.

32. Corinne Saunders, *Magic and the Supernatural in Medieval English Romance* (Cambridge, 2010), 223.

33. Siân Echard, 'Insular Romance', in *The Oxford Handbook of Medieval Literature in English*, ed. Elaine Treharne and Greg Walter (Oxford,

2010), 160-80, at 175.

34. Roger Dalrymple, 'Sir Gawain in Middle English Romance', in *A Companion to Arthurian Literature*, ed. Helen Fulton (Chichester, 2012), 265-77, at 265.

35. Jean E. Jost, 'Marshy Spaces in the Middle English *Awntyrs off Arthure at the Terne Wathelyne*', in *Rural Space in the Middle Ages and Early Modern Age*, ed. Albrecht Classen (Berlin, 2012), 589-606.

36. *Mittelenglische Artusromanzen*, ed. Jörg O. Fichte (Stuttgart, 2014), 197 n.

37. Thorlac Turville-Petre, 'The Vocabulary of the Alliterative *Morte Arthure*', in *Pursuing Middle English Manuscripts and Their Texts*, ed. Simon Horobin and Aditi Nafde (Turnhout, 2017), 43-61, at 45.

38. Walter Wadiak, *Savage Economy* (Notre Dame, 2017), 36.

39. Kenneth Hodges, 'Spenser, Malory, and Regionalism', in *The Arthurian World*, ed. Victoria Coldham-Fussell, Miriam Edlich-Muth, Renée Ward (London, 2022), 83-94, at 85.

40. A. Breeze, *The Historical Arthur and the 'Gawain' Poet* (Lanham, 2023), 117-36.

CHAPTER TEN

SIR THOMAS MALORY'S *MORTE DARTHURE*

With Malory's *Morte Darthure* we reach our story's end and take leave of medieval Britain's Arthur. It lends an image, as we look at Latin scraps on Arthur's origins and then Malory's tome, of colossal growth. A narrative acorn most unexpectedly became a massive narrative oak, of lasting qualities; for, if Sir Thomas Malory (d. 1471) was unfortunate in his life, he was fortunate thereafter. His work was printed by Caxton in 1485 and has never been forgotten; he has been admired by poets and artists; he created an enduring vision of England's past; in 1934 a manuscript copy of his book was a sensational discovery. Study of his life, sources, text, style, structure, coherence of narration, influence: they leave plenty to say, especially because Arthur is by now no longer a dominant figure. The Arthurian trunk of this oak is (even if central) often hard to see. It is obscured by dozens of leafy knightly boughs, their exploits hiding those of Arthur himself, as was not the case for earlier writers.

So we begin with a second acorn: Ker's observation on Arthur and how 'it is from Layamon, ultimately, that all the later versions – Malory's and Tennyson's – are derived.'[1] A continuity over seven centuries in English poetry, and then prose, and then poetry again. Wise (and less wise) things have been said on the way. There is an obvious amendment to Ker's dictum in pointing out Malory's debt to France. Amongst his many French sources was the very popular

Romance of Lancelot, of the thirteenth century's first quarter and later appearing as part of what was formerly called the 'Vulgate Cycle' (now the 'Lancelot-Grail Cycle').[2] That collection of tales had an interesting history, being 'conflated with a long prose Tristan in a fresh compilation' (attributed to a Robert de Boron, otherwise unknown) and surviving in substantial fragments only. Malory owed dramatic incidents to it, such as Arthur's receiving Excalibur 'from a hand in a lake', or his attempt to kill the infant Mordred by setting him adrift in a boat with 'children born on the same day' (but Mordred escapes). Chambers referred in addition to strange Celtic symptoms perceived by some in *Le Morte Darthure* (claims that would have dumbfounded its author), with Arthur, for example, seen as originally an Irish sprite or fairy-king, a notion that he rightly considered 'valueless'.[3]

Other points on Malory were made in the 1930s by the egregiously confident but otherwise dissimilar figures of C. S. Lewis (at Oxford) and G. G. Coulton (at Cambridge). Both commented on class. Lewis noted on how, while Malory's knights defend ladies, lesser women seem fair game, so that in his third book a milkmaid tells Arthur and Merlin how, when she was going to milk the cows, she met a 'stern knight' who *'half by force'* (Lewis's italics) overcame her and she was now surely a maid no longer.[4] Coulton, learned and fierce and (despite the opening words of Belloc's verses on him) in no way 'remote and ineffectual', devoted a half-chapter to Malory. His stress (natural for a historian) was not on dreams but society, its preoccupations supposedly discernable in *Le Morte Darthure*. If, in Malory's text, knights of the 'Table Round' swore 'always to flee treason' and other crimes, and 'always to do ladies, damsels, and gentlewomen succour upon pain of death', Coulton cited a 1922 pamphlet by Chambers on how Malory knew that Arthurian theory was at odds with fifteenth-century reality, as with the great gulf fixed between lord and churl (or lady and wench). Hence a masterpiece that is 'wonderful' in containing 'violent antitheses' of the moral and its opposite within 'the

harmony of a single mind'; complexities arising because by Malory's day the 'knight-errantry' of the twelfth century was dead,
killed (we are told) by 'the practical business side' of the Hundred
Years War.[5]

After generalizations, facts. Eugène Vinaver, great scholar, was
cited for identification of the authorial Sir Thomas Malory as a man
from Newbold Revel, born in about 1408 and dying in 1471. (Newbold Revel is a place by Stratton under Fosse, a village north-west
of Rugby, in the English Midlands.) Crucial for that Warwickshire
knight is *Le Morte Darthure*'s colophon, giving his name and rank
and his completing the book in the ninth year 'of the reygne of kyng
edward the fourth' (= March 1469-March 1470). Until a manuscript
(its first and last gatherings missing) was found at Winchester, the
only source was the edition printed in 1485 by William Caxton and
by him 'devyded in to xxi bookes', subdivided into chapters: convenient for readers, if creating obstacles to grasping Malory's purpose. Reprinted in 1498, 1529, 1557, 1585 (?), 1634, Caxton's version meant that Malory has never lacked readers.[6]

In his old age, Chambers provided a convenient introduction
to Malory's life, sources, style, publishing history. He began with
a familiar attitude on the waning of the medieval spirit, Caxton
allegedly putting Malory into print owing to a 'nostalgia for a de-
cayed chivalry', and added that the sole intact copy of his edition
is in the Pierpont Morgan Library, New York. Caxton, as noted
above, divided the text into books and chapters and provided its
title of *Le Morte Darthure*, which (a) does violence to French
grammar and (b) seems lifted from the alliterative *Morte Arthure*,
source for one part only. It is inaccurate twice over. Puzzlement at
Caxton's treatment of Malory was largely dispersed in 1934, when
W. F. Oakeshott (later vice-chancellor of Oxford University) discovered an almost complete manuscript (now at the British Library) in the Fellows' Library of Winchester College. Its text is so
different from Caxton's that it was hardly 'the one which he used'
(which is true, if with a further twist added in recent years).

Chambers stated that Malory's real title for his version was *The Book of King Arthur and his Noble Knights of the Round Table*, and listed its eight parts thus: the Coming of Arthur; the War with Rome; Lancelot; Gareth; Tristram; the Sangreal; the Knight of the Cart ('again on Lancelot'); the Death of Arthur. Most of this came from what Malory calls a 'Freynshe booke' which 'cannot be precisely identified' but was probably a fifteenth-century compilation deriving from an 'original prose cycle' two centuries older. That cycle incorporated work by Geoffrey of Monmouth, Wace, Chrétien de Troyes, Robert de Boron (much of it otherwise lost), Cistercian writers (on the Grail). Malory used the English alliterative *Morte Arthure* as well (in a version different from the Thornton Manuscript's), with the Winchester Malory proving that Caxton smoothed away rugged regular repetitions retained by Malory himself; who further translated the tale of Gareth from a French original of which (we hear) nothing else is known. Assimilating and coordinating materials so disparate is a task for a machine, not a human being, however gifted, and certainly not a prisoner in Newgate (which is what Malory was, apparently). He cut, he added; but anomalies and loose ends are easy to find. We never, for example, get the end of the romance of Tristram. Chambers mentioned another problem: Malory's supposed idealistic desire to restore a vanished chivalric 'curtesye and gentylnesse' to Englishmen. But Chambers (a civil servant by profession) thought that Edward IV's subjects needed 'a strong hand in the central government' rather than chivalry revived. In any case Malory was not a political analyst (despite having been an MP). He was a 'storyteller' with a 'very dramatic theme'. He possessed a gift as well for prose, noble or effective by turns. Chambers provided instances before making his last point, on Sir Thomas Malory, criminal. Before his death on 14 March 1471 and burial in the London Greyfriars (east of the present-day Old Bailey, built on the site of Newgate Prison), he had had a 'disconcerting' career of violence. Assault and robbery; cattle-rustling; escape (by swimming a moat) from prison and immediately thereafter robbery of monastic jewels; leading a murder-gang to attack the Duke of Buckingham; rape (of the same woman) in May and again in August (of the same year): records of these unedifying and unchivalrous actions by Malory have led to much biographical head-shaking and head-scratching, at which Chambers somewhat shrugged his shoulders.[7]

H. S. Bennett wrote of Malory in like manner, with stress on him as a social reactionary. He cared nothing for 'business and politics'. 'Love and war are the twin poles of men's existence' in his writings (with Bennett, Fellow-Librarian of a Cambridge college, knowing much of war, having served in the 1914-1918 conflict, which left him a cripple). Malory's art (we are told) yet survived such limitations, for he was a stylist (examples are given), telling 'some of the greatest stories of the world'. An early admirer was Caxton himself, words from whose preface on the book's 'many Ioyous and playsaunt hystoryes' (to give men and women a good example) or 'Cowardyse, Murdre, hate' and 'synne' (to be shunned by the same) are quoted as 'still the best tribute' to it.[8]

Despite comments on how Malory's readers looked back (at least out of office hours) with nostalgia for an ideal past, their author had a businesslike approach to his material. He consistently 'eliminated the supernatural and mysterious'; what he cared about was 'adventures' and the tragic 'conflict of loyalties'; while Arthur for him was 'a national hero'.[9] An interesting view of his psyche. Thereafter we come to Vinaver and an exemplary outline of our subject. He paid tribute to the US Chaucer scholar G. L. Kittredge, who in a paper of 1896 established Malory's identity (and criminality); stated that two copies only of Caxton's edition are known, one in New York City, the other (lacking eleven leaves) in the John Rylands University Library, Manchester; added that *Le Morte Darthur* was not reprinted between 1634 and 1816 (when Robert Southey, the poet, brought out an edition); and noted that the Winchester Malory lacks four leaves in its main text, as well as a gathering of eight at its beginning and another at its end. After that, Vinaver dealt with what Caxton did to Malory's original;

questions prompted by Caxton's imposing unity on material not meant as such; Malory's sources, English and French; instances of his 'matter-of-fact' attitude to both chivalry and the paranormal, including wholesale cuts of 'long theological disquisitions' in the French Grail narrative; his style; and, at the very end, a supplementary bibliography, including reference to Malory rendered into Turkish (at Istanbul in 1948).[10] It is hard to know which aspect of Vinaver's scholarship deserves highest praise: his provision of precise and relevant detail; his industry; his sensitivity on literary questions (and thus a polite scepticism concerning arguments of C. S. Lewis); his capacity to say much in little space; or his scrupulous honesty in mentioning work by others (including the Mina Urgan who turned the whole prose *Morte* into Turkish).

Which brings us to the question of Malory's royalism and a reminder in the Oxford History of England, where Vinaver is quoted on how the Arthur who (after the alliterative *Morte Arthure*) defeats the Romans was a 'victorious king "crowned Emperor by the Pope"'. He was an 'ideal chivalric prince' in whose existence Malory confidently believed. If his representation of Arthur is more 'that of an artist than that of an historian', this is needed for literary effect.[11] Had Arthur not been a great king, his fall would not have great tragedy.

Derek Brewer, in a collection of essays by various critics, took on another proposal by Vinaver, that Caxton made a unity out of writing intended to have none (so that Vinaver's Oxford edition of 1947, to which we shall return, is famously entitled *The Works of Sir Thomas Malory*). As a former pupil of C. S. Lewis (dedicated Spenserian), he concluded that the 'closest analogy' to Malory's narrative before Caxton applied Procrustean hands to it was *The Faerie Queene*. Neither Malory not Spenser made 'much attempt at organic unity'; yet each produced 'one single work of art'. For Malory, it reaches its triumph in the 'magnificent prose' and 'richness of feeling' of his 'last two books'; which (if sometimes published separately for new readers) yet 'cannot be severed' from what comes before.[12]

Any complacency on Malory amongst above writers would, however, be blown away by a chill wind from a People's Republic. Margaret Schlauch, American Marxist, who in 1951 left the USA for Poland (following a witness summons from the House Committee on un–American Activities) to become (and remain) a party member, was the very person to offer bracing views on chivalry. Yet Malory's work is less dented by her Marxist critique than we might expect. His stress on 'human relations' and *de*-stress on 'magical and mystical themes' represent an advance 'in the direction of modern fiction' (and thus, in Marxist terms, progress). Even if his 'main interest' is in an 'unreal world' oblivious to 'such mundane concerns as rents and debts' (matters on which Marx and Marxists laid justifiable emphasis), various satiric touches indicate doubts (of a kind) on courtly love. A certain Red Knight, who had hanged some forty knightly opponents, was defeated by Sir Gareth, but spared because what he did was 'at a ladyes requeste'. Hanging was a shameful death, ignominious for any knight. A 'dash of satire' appears likely. It is not alone. The comical Sir Dinadan, jubilant to miss a tournament's perils thanks to 'an untimely nap'; the sister of Sir Gareth's betrothed, who is responsible for their engagement but manages to spoil their fun; these also temper the risks of too much earnestness.[13]

Altogether different is an essay on sacred and profane love in the *Morte*, which 'inevitably issue in paradox and ambiguity'.[14] A pamphlet by Muriel Bradbrook (sometime Girton College's head of house) opens with words by Yeats on silk from a Japanese lady's dress and a Samurai sword as things 'emblematical of love and war'; a phrase also summing up Malory's twin themes (religion, a third item, being much 'subordinated'). Her essay is useful in relating Malory to the fifteenth century's violence and instability, to romance, and to the heroic tradition of English poetry (with reference to *Beowulf* and the tenth-century *Battle of Maldon*).[15] In the same year as her introduction, there appeared the second edition of Vinaver's great work, with many textual corrections, mention of a previously unknown French source (discovered in the mid-1940s) for Malory's *Tale of King Arthur*, and a new section in the Introduction on Malory as author of a collection of tales, and not of a single work.[16] More on this when we reach the third edition, of 1990.

Malory's life, one of violence in crime, violence in literature, is so strangely overlaid by Caxton's life, one of the drapery trade and publishing industry. The knight-littérateur and businessman-littérateur make an odd pair; if one that has benefited England and the world. At about this time Caxton's achievements came to the fore, thanks to Norman Blake, workmanlike scholar. He provided crucial analysis of how, in the light of the Winchester Manuscript, we can pin-point Caxton's alterations of Malory. The result is significant for Arthur (our real theme). Caxton modified what he found to make 'Christian morals and chivalry' more prominent, and he emphasized Arthur and Gawain as each being an ideal 'Christian knight', so that his breaking the narrative down into 'short episodes' was perhaps less due to a desire for 'unity' than an urge to provide brief stories 'illustrative of various Christian morals'.[17] If this got in the way of what Malory intended, it still shows how Arthur is perennially modified by admirers. No wonder that Caxton spoke in his introduction of how imitating the good deeds recounted in *Le Morte Darthur* and not the bad ones would bring readers 'to good fame and renown'.[18] They (like Caxton's deference to social superiors, something also patent in his introduction) were the way to success in society and, still more, in business.

For those who wish to go deeper into Malorian origins, there is a handy translation of the thirteenth-century *Queste del Saint Graal*.[19] Handy, too, is a modernized version of Caxton's defence of Arthur's historicity.[20] Norman Blake thereafter stated firmly that 'few have accepted' Vinaver's belief that the *Morte* was 'not designed as one composition': for Blake, it is a 'unified work' or 'cycle' on 'the rise and fall of Arthur's court', which was a noble enterprise wrecked by the sins of its members.[21] Then a new presence with an engaging analysis of Malory the writer by Peter Field (who has done so much for the Warwickshire knight), amongst whose conclusions are those that Malory was 'not a conscious artist; rather the reverse'; and that his attitudes of 'reverence' or 'fear' (due to an 'incomplete knowledge' of the narratives that he took over) offer his readers (whom he 'ignores') a 'more intimate' relationship with him than we have with (say) Thackeray, where we know pretty well what he thought of his characters (Becky Sharp, Sir Pitt Crawley, Lord Steyn, and so on).[22] In another approach to Malory's style, reviewing discussion by Vinaver and others on his use of *entrelacement* or 'interwoven episodes', it is claimed that he exploits it in (for example) his story of Balin, but less so in the narrative of Sir Lancelot and Queen Guinevere, which at his hands instead has the form of an 'exemplary tale'.[23] With wider perspectives in an entire chapter on Malory (entitled 'A New Horizon') are reflections on how his 'vast epic' concerns 'men set apart as bearers of a tragic fate' in comparisons with Aeschylus, whose *Eumenides* closes after Apollo promises 'deliverance' for Orestes, thereby re-establishing 'the eternal order of things'.[24] Malory and Aeschylus: a lofty comparison for an English knight's fictions.

Caxton's prologue and epilogue to his edition were then neatly presented by Norman Blake.[25] He followed it with a prose anthology, including a passage on Arthur's wars against Rome, with mention of 'the mount of Arabé' where Arthur killed a disagreeable giant ('Arabé' here ultimately from Welsh *Eryri* or Snowdonia).[26] So Arthur's archaic reputation as fighter and giant-killer has met the new technology of printing. More imaginative than Blake was Derek Pearsall, comparing (John Stanley's) *Sir Gawain and the Green Knight* (of 1387) with Malory's *Morte Darthur* (completed 1469-70) to the latter's disadvantage. Malory lacked the earlier writer's 'certainty of touch'. He was 'overwhelmed by the multifarious nature of his sources' (often contradicting each other). Only in the last three books did Malory show 'clear direction' by providing a 'humane and tragic' interpretation of his material, wherein he rejected the 'transcendental' aspects of his French monastic originals, also refusing to accept that chivalry, despite terrible failure, was in itself 'worthless and doomed'. For him, the Round Table falls because of 'a human conflict of loyalties' with Lancelot acquiring therein 'the lineaments of a genuine tragic hero'.[27] The Arthur and his henchmen of Welsh chronicle and saga had been the stuff of folk-tale. Malory went far beyond that to the world of epic and tragedy. A remarkable ascent. A final and still more imaginative response to his text was that of John Stevens (known, like Blake and Pearsall, to the present writer). He had a warm receptiveness to medieval religion (as Blake and Pearsall did not), and selected a passage from the Grail romance on the elevation at mass (celebrated by a bishop) of the 'ubble' or *oblatio* or consecrated host, with the miracles that accompanied it. Despite Malory's 'inadequacies (or disinclinations)' for anything mystical, the episode retains a 'primitive power' (aided by the 'sheer quality' of Malory's prose).[28] From books published in one year, readers find quite different impressions of Malory. It says much about the three critics concerned. Which of them was nearest the truth, readers may determine for themselves.

Peter Field's study of 1971 began a series of such monographs. The author of one of them anatomizes features or topoi of Malorian discourse that are sometimes unfamiliar to us: formal speech, superlatives, catalogues, landscapes, the good place, shame, love's language.[29] Another book is a general introduction, going through the tales in order, but with chapters as well on fifteenth-century prose romance, chivalry, knighthood. Malory's world is there considered in an actual one, that of decisions good and bad by Henry VI and Edward IV; or else by men of the Paston family: writing a love-letter, jousting at Eltham (near London), reading romances, seeing (at Bruges) a chivalric gathering of the Duke of Burgundy.[30] Plenty of material on real and unreal. One very real thing is death, whereon a further writer (noting that Merlin even at the Round

Table's foundation 'constantly prophesies the collapse to come') contrasts shifts in tone and emphasis between *Le Morte Darthur* and slightly earlier English poems on Arthur.[31] Moving from the Great Reaper to editing, we find practical remarks on Malory and how for most students the 'set edition will be accepted at face value', with salutary results for those who go to the same text edited by someone else.[32] Indeed. When young scholars begin to see that almost all university handbooks contain untruths, an unforgettable day of revelation will arrive.

On that very subject, an edition by Peter Field is a model of clear and informative work, with accessible notes and accounts (in its introduction) of medieval war, thought, kingship, chivalry, religion, tragedy, mystery.[33] More advanced, but useful in showing the way ahead for Malory's ultimate sources, is a passage on Arthur's death from 'the vast thirteenth-century prose romance known as the *Prose Lancelot* or the *Vulgate Cycle*'.[34] Progress is shown indirectly by a thoughtful essay of Derek Brewer on the tale of Sir Gareth, noting the discovery of its source by Peter Field (it is therefore not Malory's invention), and relating it to 'the family drama' of growth 'from childhood to adulthood' and the 'new equal relationships' that come with maturity.[35] In a volume containing important advances is an essay on the prose *Morte*'s real author as a Thomas Malory of Papworth St Agnes, Cambridgeshire (not his Warwickshire namesake).[36] It has not fared well. All the same, biographical enquiries are usually worth the effort, because they make us look at preconceptions. In a warm and appreciative survey of Malory, Derek Brewer deals with the 'exciting quests and conflicts' provided by knighthood as a subject, the problems of texts and authorship, the nature of traditional story, and how the *Morte*'s 'internal contradictions' are intrinsic to 'Gothic' aesthetics or art.[37] Which is a provoking insight. Provoking too are Blake's comments on Caxton's introduction, with the conclusion that most of what he claimed about 'certain gentlemen' who urged him to publish the text is 'fictitious'. Its sole purpose was 'to arouse interest in Arthur' and sell the book.[38] In a publisher's blurb, then as now, one is not upon oath.

Douglas Gray had acute comments on Malory, citing Peter Field for him as political victim rather than 'picturesque ruffian'; praising the 'extraordinary range of incident and emotion' in his work (almost encyclopaedic in its scope), whether comic, pathetic, violent, uncanny; noting that Malory's gift is not usually for character analysis, but for 'vivid scenes', 'dialogue', 'direct speech'; and citing sensational new evidence (published in 1977 and again discussed in Takamiya and Brewer's 1981 volume) for the Winchester manuscript as having been in Caxton's workshop, but not used by him.[39] For those bewildered by Malory's French sources, there is clear guidance from a Leeds University teacher.[40]

Of value for the ongoing metamorphoses of Arthur in time is consideration of him (along with much else) in Malory's *Morte*. It underscores his development there. In the first tale, he comes to the foreground with Britain in the midst of a 'despicable civil war', although he at first displays few of his 'qualities'. That changes. In wars against Lot of Lothian and Orkney he acquires fame as a 'fierce warrior' possessing a 'rash enthusiasm for battle'; but not those of kingly 'discretion' or wisdom. He is also 'self-centred'. A long way to go before we reach the Quest for the Grail, where he now displays 'love and concern for his knights for *their* sakes'. At the earlier date he also 'stubbornly insists' on marrying Guinevere, despite Merlin's doom-laden warnings on her. Then too is the 'barbaric and savage' episode of innocent children put to sea and left to die in a boat. The later Arthur is other. If he now fully understands that his responsibilities as king mean 'always to make peace when he can', he yet fails to 'exercise effective leadership' in the last crisis. He is 'fatally weak'. 'The human weakness of King Arthur is the single most important reason for the downfall of the Round Table.'[41] Within Malory's text is material on the theory and practice of kingship. The theme of Arthur is, once more, remolded and remade.

After these significant observations is a summary account, with emphasis on how 'Lancelot, "the greatest knight of a sinful man" as Malory calls him', brings an evil fate to Camelot.[42] The thirteenth-century French text on the flowering of Lancelot's love for Guinevere (a flowering with a grim and bloody outcome) in the same year came out in fresh translation.[43] In an article appearing posthumously is acceptance that the Winchester Manuscript 'was in Caxton's printshop' and yet was not his 'exemplar', with the further proposition that what he used instead was 'a revision by Malory' himself, including 'a shorter account of the Roman war' and many 'minor improvements'.[44] A point worth making, if only to give academic inertia a jolt. Elsewhere is consideration of genres (romance, history, tragedy) in our narrative.[45] For a change is examination of nineteenth-century tampering with it, where Victorian editors saw knightly *amours* (and so on) much as Roger Ascham (d. 1568) did when he called them 'bold bawdrye'.[46]

In 1990 came another milestone on the Malorian highway, with publication under a new editor (Peter Field) of Vinaver's *opus magnum*. It takes us on a stately way (and with added precision) from 'Hit befel in the dayes of Uther Pendragon' of its opening words to the closing ones of its imprisoned author, 'SERVAUNT OF JESU BOTHE DAY AND NYGHT'. Changes are numerous but minor. As the reviser puts it, the edition is 'Vinaver's rather than mine', his own priority being to make text and supporting material 'factually accurate'.[47] Readers can go their way with enhanced confidence. This splendid three-volume edition was soon accompanied by a thorough examination of the author, with the jailbird of Newbold Revel retaining his place against contending namesakes, if with careful remarks on the limits of our knowledge. In the absence of personal documents (letters, diaries, anecdotes), Malory's personality will always be elusive, although Field is surely right when he defines it as 'unacademic'. Questions of free will or the salvation of virtuous pagans did not interest him (as they did Chaucer, Langland, or the John and William Stanley to whom we attribute *Pearl* and other Cheshire poems). His reading hardly 'extended much beyond Arthurian literature'. He yet felt strongly about 'the dignity of knighthood', a consequence being that the gap between the chivalric ideals and degrading realities of fifteenth-century England perhaps created ongoing 'problems' for Malory. A third feature is 'historical allusiveness'. Unlike its sources, the *Morte* has much on how 'noble houses could ruin a kingdom', so that Field even proposes that Malory, in the midst of noble houses doing just that, deserted York for Lancaster, winner for loser, owing to 'a bad conscience'.[48] Under pressures social and personal, Arthurian tradition once more shifted a few degrees. In another admirable and perceptive piece, Field lays emphasis (after R. H. Wilson) on Malory's skill as narrator, the proof of that being the myriad present-day Arthurian creations 'directly or indirectly based on his work'.[49]

In a book first published in 1985, a Canadian critic here related questions of narrative unity to 'post-structuralist literary theory' and questions of genre to Northrop Frye (another Canadian) on epic.[50] North America on this rightly offered its own insights. At a different level is a survey of how Malory treated his sources, with the paradoxical conclusion that he created 'a sense of specifically English history' even though most of his book is a translation from French.[51] Different again is a voice from Tel Aviv, weighing Arthurian ideals in the prose *Morte* and finding them wanting. Its author had seen too much 'violence, greed, hatred, dishonor, lying, and ordinary human lust' to see humankind as anything but 'dark'.[52] Character was thereby Camelot's destiny; and that fate was hard. In a further examination of what Malory did to the texts before him, Peter Field itemizes authorial lapses such as the 'child-killing episode'; or the promise (never fulfilled) in the fifth tale to relate what happened to Keyhydyns, 'hapless suitor' of La Beale Isode; or the 'duplicated account of the arrival of the Roman ambassadors'. They are flaws. Malory was not writing a 'twentieth-century experimental novel' (or, for that matter, *Don Quixote* or

Tristram Shandy, with their own proto-modernist narrative tricks).[53] As for evil in art and life alike, Malory's own words are quoted from his lament on how Arthur, 'noblest Knight', was betrayed by his knights, Englishmen ever having the defect that 'there may us nothing please no term'.[54] Yet others might think (after the Oxford historian Bruce McFarlane) that the real problem for both Camelot and Henry VI's England was not overmighty subjects, but 'undermighty kings'.

Which brings us to warfare and an observation that the 'grete gunnes' used by Mordred when attacking Guinevere in the Tower of London were not cannon but traditional siege-engines.[55] Not quite as modern as imagined. In a clear and sensible discussion of how Malory dealt with his material and the unity that he aimed at are also surprises. One is Caxton's substituting 'buttocks' for the blunter and more soldierly word found in the Winchester Manuscript. Another is a nod to John Speirs, who in 1954 condemned Malory for a 'lifeless' style and for reducing a magnificent original to cheap sensations.[56] Still, it is easy to condemn writers for not writing as one would have written oneself. Returning to warfare, we find an exhaustive study of fighting in *Le Morte Darthure*.[56] It provides minutiae on what Milton in *Paradise Lost* (book nine) styled the 'long and tedious havoc' of 'fabled knights / In battle feigned'. He, like others, clearly found armed combat a dreary subject. Derek Pearsall had a more subtle theme in typifying the prose *Morte* as reflecting not a guilt culture but a shame culture (where the eleventh commandment is 'Thou Shalt Not Get Found Out'). That gives an additive to privacy. Arthur, despite a notion of Guinevere's unfaithfulness, 'wold nat here thereoff'. He ignored everything until his hand was forced by 'the malice of Agravaine and Mordred'. It is later imitators (Tennyson, T. H. White, John Steinbeck) who try to explain everything, and so 'change the whole nature of the story'.[58]

Then a startling comparison of Guinevere at the stake in Camelot to Joan of Arc at the stake in Rouen, argued with learned references to original sources (and worth reading for that reason).[59] But the proposition (that Malory had Joan in mind when writing of Guinevere) does not convince. Guinevere, a faithless wife, was to be burnt for petty treason. (In English law, to be burnt alive was for women the penalty for petty treason. It took place as late as 1786, when Phoebe Harris was burnt at Newgate before 20,000 spectators. In 1790, Parliament replaced burning a woman alive with the more conventional penalty of hanging.) Joan's offence was (despite what some claim) not matrimonial but political. She was a threat to English power in France and, under English government pressure, had to be eliminated. All the same, Ann W. Astell's gift for lobbing literary bombshells is commendable. She makes us sit up. More reassuring is a further and updated statement by Field, coming down (against Lumiansky) for the Winchester text as 'appreciably closer to what Malory wrote' than Caxton's.[60] Also illuminating for Malory's *Nachleben* are observations on how his book was in the 'tiny corpus' of medieval English ones 'read beyond the sixteenth century' (in 'black-letter reprintings'), the last being of 1634. Then, a long gap followed by a rush of appreciation: two editions of 1816, another by the poet Robert Southey in 1817. A romanticism headed by Sir Walter Scott pushed the first of these, followed in a different mode by Southey's gentlemanly neo-conservative antiquarianism. The impulse was in no way philological or academic. That had to wait for the later nineteenth century.[61] Such is the whirligig fate of a literary classic.

An exploration of Malory's religious language shows it to be very often stereotyped, an 'institutional discourse' of formulae natural in a society where belief was almost as normal as breathing.[62] Regarding women, results are disappointing. They are persistently 'marginalized'. They are 'secondary to men's ongoing struggles to construct their knightly identities'.[63] We shall see more of Malory's unenlightened attitudes when we come to remarks by Derek Pearsall on Arthur. Also on Arthur, in a thoughtful and well-considered chapter, is his duality, or one of his dualities. Specifically it is the question of whether he belonged to history or to romance? By 1485 it was an issue, Arthur's historicity having by then 'been opened to challenge', with Caxton in his prologue coming to the defence. It was a different and more artistic difficulty for Malory, most obviously for his book's end and the Passing of Arthur, where he effectively has it both ways: the 'paradox' of 'a king who was, and who may yet be'. Blending of the historical–factual with the romance–fantastic is one of the prose *Morte*'s various dual or two-fold aspects, like its use of French narratives to create 'a sense of English history and identity'.[64] Our focus in this book being on Arthur, a collection of seventeen studies on Merlin may be mentioned only briefly, despite their abundance of discussion on Malory.[65] What must be mentioned, though, is Arthur's attitude to women. It is ugly. There are two aspects.

First is royal seduction. The King could in that be 'disconcerting abrupt' and 'brutal'. He and Lionors fall for each other; 'the King had ado with her and begot on her a child' (the future Sir Borre), after which Pearsall remarks 'And that's all we ever hear of her'. A week later, Arthur has fallen for Guinevere; in the chapter after *that*, he beds Margawse of Orkney (wife to King Lot) and 'begot upon her Sir Mordred'. After those brisk wooings there follow, at the Pentecostal feast, the high–flown 'principles of the Round Table' (filling us with a certain puzzlement). Second, however, is Arthur the reverse of 'abrupt' or decisive as regards Guinevere's matrimonial tangles. He was 'reluctant to act' when Agravain voiced suspicions, or, in Malory's words, 'For, as the French book saith, the King was full loath that such a noise should be upon Sir Lancelot and his queen.' On that, Pearsall draws attention to Malory's habit of assigning comment to 'the French book' (even if no French source is known for it, as here) whenever interpretation is 'enigmatic' or 'ambiguous'.[66] In any case, Malory has unenlightened male views of women, and of the thoughts or feelings of women. He was no feminist icon.

If researchers (cited above) took on Malory and combat, or

Malory and popular religion, a third relates him to the gentry class, with reflections on 'the complex perspective of contemporary political gentry attitudes' and 'the importance of assessing cultural processes' as regards 'the gentlemen and gentlewomen of England' who were Malory's readers.[67] Nothing, however, on what those 'gentlewomen' might have thought about some of the text's episodes (on rape, adultery, seduction, sexual betrayal), which together suggest (after a quip of Quiller-Couch on *Two Gentlemen of Verona*) that there were *no* gentlemen in Camelot. Something similar may be said of Helen Cooper's assertions on how what matters for Malory is that 'love should be true, singular, and faithful' and that 'he reserves his strongest disapproval for lust'.[68] Somewhat at odds with Arthur's behaviour as described by Derek Pearsall. Perhaps we are better off with considerations on whether Malory was 'writing romance, or reverting to chronicle'.[69] If what is called 'romance' might bluntly be termed 'male fantasy' (as in some spy-thriller or production of Hollywood), it could sum up a great deal of *Le Morte Darthur*. It also puts us on surer ground with 'recuperation of the ancient Celtic past' (as a ploy of medieval and Tudor regimes) for fantasies of a political kind anatomized in a volume containing much that is startling. It reproduces a propaganda picture of Adolf Hitler, 'in profile, armored and on horseback', and bearing aloft a 'large swastika flag of the Third Reich', the 'knight function' having now become 'a player in fascist fantasy'.[70] Even a sober account of relics of Christ's blood at a Gloucestershire monastery reminds us that the quest for the Holy Grail told by Malory is not so far from the murky hinterlands of recent best-sellers.[71] Given such excesses, no surprise if war and knightly ideals should clash. The Malory described as *valens miles* who was likewise 'thief, prisoner, prison-breaker' (also rapist, author) would be more of a piece than we suppose.[72]

After propaganda and sins of the flesh, Malory the MP. His experience in the House of Commons hardly shifted his archaic or backward-looking mentality. To judge from the prose *Morte*, a parliamentary gathering was an entity deserving 'little attention' and, when he did notice it (in alterations to his sources), it resembles more a 'baronial assembly' than a 'communal' legislature.[73] Rather different (in an unusual and original study) is the subject of names, providing curious narratives with (for example) two people of the same name, or persons who change their name. Such words being fundamental to identity, analysis of their function (in tales of Sir Balin, Tristram, the Fair Maid of Astolat, Sir Gareth) brings out their at times uncanny or disturbing effect.[74] Certainly a subject that merits examination. After parliaments and names, printing and translation. Both inform us on *Le Morte Darthur*. With the former, the point is made that its last reprint before the nineteenth century was in 1634; as if it were the Civil War and Cromwell that really finished off medieval England. Malory was yet luckier than Gower (last full edition in 1554) or Langland (1561); not so lucky as Chaucer, always in favour with publishers.[75] With the latter subject, translation offers plenty to say, on Malory's treatment or transformation of French prose or English verse, and then also Caxton's own literary surgery on Malory. Each raises questions of selection, potential readership, linguistic competence. The result is welcome. Malory and Caxton had it both ways, making 'something new out of inherited material' while retaining a 'status conferred by antiquity'.[76]

Just as with Kenneth Sisam or J. A. W. Bennett (each of New Zealand and Oxford), we gather a harvest of the medieval with Douglas Gray (also of New Zealand and Oxford). Malory (as one would expect) brought his sympathies for medieval England (and Scotland) to the fore. From him we learn of the author's chequered or equivocal career. If the knight of Newbold Revel was not 'a flower of chivalry', neither was he 'an old fighter turned gangster' nor a 'picturesque ruffian sitting in prison' and writing in nostalgic vein about knighthood. Gray also thought him gaoled in the Tower of London, not Newgate, where Malory evidently made full use of the prison (or another) library. There are further comments on the book as echoing its author's life ('well disguised' if so); his times (many speculative 'suppositions' and things 'unproven'); how the manuscript used by Caxton perhaps belonged to Earl Rivers, beheaded in 1483 by Richard III, so that Caxton in 1485 erased his patron's identity; the relation of manuscript to printed book, with Gray coming down against Vinaver's 'rather tendentious title' *The Works of Sir Thomas Malory*, citing evidence for 'some sense of "unity"' given by the author-translator; Caxton's preface, 'very interesting' for what people in 1485 thought of Arthur; the eight tales of the original; the 'powerful fascination' which helps makes them 'an extraordinary achievement' (with mesmerizing effects on, of all people, Mark Twain, himself a storytelling genius); the tricks and rhythms and magic of their style; the lash of censure from Roger Ascham and his like; genuine problems on knights who fall short of their ideals; the religious element, where Malory 'acquits himself very well'; and questions equally deep on how his masterpiece is 'a tragedy of humanity'.[77] Those who seek commentary could not do better than read and meditate on the words of this wise New Zealander.

There are still points to be made. Wales has a minor presence in the prose *Morte*, unlike (say) Cornwall, but tells us things just the same, South Wales ('loyal to Arthur') being contrasted with North Wales (varying between the 'moderately subversive' and 'overtly hostile').[78] Elsewhere is encyclopaedic information on adventure, characterization, chivalry, death, destiny, epic, free will, humour, justice, kingship (so that Arthur insists that Roman legates 'be treated well', if only for his own *worshyp*: a complex word), marriage, nobility, sense of loss, violence, war, women, antiquity.[79] Quite a catalogue, quite an ensemble of complexities.

As our century progresses, new critical fashions emerge. Assumptions on gender have changed, with many affirming it to be a 'construct'. A complete book on the subject thus ends with declarations on how it has 'followed the text's many sightlines between images and viewers to highlight positive and negative

impacts that intromissive vision has on the productions of femi-
ninity and especially masculinity'.[80] Perhaps easier to grasp is ex-
plication of signs and wonders: Merlin's knowledge of what is to
come; marvels, enchantments, sorceries; the miracles and demons
of the Grail quest; the hand of destiny.[81] For, despite his soldierly
life and (sometimes) language, Malory would be a lesser writer
without the *frisson* of the unseen. Indubitably soldierly, however,
is his attitude to women. In a 'much-discussed digression' he
speaks of 'vertuouse love'; where Catherine Batt is yet cited on
how the entire passage 'assumes a male audience' or readership
and 'does not comment' on what a woman might feel.[82] Which is
true.

It brings us to the subject of rape, the very opposite of 'vertuouse love' and a repellent feature of his narrative. Catherine Batt
is once more quoted on it for a consistent lack of reference to
'women's pain' or 'reactions', the author being far more concerned
with 'male responses'.[83] Malory is a man, writing for men. In more
adventurous vein is a study where Sir Thomas Malory encounters
Sigmund Freud, with startling results on (for example) the
'Oresteian Mother' and Morgause, who is 'decapitated by her
son'.[84] After rape and matricide one moves to a pleasanter matter,
Malory and Cornwall. He has been good news for the place, helping put billions of pounds (with the aid of Tennyson the poet) into
its tourist industry (and prompting visits to Tintagel or the court
of King Mark or the site of Arthur's supposed last battle), all
thanks to his awareness of 'fifteenth-century Cornish distinctive-
ness'.[85] Such are the socio-economic effects of literature as commodity.

If Cornwall is one Celtic realm, Ireland is another; and provides unexpected information on sources. *Lorgaireacht an
tSoidhigh Naomhtha* ('Quest of the Holy Grail') is a translation
predating Malory, made either from English or from French (perhaps Anglo-French). Because it agrees with his text on details unknown elsewhere, it is a 'witness' to the lost narrative which he

used.[86] It is a welcome reminder of Britain and Ireland's varied languages and peoples. Another one is on how those peoples were represented by Malory. Wales and Cornwall have here already been cited, but he writes as well on the Orkneys (islands little known to the English), presenting further questions on 'loyalties' and 'sovereignty', because Orcadian knights had no obvious 'allegiance to Arthur and England'.[87] *Vive la différence* is bad news for ministers of trade or defence. But for writers it opens artistic doors. In contrast to the Northern Isles is Winchester, which Malory deliberately chose as Arthur's capital (even though Caxton sided for Caerleon, Wales). His reasons are interesting, for they show his awareness of earlier myth-making, most substantially represented in the 'replica wooden Round Table' commissioned (it seems) in 1290 by Edward I (effective propagandist) and hanging to this day on a wall inside Winchester Castle.[88] Underlining further the truism that to edit is to interpret is a chapter on how the prose *Morte* will be presented in the future, with the arresting remark that C. S. Lewis (good lawyer for unwinnable cases) preferred Caxton's text to that of Vinaver; no doubt because of the 'emotional connection' that he gained from reading it as a child in Belfast.[89]

And so we make an end. Meagre facts on the real Arthur, a North British historical acorn, have swelled into Malory's towering narrative oak. It is not alone. Around it is a whole stand or honour of oak trees, being the works of poets and novelists and painters and critics and Hollywood film-directors who have taken and reshaped and recreated Arthurian fictions. A remarkable proliferation, in which an ending is really an endless or eternal beginning, as hinted even in Malory's own superlative and unforgettable ending, when Bedivere, 'lone survivor' of the last battle, cast the sword Excalibur away, 'and Morgan and Nimue then took Arthur, dying from his wounds, to Avalon.'[90]

Notes

1. W. P. Ker, *English Literature: Medieval* (London, 1912), 118.

2. *Historical French Reader: Medieval Period*, ed. Paul Studer and E. G. R. Waters (Oxford, 1924), 149-58.

3. E. K. Chambers, *Arthur of Britain* (London, 1927), 163-4, 167, 206.

4. C. S. Lewis, *The Allegory of Love* (Oxford, 1936), 35 n. 1.

5. G. G. Coulton, *Medieval Panorama* (Cambridge, 1938), 240, 242-3, 253, 257.

6. W. L. Renwick and Harold Orton, *The Beginnings of English Literature to Skelton* (London, 1939), 287-8.

7. E. K. Chambers, *English Literature at the Close of the Middle Ages* (Oxford, 1945), 185-205.

8. H. S. Bennett, *Chaucer and the Fifteenth Century* (Oxford, 1947), 200-3.

9. A. R. Myers, *England in the Late Middle Ages* (Harmondsworth, 1952), 251.

10. Eugène Vinaver, 'Sir Thomas Malory', in *Arthurian Literature in the Middle Ages*, ed, R. S. Loomis (Oxford, 1959), 541-52.

11. E. F. Jacob, *The Fifteenth Century* (Oxford, 1961), 657.

12. D. S. Brewer, 'the hoole book', in *Essays on Malory*, ed. J. A. W. Bennett (Oxford, 1963), 41-63.

13. Margaret Schlauch, *Antecedents of the English Novel* (Warszawa, 1963), 75-7.

14. R. T. Davies, 'The Worshipful Way in Malory', in *Patterns of Love and Courtesy*, ed. John Lawlor (London, 1966), 157-77.

15. M. C. Bradbrook, *Sir Thomas Malory*, 2nd edn (London, 1967).

16. *The Works of Sir Thomas Malory*, ed. Eugêne Vinaver, 2nd edn (Oxford, 1967), v-vi.

17. Norman Blake, *Caxton and His World* (London, 1969), 113.

18. J. R. Lander, *Conflict and Stability in Fifteenth-Century England* (London, 1969), 149.

19. *The Quest of the Holy Grail*, tr. P. M. Matarasso (Harmondsworth, 1969).

20. *English Historical Documents 1327-1485*, ed. A. R. Myers (London, 1969), 1135-7.

21. N. F. Blake, 'Late Medieval Prose', in *The Middle Ages*, ed. W. F. Bolton (London, 1970), 371-403, at 397.

22. P. J. C. Field, *Romance and Chronicle: A Study of Malory's Prose Style* (London, 1971), 7, 158.

23. Pamela Gradon, *Form and Style in Early English Literature* (London, 1971), 149.

24. Eugène Vinaver, *The Rise of Romance* (Oxford, 1971), 137, 138.

25. N. F. Blake, *Caxton's Own Prose* (London, 1973), 106-11.

26. N. F. Blake, *Selections from William Caxton* (London, 1973), 43-8, 126-7.

27. D. A. Pearsall, 'The Story and its Setting', in *The Mediaeval World*, ed. David Daiches and Anthony Thorlby (London, 1973), 371-406, at 404.

28. John Stevens, *Medieval Romance* (London, 1973), 122-3.

29. Mark Lambert, *Malory: Style and Vision in 'Le Morte Darthur'* (New Haven, 1975).

30. Larry D. Benson, *Malory's 'Morte Darthur'* (Cambridge, Mass., 1976).

31. Philippa Tristram, *Figures of Life and Death in Medieval English Literature* (London, 1976), 124.

32. N. F. Blake, *The English Language in Medieval Literature* (London, 1977), 56.

33. Thomas Malory, *Le Morte Darthur: The Seventh and Eighth Tales*, ed. P. J. C. Field (London, 1978).

34. *A Medieval French Reader*, ed. C. W. Aspland (Oxford, 1979), 132-7.

35. Derek Brewer, *Symbolic Stories* (Cambridge, 1980), 100-11.

36. Richard R. Griffith, 'The Authorship Question Reconsidered', in *Aspects of Malory*, ed. Toshiyuki Takamiya and Derek Brewer (Cambridge, 1981), 159-77.

37. Derek Brewer, *English Gothic Literature* (London, 1983), 264-76.

38. N. F. Blake, 'William Caxton', in *Middle English Prose*, ed. A. S. G. Edwards (New Brunswick, 1984), 389-412, at 403.

39. *The Oxford Book of Late Medieval Verse and Prose*, ed. Douglas Gray (Oxford, 1985), 204, 460.

40. Lynette R. Muir, *Literature and Society in Medieval France* (Basingstoke,

1985).

41. Christopher Dean, *Arthur of England* (Toronto, 1987), 93-4, 100-1.

42. Stephen Coote, *English Literature of the Middle Ages* (Harmondsworth, 1988), 330-2.

43. *Lancelot of the Lake*, tr. Corin Corley (Oxford, 1988).

44. R. M. Lumiansky, 'Concerning Three Names in *Le Morte Darthur*', in *Medieval English Studies Presented to George Kane*, ed. E. D. Kennedy, Ronald Waldron, Joseph S. Wittig (Woodbridge, 1988), 301-8.

45. Terence McCarthy, '*Le Morte Darthur* and Romance', in *Studies in Medieval English Romances*, ed. Derek Brewer (Cambridge, 1988), 148-75.

46. Marylin Jackson Parins, 'Malory's Expurgators', in *The Arthurian Tradition*, ed. Mary Flowers Braswell and John Bugge (Tuscaloosa, 1988), 144-62.

47. *The Works of Sir Thomas Malory*, ed. Eugêne Vinaver, 3rd edn, rev. P. J. C. Field (Oxford, 1990), 7, 1260, 1747.

48. P. J. C. Field, *The Life and Times of Sir Thomas Malory* (Cambridge, 1991), 172-3.

49. P. J. C. Field, 'Malory, Sir Thomas', in *The New Arthurian Encyclopedia*, ed. Norris J. Lacy (Chicago, 1991), 294-7.

50. Beverly Kennedy, *Knighthood in the Morte Darthur*, 2nd edn (Cambridge, 1992), 348.

51. William Calin, *The French Tradition and the Literature of Medieval England* (Toronto, 1994), 510.

52. Jerome Mandel, 'The Dark Side of Camelot', *Chaucer Yearbook*, ii (1995), 77-93.

53. P. J. C. Field, 'Malory's Mordred and the *Morte Arthure*', in *Romance Reading on the Book*, ed. Jennifer Fellows, Rosalind Field, Gillian Rogers, Judith Weiss (Cardiff, 1996), 77-93, at 90.

54. Simon Walker, 'Civil War and Rebellion', in *An Illustrated History of Late Medieval England*, ed. Chris Given-Wilson (Manchester, 1996), 229-47.

55. Malcolm Hebron, *The Medieval Siege* (Oxford, 1997), 31-2.

56. Norris J. Lacy and Geoffrey Ashe, *The Arthurian Handbook*, 2nd edn (New York, 1997), 128-31.

57. Andrew Lynch, *Malory's Book of Arms* (Cambridge, 1997).

58. Derek Pearsall, 'Courtesy and Chivalry', in *A Companion to the 'Gawain' Poet*, ed. Derek Brewer and Jonathan Gibson (Cambridge, 1997), 351-62, at 358.

59. Ann W. Astell, *Political Allegory in Late Medieval England* (Ithaca, 1999), 138-60.

60. P. J. C. Field, 'Sir Thomas Malory's *Le Morte Darthur*', in *The Arthur of the English*, ed. W. R. J. Barron (Cardiff, 1999), 225-46, at 229.

61. David Matthews, *The Making of Middle English* (Minneapolis, 1999), 92-3.

62. Roger Dalrymple, *Language and Piety in Middle English Romance* (Cambridge, 2000), 1-34.

63. Sheila Fisher, 'Women and Men in Late Medieval English Romance', in *The Cambridge Companion to Medieval Romance*, ed. Roberta L. Krueger (Cambridge, 2000), 150-64, at 158.

64. Andrew King, *'The Faerie Queene' and Middle English Romance* (Oxford, 2000), 117, 124, 125.

65. *Merlin: A Casebook*, ed. Peter H. Goodrich and Raymond H. Thompson (New York, 2003).

66. Derek Pearsall, *Arthurian Romance* (Oxford, 2003), 90, 104.

67. Raluca L. Radulescu, *The Gentry Context for Malory's 'Morte Darthur'* (Cambridge, 2003), 147.

68. Helen Cooper, *The English Romance in Time* (Oxford, 2004), 302.

69. Tony Davenport, *Medieval Narrative* (Oxford, 2004), 147.

70. Laurie A. Finke and Martin B. Schichtman, *King Arthur and the Myth of History* (Gainesville, 2004), 159-60, 188.

71. Richard Barber, 'Sir Thomas Malory and the Holy Blood of Hailes', in *The Medieval Book and a Modern Collector*, ed. Takami Matsuda, Richard A. Linenthal, John Scahill (Cambridge, 2004), 279-84.

72. K. S. Whetter, 'Warfare and Combat in *Le Morte Darthur*', in *Writing War*, ed. Corinne Saunders, Françoise Le Saux, Neil Thomas (Cambridge, 2004), 169-86.

73. Matthew Giancarlo, *Parliament and Literature in Late Medieval England* (Cambridge, 2007), 255.

74. Jane Bliss, *Naming and Namelessness in Medieval Romance* (Cambridge, 2008), 44-5.

75. Siân Echard, *Printing the Middle Ages* (Philadelphia, 2008), 101.

76. Rosalind Field, 'Romance', in *The Oxford History of Literary Translation in English: To 1550*, ed. Roger Ellis (Oxford, 2008), 296-331, at 327.

77. Douglas Gray, *Later Medieval English Literature* (Oxford, 2008), 184-204.

78. Cory James Ruston, 'Malory's Divided Wales', in *Authority and Subjugation in Writing of Medieval Wales*, ed. Ruth Kennedy and Simon Meecham-Janes (New York, 2008), 175-89, at 186.

79. K. S. Whetter, *Understanding Genre and Medieval Romance* (Aldershot, 2008), 116, 196-8.

80. Molly Martin, *Vision and Gender in Malory's 'Morte Darthur'* (Cambridge, 2010), 175.

81. Corinne Saunders, *Magic and the Supernatural in Medieval English Romance* (Cambridge, 2010), 234-60.

82. Elizabeth Archibald, 'Malory's Lancelot and Guenevere', in *Companion to Arthurian Literature*, ed. Helen Fulton (Chichester, 2012), 312-25, at 316.

83. Fiona Tolhurst, *Geoffrey of Monmouth and the Feminist Origins of the Arthurian Legend* (New York, 2012), 112.

84. Kristina Pérez, *The Myth of Morgan la Fey* (New York, 2014), 187.

85. S. J. Drake, *Cornwall, Connectivity and Identity in the Fourteenth Century* (Woodbridge, 2019), 91.

86. Aisling Byrne, 'Irish Translations and Romances', in *Arthur in the Celtic Languages*, ed. Ceridwen Lloyd-Morgan and Erich Poppe (Cardiff, 2019), 344-57, at 346.

87. Kenneth Hodges, 'Spenser, Malory, and Regionalism', in *The Arthurian World*, ed. Victoria Coldham-Fussell, Miriam Edlich-Muth, Renée Ward (London, 2022), 83-94, at 84.

88. Mary Bateman, *Local Place and the Arthurian Tradition* (Cambridge, 2023), 124.

89. Fiona Tolhurst and K. S. Whetter, 'The Ethics of a New Edition', in *Ethics of the Arthurian Legend*, ed. Melissa Ridley Elmes and Evelyn Meyer (Cambridge, 2023), 325-56, at 329.

90. Bernard Mees, *King Arthur and the Languages of Britain* (London, 2025), 138.

AFTERWORD

Following ten chapters and a thousand Arthurian years or so from the 530s (with Rome's Empire then still a vivid memory) to 1485 (with printing a fact and the New World awaiting discovery), we may now look back and look forward. Looking back lets us trace themes of what has gone before; looking forward will suggest how others may develop and correct them.

As concerns the former, perhaps a chief use of this book is in presenting not so much Arthur, as what critics have thought about Arthur. Schools have arrived in sequence (each with an agenda, whether patriotic, nationalist, mystical, imperialistic, neo-pagan, post-colonial, even feminist). In this book their authors are on chronological display, so that readers can take critics not mentioned and place them within a context; or add future writers (with new insights or new misconceptions) to them, and see if they advance our understanding or obstruct it; for the task of inter-preting early Arthurian literature will surely go on for all time.

Besides that are specific projects ready to take on. Here are some indicators. Arthur the North Briton provides work for archaeologists and historians alike. Leslie Alcock's investigations at Cadbury Castle, Somerset (in England's south-west), set out by his *Arthur's Britain* (Harmondsworth, 1971) and other books, have dominated accounts of fifth- and sixth-century Britain. Now that we can be sure that Arthur fought a long way from Cadbury, all histories of early England and Wales and Scotland will have to be rewritten. There is also the tantalizing hope that physical remains (spears, trappings, insignia) of his conflicts will be found at battlefields here identified on each side of the present-day Anglo-Scottish border.

There is plenty in addition. For Welsh scholars, there is still much to be done before the dating of *Mabinogion* texts is settled rationally, with the tale of Culhwch in the late eleventh century, those of the Three Romances squarely in the thirteenth. As regards the commentary on Laʒamon's *Brut*, when it is at last published by the EETS, it will also take us forwards, even if it is perhaps not the last word on restoring the poet's original text.

For later Arthurian poetry in English, there are likewise great enterprises in the offing. The first concerns Sir John Stanley as author of *Sir Gawain and the Green Knight* and its three associated poems. The proposition that he was a poet, as well as an astute Cheshire-Lancashire magnate and court politician, must transform our perceptions of Richard II's age and of Ricardian poetry. A study is thus now needed on Stanley's life and career. There is no shortage of material in official archives, including at least one letter (in Anglo-French) by him to Henry IV. The result would be a dossier comparable to the ample one that we possess for Geoffrey Chaucer. It has the surprising consequence that the *Gawain* Poet would not be some obscure and anonymous clerk or priest, but amongst the best-documented writers from the whole of England's early literature. Fresh material in abundance, one might think, for a string of doctoral dissertations. One of them should explore the literary and other relations between Stanley as the *Gawain* Poet, whose concern for Arthurian tradition was obsessive (if less so than his zeal for hunting deer or foxes or wild boar) and his associate Geoffrey Chaucer, a civil servant who (it seems) had little enthusiasm for Arthurian romance (or chasing after wild animals), even if he stole aspects of the Green Knight poem for his own tales of Squire and Wife of Bath.

Still more fundamental is the quest for the author of the alliterative *Morte Arthure*. Its text presents clues on who he was: a man active in about 1400, of high status, a veteran of the King's French wars, having a long military and diplomatic experience (perhaps even in Italy?), and speaking Lincolnshire dialect. That part of England's north-east Midlands cannot have had too many landowners or other men of rank to fit such a description. Those with access to records of Lincolnshire gentry in the late fourteenth century might soon discover a possible candidate, or candidates. If we knew who this gifted poet was, the implications for English poetry will be considerable. Much the same might be said for the Carlisle cleric, perhaps a member of one of its religious communities, who in about 1425 wrote *The Awntyrs off Arthure*. On such questions we are evidently far from the evening of our labours. If, then, *King Arthur* sets off dozens of scholarly rabbits, its author will wish every success to researchers (especially young ones) in catching them.

www.ingramcontent.com/pod-product-compliance
Lightning Source LLC
Chambersburg PA
CBHW021221130626
46554CB00004B/1309